2 ★ All-Star

Linda Lee

Kristin Sherman ★ Grace Tanaka ★ Shirley Velasco

Second Edition

Mc Graw Hill

Connect
Learn
Succeed™

ALL-STAR 2 STUDENT BOOK

Published by McGraw-Hill, a business unit of The McGraw-Hill Companies, Inc., 1221 Avenue of the Americas, New York, NY, 10020. Copyright © 2011, 2006 by The McGraw-Hill Companies, Inc. All rights reserved. No part of this publication may be reproduced or distributed in any form or by any means, or stored in a database or retrieval system, without the prior written consent of The McGraw-Hill Companies, Inc., including, but not limited to, in any network or other electronic storage or transmission, or broadcast for distance learning.

Some ancillaries, including electronic and print components, may not be available to customers outside the United States.

This book is printed on acid-free paper.

1 2 3 4 5 6 7 8 9 0 WDQ/WDQ 1 0 9 8 7 6 5 4 3 2 1 0

ISBN   978-0-07-719711-7

MHID   0-07-719711-9

ISE ISBN 978-0-07-131383-4

ISE MHID 0-07-131383-4

Vice president/Editor in chief: *Elizabeth Haefele*
Vice president/Director of marketing: *John E. Biernat*
Director of sales and marketing, ESL: *Pierre Montagano*
Director of development: *Valerie Kelemen*
Developmental editors: *Amy Lawler, Laura LeDrean, Nancy Jordan*
Marketing manager: *Kelly Curran*
Lead digital product manager: *Damian Moshak*
Digital developmental editor: *Kevin White*
Director, Editing/Design/Production: *Jess Ann Kosic*
Lead project manager: *Susan Trentacosti*
Senior production supervisor: *Debra R. Sylvester*
Designer: *Srdjan Savanovic*
Senior photo research coordinator: *Lori Kramer*
Photo researcher: *Allison Grimes*
Digital production coordinator: *Cathy Tepper*
Illustrators: *Alyta Adams, Anna Divito, Jerry Gonzalez, Mike Hortens, Andrew Lange, Bot Roda, Daniel Rubenstein, Blanche Simms, Chris Winn, Laserwords*
Typeface: *11.5/12.5 Frutiger LT Std 45 Light*
Compositor: *Laserwords Private Limited*
Printer: *Worldcolor*
Cover credit: *Andrew Lange*
Credits: The credits section for this book begins on page 222 and is considered an extention of the copyright page.

The Internet addresses listed in the text were accurate at the time of publication. The inclusion of a Web site does not indicate an endorsement by the authors or McGraw-Hill, and McGraw-Hill does not guarantee the accuracy of the information presented at these sites.

www.mhhe.com

ACKNOWLEDGMENTS

The authors and publisher would like to thank the following individuals who reviewed *All-Star Second Edition* at various stages of development and whose comments, reviews, and field-testing were instrumental in helping us shape the second edition of the series:

Carlos Alcazar, Newport-Mesa USD Adult School, Costa Mesa, CA ★ Isabel V. Anderson, The English Center, Miami, FL ★ Carol Antunano, The English Center, Miami, FL ★ Ted Anderson ★ Josefina Aucar, Miami Beach Adult and Community Education Center, Miami, FL ★ Veronica Pavon-Baker, Miami Dade County Public Schools, Miami, FL ★ Barry Bakin, Pacoima Skills Center, Pacoima, CA ★ Michael Blackman, Reseda Community Adult School, Reseda, CA ★ Taylor H. Blakely, Newport-Mesa USD Adult School, Costa Mesa, CA ★ Marge Bock, Sweetwater USD Adult Education, Chula Vista, CA ★ Lusine Bokhikyan ★ Rothwell H Bouillon, Pacoima Skills Center, Pacoima, CA ★ Ian Brailsford, South Piedmont Community College, Monroe, NC ★ Roy Carl Brungardt, Riverside Adult School, Riverside, CA ★ Paul Buczko, Pacoima Skills Center, Pacoima, CA ★ Gemma S Burns, Riverside Adult School, Riverside, CA ★ Kathleen Bywater, Riverside Adult School, Riverside, CA ★ Helen Canellos, Milwaukee Area Technical College, Milwaukee, WI ★ Richard H Capet, Pimmit Hills Adult Education Center, Falls Church, VA ★ Waldo Cardenas, Miami Dade County Public Schools, Miami, FL ★ Gemma Santos Catire, Miami Beach Adult and Community Education Center, Miami, FL ★ Julio Chow, Pacoima Skills Center, Pacoima, CA ★ Claire Cirolia, Fairfax County Adult ESL Program, Fairfax, VA ★ Sabine Cooke, Riverside Adult School, Riverside, CA ★ Jeffrey R Corrigan, Newport-Mesa USD Adult School, Costa Mesa, CA ★ Don Curtis, Oakland USD Adult Education, Neighborhood Centers, Oakland, CA ★ Angela DeRocco, Sweetwater USD Adult Education, Chula Vista, CA ★ Jorge de la Paz, Miami Sunset Adult Center, Miami, FL ★ Deborah Ebersold, Pacoima Skills Center, Pacoima, CA ★ Fernando Egea, Miami Sunset Adult Center, Miami, FL ★ Marilyn Farrell, Riverside Adult School, Riverside, CA ★ Lora Finch, Newport-Mesa USD Adult School, Costa Mesa, CA ★ Pat Fox, Montgomery College, Rockville, MD ★ Antoinette Galaviz, Reseda Community Adult School, Reseda, CA ★ Elizabeth Gellatly, Newport-Mesa USD Adult School, Costa Mesa, CA ★ Dennys Gonzalez, Miami Dade College, Miami, FL ★ Amber G Goodall, South Piedmont Community College, Monroe, NC ★ Amy Grodzienski, Reseda Community Adult School, Reseda, CA ★ Ana Guadayol, Miami-Dade College VESOL, Miami, FL ★ Diane Helvig, Sweetwater USD Adult Education, Chula Vista, CA ★ Kristine Hoffman, Newport-Mesa USD Adult School, Costa Mesa, CA ★ Dr. Coral Horton, Miami-Dade College, Miami, FL ★ Valerie Johnson, Reseda Community Adult School, Reseda, CA ★ Ali Kiani, Reseda Community Adult School, Reseda, CA ★ Donna Kihara, Reseda Community Adult School, Reseda, CA ★ Angela Kosmas, Wilbur Wright College, Chicago, IL ★ Alida Labiosa, Newport-Mesa USD Adult School, Costa Mesa, CA ★ Lourdes A. Laguilles, Reseda Community Adult School, Reseda, CA ★ Holly Lawyer, Elgin Community College, Elgin, Illinois ★ Lia Lerner, Burbank Adult School, Burbank, CA ★ Mae F Liu, Chinese American Planning Council, New York, NY ★ Levia Loftus, College of Lake County, Grayslake, IL ★ Nancy Magathan, Reseda Community Adult School, Reseda, CA ★ Monica Manero-Cohen, Miami Beach Adult and Community Education Center, Miami, FL ★ Matilda Martinez, Miami Beach Adult and Community Education Center, Miami, FL ★ Suzette Mascarenas, Newport-Mesa USD Adult School Costa Mesa, CA ★ Sara McKinnon, College of Marin, Kentfield, CA ★ Ibis Medina, Miami Sunset Adult Center, Miami, FL ★ Alice-Ann Menjivar, Carlos Rosario International Public Charter School, Washington, DC ★ Kathleen Miller, Reseda Community Adult School, Reseda, CA ★ Kent Minault, Pacoima Skills Center, Pacoima, CA ★ Pedro Monteagudo, Miami Beach Adult and Community Education Center, Miami, FL ★ Jose Montes, The English Center, Miami, FL ★ Ilene Mountain, Newport-Mesa USD Adult School Costa Mesa, CA ★ Mary Murphy-Clagett, Sweetwater USD Adult Education, Chula Vista, CA ★ Fransisco Narciso, Reseda Community Adult School, Reseda, CA ★ Anita Nodarse, Miami Dade College, Miami, FL ★ Zoila Ortiz, Miami Sunset Adult Center, Miami, FL ★ Phil Oslin, Sweetwater USD, Adult Education, Chula Vista, CA ★ Nancy Pakdel, Newport-Mesa USD Adult School, Costa Mesa, CA ★ Eduardo Paredes-Ferro, Miami Sunset Adult Center, Miami, FL ★ Virginia Parra, Miami Dade College, Interamerican Campus, Miami, FL ★ Elaine S Paris, Chinese American Planning Council, New York, NY ★ Ellen R. Purcell, Public Schools/Pimmit Hills, Falls Church, VA ★ Michelle R Quiter, Austin Community College, Austin, TX ★ Sandra Ramirez, Pacoima Skills Center, Pacoima, CA ★ Corinne Rennie, Newport-Mesa USD Adult School, Costa Mesa, CA ★ Barbara Rinsler ★ Ray Rivera, South Dade Adult Education Center, Homestead, FL ★ Abdali Safaei, Reseda Community Adult School, Reseda, CA ★ Bernard Sapir, Reseda Community Adult School, Reseda, CA ★ Amy Schneider, Pacoima Skills Center, Pacoima, CA ★ Delisa Sexton, Pacoima Skills Center, Pacoima, CA ★ Norma S Smith, Pacoima Skills Center, Pacoima, CA ★ Mandi M Spottsville, Newport-Mesa USD Adult School ★ Helen G Stein, Miami Dade College, Miami, FL ★ Jennifer C Storm, College of Lake County, Grayslake, IL ★ Terri L Stralow, South Piedmont Community College, Monroe, NC ★ Dina P Tarrab, Reseda Community Adult School, Reseda, CA ★ Maliheh Vafai, East Side Adult Education, San Jose, CA ★ Rosanne Verani, Riverside Adult School, Riverside, CA ★ Kermey Wang, Riverside Adult School, Riverside, CA ★ Cynthia Whisner, Riverside Adult School, Riverside, CA ★ Duane Wong, Newport-Mesa USD Adult School, Costa Mesa, CA

SCOPE AND SEQUENCE

LIFE SKILLS

UNIT	Listening and Speaking	Reading and Writing	Critical Thinking	Vocabulary	Grammar
Pre-Unit **Getting Started** *page 2*	• Introduce yourself • Use useful expressions • Follow and give classroom instructions • **WB:** Explain how to set up an e-mail account			• Introductions • Useful expressions • Classroom instructions • **WB:** Parts of a computer	
Unit 1 **Describing People** *page 4*	• Exchange personal information • Describe people • Greet a friend • Make introductions • Take phone messages • Pron: Vowel sounds in *slip* and *sleep*	• Read and interpret personal documents (birth certificate, driver's license, diploma) • Read and write bio poems • Write about likes and dislikes • Interpret personal information forms • **WB:** Complete an application for a driver's license • **WB:** Write a note to a child's teacher regarding an absence	• Interpret information • Reasoning	• Personal information (name, address, date of birth) • Physical descriptions • Moods and emotions • Forms of identification • Adverbs of time	• Simple present of *be*, statements • Simple present of *have*, statements • Simple present, questions • Simple present, statements
Unit 2 **Going Places** *page 18*	• Ask about places in the community • Ask for and give directions • Ask for information at a train station • Pron: Word stress	• Read a map • Read a train schedule • Read a telephone directory • **WB:** Read an excerpt from a government website • **WB:** Read a story	• Interpret a map • Make inferences	• Places and activities in the community • Directions • People and things in a train station • **WB:** Parts of a car	• Present continuous, statements and questions • Prepositions of place and direction • Simple present, *Wh*-questions review • Prepositions of time
Unit 3 **Dollars and Cents** *page 32*	• Talk about expenses • Talk about purchases • Talk about money • Talk about banking services • Listen to an automated phone message • Pron: *Ng* versus *Nk*	• Read and complete a check register • Read and interpret a pay stub • Read and interpret a cable bill	• Classify information • Apply knowledge to new situations	• Personal expenses • Money: coins and bills • Banking • Utilities	• Simple past, statements • Simple past of *be*, statements • Simple past, *Yes/No* questions • Simple past, *Wh*-questions

CORRELATIONS TO STANDARDS

Civics Concepts	Math Skills	CASAS Life Skills Competencies	SCANS Competencies (Workplace)	EFF Content Standards	Florida	LAUSD
• Set up an e-mail account		• 0.1.4, 0.1.6, 0.2.1, 0.2.4	• Sociability • See things in the mind's eye	• Speak so others can understand	• **WB:** 3.03.16	• 5, 7 (a), 11 (d, e), 15 • **WB:** 60, 61
	• Calculate time	• **1:** 0.1.2, 0.2.1 • **2:** 0.1.2 • **3:** 0.1.8, 0.2.4 • **4:** 0.1.2, 2.7.5 • **5:** 0.1.4 • **6:** 2.1.7, 2.3.4, 6.1.3, 6.6.6 • **WB:** 2.5.5	• See things in the mind's eye • Creative thinking • Reasoning • Sociability • Acquire and evaluate information • Organize and maintain information • Use technology to complete tasks	• Speak so others can understand • Reflect and evaluate • Use information and communications technology • Use math to solve problems and communicate	• **1:** 3.01.01 • **2:** 3.01.01 • **5:** 3.01.03 • **6:** 3.01.07	• **1:** 1, 3, 5, 7, 62 (all), G1a • **2:** 3 • **3:** 7b, G1a • **4:** 3 • **5:** 7 • **6:** 21 • **WB:** 12, 16
• Identify places and activities in the community • Give directions to places in the community • Identify addresses and telephone numbers of places in the community • **WB:** Identify safe driving practices	• Measure time • Interpret schedules • Tell the time • Calculate distance • Convert units of measurement	• **1:** 0.1.2 • **2:** 2.2.1 • **3:** 2.2.2, 2.2.3, 2.2.4 • **4:** 2.2.4, 2.2.5, 6.2.4, 6.6.1, 6.6.2, 6.6.6 • **5:** 2.2.4, 2.3.1 • **6:** 2.1.1, 2.5.1, 2.5.8 • **WB:** 1.9.2, 3.4.2	• Use resources • Acquire and evaluate information • See things in the mind's eye • Use technology to complete tasks • Reasoning	• Use information and communications technology • Speak so others can understand • Use math to solve problems and communicate	• **2:** 3.02.02, 3.06.03 • **4:** 3.06.01 • **5:** 3.04.01, 3.06.01 • **6:** 3.01.10, 3.02.01 • **WB:** 3.06.05, 3.01.06, 3.01.08, 3.06.04	• **1:** G2a • **2:** 23 (a, b), G22a-b, • **3:** 23, G28c • **4:** 23 (c), 31 (b), G22c • **5:** 11c and e, 22 • **6:** 19, 20, 58 • **WB:** 41 • **RC:** 25
• Distinguish U.S. coins and bills • **WB:** Understand procedure for obtaining a home loan • **WB:** Create a budget • **WB:** Pay a bill	• Use coins and bills • Calculate change • Balance a check register • Compute deductions	• **1:** 1.5.1 • **2:** 1.1.6, 6.2.1, 6.2.2 • **3:** 1.8.1 • **4:** 1.8.1 • **5:** 1.8.7 • **6:** 4.2.1, 6.4.3 • **WB:** 1.2.5, 1.4.6, 1.5.1, 1.5.2, 1.5.3	• Acquire and evaluate information • Organize and maintain information • Analyze and communicate information • Use resources wisely	• Use math to solve problems and communicate	• **1:** 3.04.06, 3.04.07 • **2:** 3.04.06 • **3:** 3.04.07 • **4:** 3.04.07 • **5:** 3.04.07 • **WB:** 3.04.08	• **1:** G5b-c • **2:** 27, G5a • **3:** 11a, G5a-c, G25, G28a • **4:** 28, G5a-c, G25, G28c • **5:** 18 • **6:** 56 • **RC:** 29, 37, 38

CASAS, Florida, and LAUSD standards: Numbers in bold indicate lesson numbers. • **G:** Grammar • **WB:** Workbook • **RC:** Online Teacher Resource Center

SCOPE AND SEQUENCE

LIFE SKILLS

UNIT	Listening and Speaking	Reading and Writing	Critical Thinking	Vocabulary	Grammar
Unit 4 **Plans and Goals** *page 46*	• Talk about goals • Talk about plans • Describe the workplace • Ask for and give advice • Listen to a recorded message • Pron: Past tense endings	• Read and interpret a website • Read a biography • Read a timeline • **WB**: Read an article • **WB**: Read a school calendar • **WB**: Complete a school registration form	• Classify information • Sequence events	• Personal, educational, and work goals • People in the workplace	• *Want to, like to, would like to* • Future with *be going to* • Future with *will* • *Because* and *to* for reasons
Unit 5 **Smart Shopping** *page 60*	• Talk about common purchases • Talk about shopping • Make exchanges, returns, and purchases • Pron: Stress	• Read advertisements • Read an article about shopping • Read and write shopping tips • **WB**: Read warning labels	• Choose the best alternative • Compare	• Things and activities in a shopping mall • Items of clothing • Items in a kitchen • **WB**: Uniforms and work apparel • **WB**: Cleaning and laundry supplies • **WB**: Small appliances	• *Go* + verb + *ing* • Comparative adjectives • *There was* and *There were* • Superlative adjectives
Unit 6 **Food** *page 74*	• Talk about food • Ask for things in a restaurant • Order from a menu • Take food orders • Pron: Intonation patterns in sentences and questions	• Read and interpret a bar graph • Read a menu • Read and write a recipe • Read and interpret an article about food groups • Read an article about Thanksgiving • **WB**: Read an article about the FDA and food labels	• Sequence events • Make inferences • Choose the best alternative	• Food • People and things in a restaurant • Food preparation • **WB**: Food containers and measurements	• Count and noncount nouns • *One, each, some, another* and *the other(s)* • Quantifiers • Adjective + noun

Civics Concepts	Math Skills	CASAS Life Skills Competencies	SCANS Competencies (Workplace)	EFF Content Standards	Florida	LAUSD
• **WB:** Understand a school schedule • **WB:** Register for school	• Calculate grade point average	• **1:** 4.1.9, 7.1.1 • **2:** 4.1.9, 7.1.1, 7.1.2 • **3:** 4.1.6, 4.4.1, 4.4.2 • **4:** 7.2.1 • **5:** 0.1.3 • **6:** 2.8.8, 2.8.9 • **WB:** 2.5.5, 4.4.1, 4.4.2, 4.4.5, 4.6.2	• See things in the mind's eye • Responsibility • Self-management • Organize and maintain information • Use technology to complete tasks	• Use information and communications technology • Speak so others can understand • Observe critically • Plan • Take responsibility for learning	• **1:** 3.03.14 • **2:** 3.01.02, 3.03.14 • **3:** 3.03.06 • **5:** 3.03.09 • **6:** 3.02.08 • **WB:** 3.03.06, 3.03.09, 3.03.13, 3.03.14, 3.03.15	• **1:** 64, G1b • **2:** G3 • **3:** G4 • **4:** 63, G24 • **5:** 18, G25 • **WB:** 6, 14, 22, 55a • **RC:** 40
• Explore a shopping mall • Understand shopping terms • Shop online	• Calculate percentages • Calculate savings	• **1:** 1.4.1 • **2:** 1.2.6, 1.3.1 • **3:** 1.2.1, 1.2.2, 1.2.3 • **4:** 1.2.5 • **5:** 1.2.2, 1.3.3 • **6:** 1.2.6, 1.3.1, 1.3.5, 1.6.3, 1.7.1 • **WB:** 1.2.2, 1.3.3, 1.3.9, 1.7.3, 3.4.1, 3.4.2, 4.3.1, 7.2.3	• Decision making • Use resources wisely • Acquire and evaluate information • Organize and maintain information • Analyze and communicate information • Use technology to complete tasks	• Learn through research • Use information and communications technology	• **1:** 3.01.02 • **3:** 3.04.01, 3.04.02 • **4:** 3.04.02 • **6:** 3.04.02 • **WB:** 3.03.04, 3.03.08, 3.07.01 • **RC:** 3.04.03	• **1:** G26 • **2:** 30, G20c • **3:** 27, G21b, 32 • **4:** G20d • **5:** 33 • **WB:** 64
• Understand eating habits in the U.S. • Understand food groups • Learn about Thanksgiving • **WB:** Understand food labels	• Compute a tip • Compute the cost of a meal • **WB:** Compute the cost of a catering order	• **1:** 1.2.8 • **2:** 0.1.7 • **3:** 6.2.3, 6.4.3 • **4:** 1.1.1, 2.7.1, 5.2.1 • **5:** 6.2.1 • **6:** 3.5.1, 3.5.2 • **WB:** 1.1.4, 1.1.7, 1.2.1, 1.3.8, 1.6.1, 4.7.2	• Decision making • Reasoning • See things in the mind's eye • Teach others new skills • Serve clients or customers • Use technology to complete tasks • Acquire and evaluate information	• Use information and communications technology • Speak so others can understand • Use math to solve problems and communicate	• **3:** 3.04.06 • **4:** 3.02.03 • **5:** 3.04.06 • **6:** 3.05.06 • **WB:** 3.04.06, 3.04.09	• **1:** 31 (a), G16d • **2:** 8 (a), G18 • **3:** 36, G17e • **4:** G20b • **5:** 36, G14 • **WB:** 31a, 34, 35

CASAS, Florida, and LAUSD standards: Numbers in bold indicate lesson numbers. • **G:** Grammar • **WB:** Workbook • **RC:** Online Teacher Resource Center

SCOPE AND SEQUENCE

CORRELATIONS TO STANDARDS

Civics Concepts	Math Skills	CASAS Life Skills Competencies	SCANS Competencies (Workplace)	EFF Content Standards	Florida	LAUSD
• **WB:** Use postal services	• Calculate time changes	• **1:** 0.1.2 • **2:** 0.1.8 • **3:** 0.1.2, 0.1.3, 0.1.4 • **4:** 2.3.5, 2.7.2, 2.7.6 • **5:** 0.1.2, 0.1.6 • **6:** 4.4.1	• Decision making • See things in the mind's eye • Work with people of diverse backgrounds • Organize and maintain information • Acquire and evaluate information • Use technology to complete tasks	• Use information and communications technology • Speak so others can understand	• **3:** 3.01.02 • **4:** 3.02.07 • **5:** 3.01.02, 3.03.07 • **6:** 3.01.04, 3.03.11 • **WB:** 2.4.2, 2.4.4 • **RC:** 3.07.02	• **1:** 4 , G17c, G19b • **2:** 6, G19a • **3:** 10 (all), G19c • **4:** 4, G12 • **5:** 9 (a, b, c) • **WB:** 24 • **RC:** 8b, 11b
• Explore an emergency room • **WB:** Complete an accident report • **WB:** Complete a medical history form	• Calculate ounces, tablespoons, and teaspoons	• **1:** 3.6.1 • **2:** 3.6.3, 3.6.4 • **3:** 2.5.1, 3.1.3, 3.6.2 • **4:** 3.3.1, 3.3.2, 3.3.4, 3.4.1 • **5:** 3.1.2, 3.1.3, 3.6.3, 3.6.4 • **6:** 3.5.9, 3.6.5, 3.6.9 • **WB:** 3.1.1, 3.2.1, 4.3.4	• See things in the mind's eye • Use resources wisely • Use technology to complete tasks • Organize and maintain information • Acquire and evaluate information • Work within the system	• Use information and communications technology	• **1:** 3.05.01 • **2:** 3.05.01 • **3:** 3.05.01 • **4:** 3.07.03 • **5:** 3.05.03, 3.05.04 • **6:** 3.05.02 • **WB:** 3.05.01 • **RC:** 3.05.05	• **1:** 43, G9, G10 • **2:** 45 (a), G15 • **3:** G23a • **4:** 46, 47, G23f • **5:** 44, 45 • **WB:** 43, 45, 57, 62 • **RC:** 50
• Understand emergency procedures • Practice fire safety in the home	• Converting temperatures	• **1:** 1.7.3, 3.4.2 • **2:** 1.4.7 • **3:** 2.1.2 • **4:** 1.7.3, 6.6.1 • **5:** 1.7.4, 2.1.2 • **WB:** 2.5.4, 3.4.2, 4.3.3	• Reason • See things in the mind's eye • Use technology to complete tasks • Organize and maintain information	• Use information and communications technology • Use math to solve problems and communicate	• **2:** 3.04.05 • **4:** 3.02.05, 3.02.09 • **WB:** 3.01.05, 3.02.05, 3.03.08 • **RC:** 3.01.09	• **1:** 59, G5a-c • **2:** 39, • **3:** 20, 48, G8 • **4:** 26, 48, G23b • **5:** 20 • **6:** 48 • **WB:** 48 • **RC:** 42

CASAS, Florida, and LAUSD standards: Numbers in bold indicate lesson numbers. • **G:** Grammar • **WB:** Workbook • **RC:** Online Teacher Resource Center

SCOPE AND SEQUENCE

LIFE SKILLS

UNIT	Listening and Speaking	Reading and Writing	Critical Thinking	Vocabulary	Grammar
Unit 10 **Work** *page130*	• Talk about jobs and job skills • Talk about work experience and job skills • Communicate with an employer • Talk about work schedules • Pron: Intonation in *Yes/No* and *Wh-* questions	• Read and write job tips • Read job advertisements • Read and interpret a job application • Read about federal holidays	• Evaluate	• Occupations and skills • Job advertisements • **WB:** U.S. holidays	• *Have to, don't have to*, and *must* • Adverbs of manner • Compound sentences with *and, but*, and *or* • Negative compound sentences with *and ... not either* and *neither...nor*

CORRELATIONS TO STANDARDS

Civics Concepts	Math Skills	CASAS Life Skills Competencies	SCANS Competencies (Workplace)	EFF Content Standards	Florida	LAUSD
• Recognize appropriate work behavior • Understand how to look for and apply for a job • **WB:** Understand time cards • **WB:** Understand the historical origins of U.S. holidays	• Compute overtime pay	• **1:** 4.1.8 • **2:** 4.1.7, 4.1.8 • **3:** 4.1.3, 4.1.7 • **4:** 4.1.7, 4.4.1, 4.4.2, 6.1.3 • **5:** 4.1.5, 4.1.7, 4.1.8, 4.4.1 • **6:** 4.1.2, 4.1.3, 4.1.8 • **WB:** 2.7.1, 4.2.1, 5.1.4, 5.2.1,	• Integrity and honesty • Acquire and evaluate information • Organize and maintain information	• Use math to solve problems and communicate	• **1:** 3.03.01 • **2:** 3.03.01, 3.03.05 • **3:** 3.03.01 • **4:** 3.03.06, 3.03.09, 3.03.11 • **5:** 3.03.02, 3.03.04, 3.03.05, 3.03.10 • **6:** 3.03.02, 3.03.05 • **WB:** 3.02.03, 3.02.04 • **RC:** 3.03.03, 3.03.12	• **2:** 54a-b, G23e • **3:** 51, 53, 54a-c, G30 (a, d) • **4:** 55, G30c • **5:** 8b, 10 (b), 54 (a, b, c), 55 G11a-b (a, b, c) • **6:** 51, 52 • **WB:** 3.04.01

CASAS, Florida, and LAUSD standards: Numbers in bold indicate lesson numbers. • **G:** Grammar • **WB:** Workbook • **RC:** Online Teacher Resource Center

TO THE TEACHER

All-Star Second Edition is a four-level, standards-based series for English learners featuring a picture-dictionary approach to vocabulary building. "Big picture" scenes in each unit provide springboards to a wealth of activities developing all of the language skills.

An accessible and predictable sequence of lessons in each unit systematically builds language and critical thinking skills around life-skill topics. *All-Star* presents family, work, and community topics in each unit and provides alternate application lessons in its workbooks, giving teachers the flexibility to customize the series for a variety of student needs and curricular objectives. *All-Star* is tightly correlated to all of the updated major national and state standards for adult instruction.

New to the Second Edition

- **Updated content** provides full coverage of all major *revised* standards including CASAS, Florida, LAUSD, EFF, and Texas.

- **NEW comprehensive, carefully sequenced grammar program** connects target grammar to the content to enrich learning and provide full coverage of grammar standards.

- **NEW robust listening program** addresses the latest CASAS standards and prepares students for the types of listening items on CASAS tests.

- **NEW Work-Out CD-ROM with complete student audio** provides a fun, rich environment with over 25 hours of interactive learning and the entire *All-Star Second Edition* student audio program in downloadable MP3 files.

- **NEW Teacher Resource Center** offers downloadable and printable Study Guides and Learner Persistence Worksheets, EZ Tests, Big Picture PowerPoint Slides, full Teacher Audio for Tests in downloadable MP3 files, and other materials to support teaching.

- **NEW Interactive Correlations Chart** allows teachers to easily cross-reference standards with Student Book, Workbook, and Study Guide pages.

Hallmark *All-Star* Features

- Dynamic Big Picture scenes present life-skills vocabulary and provide lively contexts for activities and discussions that promote all-skills language development.

- Predictable sequence of seven two-page lessons in each unit reduces prep time for teachers and helps students get comfortable with the format of each lesson.

- Flexible structure, with application lessons addressing family, work, and community topics in both the Student Book and Workbook, allows teachers to customize each unit to meet a variety of student needs and curricular objectives.

- Comprehensive coverage of key standards, such as CASAS, Florida, LAUSD, EFF, and Texas, prepares students to master a broad range of critical competencies.

- Multiple assessment measures like CASAS-style tests and performance-based assessment offer a variety of options for monitoring and assessing learner progress.

The Complete *All-Star* Program

- The **Student Book** features ten 14-page units that integrate listening, speaking, reading, writing, grammar, math, and pronunciation skills with life-skills topics, critical thinking activities, and civics concepts.

- The **Student Work-Out CD-ROM with full student audio** extends the learning goals of each Student Book unit with interactive activities that build vocabulary, listening, reading, writing, and test-taking skills. The CD-ROM also includes the full Student Book audio program.

- The **Teacher's Edition with Tests** includes:
  - Step-by-step procedural notes for each Student Book activity
  - Notes on teaching the Target Grammar Pages
  - Expansion activities addressing multi-level classes, literacy, and students that need to be challenged
  - Culture, Grammar, and Pronunciation Notes
  - Two-page written test for each unit (*Note:* Listening passages for the tests are available on the Teacher Audio with Testing CD and on the Online Teacher Resource Center.)
  - Audio scripts for all audio program materials
  - Answer keys for Student Book, Workbook, and Tests

- The **Workbook** includes supplementary practice activities correlated to the Student Book. As a bonus feature, the Workbook also includes two alternate application lessons per unit that address the learner's role as a worker, family member, and/or community member. These lessons may be used in addition to, or as substitutes for, the application lessons found in Lesson 6 of each Student Book unit.

- The **Teacher Audio with Testing CD** contains recordings for all listening activities in the Student Book as well as the listening passages for each unit test.

- The **Online Teacher Resource Center** provides teachers with the tools to set goals for students, customize classroom teaching, and better measure student success. It includes:
  - EZ Tests that allow teachers to create customized online tests
  - An Interactive Correlations Chart that allows teachers to easily cross-reference standards with Student Book, Workbook, and Study Guide pages
  - Big Picture PowerPoint slides that present the Student Book Big Picture scenes
  - A Learner Persistence Kit that sets and tracks student achievement goals
  - A Post-Testing Study Guide that moves students toward mastery and tracks their progress using the reproducible Study Guide Worksheets
  - Downloadable MP3 files for the Testing audio program

Overview of the *All-Star Second Edition* Program

UNIT STRUCTURE

The Welcome to *All-Star Second Edition* guide on pages xvi–xxi offers teachers and administrators a visual tour of one Student Book unit and highlights the exciting new features of the Second Edition.

All-Star Second Edition is designed to maximize flexibility. Each unit has the following sequence of seven two-page lessons:

- Lesson 1: Vocabulary
- Lesson 2: Vocabulary in Action
- Lesson 3: Talk about It
- Lesson 4: Reading and Writing
- Lesson 5: Conversations
- Lesson 6: Application
- Lesson 7: Review and Assessment

Each unit introduces several grammar points. A Target Grammar icon in the lessons refers teachers and student to the Target Grammar Pages at the back of the book where they can find explanations of the grammar points and contextualized practice.

SPECIAL FEATURES OF EACH UNIT

- **Target Grammar Pages:** Throughout each unit, students are directed to the Target Grammar Pages in the back of the book, where the grammar point they have been exposed to in the lesson is presented and practiced in manageable chunks. Students learn the target grammar structure with clear charts, meaningful examples, and abundant practice activities.

    This approach gives teachers the flexibility to introduce grammar in any of several ways:
    - At the beginning of a lesson
    - At the point in the lesson where the grammar appears in context
    - As a follow-up to the lesson

- **CASAS Listening:** Each unit has at least two activities that simulate the CASAS listening experience.

- **Pronunciation.** The introductory activity in Lesson 5 (Conversation) of each unit is Pronunciation. This special feature has two major goals: (1) helping students hear and produce specific sounds, words, and minimal pairs of words so they become better listeners and speakers; and (2) addressing issues of stress, rhythm, and intonation so that the students' spoken English becomes more comprehensible.

- **Window on Math.** Learning basic math skills is critically important for success in school, on the job, and at home. As such, national and state standards for adult education mandate instruction in basic math skills. In each unit, a box called Window on Math is dedicated to helping students develop the functional numeracy skills they need for basic math work.

TWO-PAGE LESSON FORMAT

The lessons in *All-Star* are designed as two-page spreads. Lessons 1–4 follow an innovative format with a list of activities on the left-hand page of the spread and picture dictionary visuals supporting these activities on the right hand page. The list of activities, entitled Things to Do, allows students and teachers to take full advantage of the visuals in each lesson, enabling students to achieve a variety of learning goals.

"BIG PICTURE" SCENES

Each unit includes one "big picture" scene in either Lesson 2 or Lesson 3. This scene is the visual centerpiece of each unit, and serves as a springboard to a variety of activities in the Student Book, Teacher's Edition, and Work-Out CD-ROM. In the Student Book, the "big picture" scene introduces key vocabulary and serves as a prompt for classroom discussion. The scenes feature characters with distinct personalities for students to enjoy, respond to, and talk about. There are also surprising and fun elements for students to discover in each scene.

The Teacher's Edition includes a variety of all-skills "Big Picture Expansion" activities that are tied to the Student Book scenes. For each unit, these expansion activities address listening, speaking, reading, writing, and grammar skills development, and allow teachers to customize their instruction to meet the language learning needs of each group of students.

CIVICS CONCEPTS

Many institutions focus direct attention on the importance of civics instruction for English language learners. Civics instruction encourages students to become active and informed community members. Throughout each *All-Star* unit, students and teachers will encounter activities that introduce civics concepts and encourage community involvement. In addition, Application lessons provide activities that help students develop in their roles as workers, parents, and citizens. Those lessons targeting the students' role as citizen encourage learners to become more active and informed members of their communities.

CASAS, SCANS, EFF, FLORIDA, TEXAS, LAUSD, AND OTHER STANDARDS

Teachers and administrators benchmark student progress against national and/or state standards for adult instruction. With this in mind, *All-Star* carefully integrates instructional elements from a wide range of revised standards including CASAS, SCANS, EFF, LAUSD, Texas, and the Florida Adult ESOL Standards. Unit-by-unit correlations of these standards appear in the scope and sequence in the front of this book and in the Online Teacher Resource Center. Here is a brief overview of our approach to meeting the key national, state, and district standards.

- **CASAS.** Many U.S. states, including California, tie funding for adult education programs to student performance on the Comprehensive Adult Student Assessment System (CASAS). The CASAS (www.casas.org) competencies identify more than 300 essential skills that adults need in order to succeed in the classroom, workplace, and community. Examples of these skills include identifying or using appropriate nonverbal behavior in a variety of settings, responding appropriately to common personal information questions, and comparing price or quality to determine the best buys. *All-Star* comprehensively integrates all of the CASAS Life Skill Competencies throughout the four levels of the series.

- **SCANS.** Developed by the United States Department of Labor, SCANS is an acronym for the Secretary's Commission on Achieving Necessary Skills (wdr.doleta.gov/SCANS/). SCANS competencies are workplace skills that help people compete more effectively in today's global economy. The following are examples of SCANS competencies: works well with others, acquires and evaluates information, and teaches others new skills. A variety of SCANS competencies is threaded throughout the activities in each unit of *All-Star*. The incorporation of these competencies recognizes both the intrinsic importance of teaching workplace skills and the fact that many adult students are already working members of their communities.

- **EFF.** Equipped for the Future (EFF) is a set of standards for adult literacy and lifelong learning developed by The National Institute for Literacy (www.nifl.gov). The organizing principle of EFF is that adults assume responsibilities in three major areas of life—as workers, as parents, and as citizens. These three areas of focus are called "role maps" in the EFF documentation. In the parent role map, for example, EFF highlights these and other responsibilities: participating in children's formal education and forming and maintaining supportive family relationships. *All-Star* addresses all three of the EFF role maps in its *Application* lessons.

NUMBER OF HOURS OF INSTRUCTION

The *All-Star* program has been designed to accommodate the needs of adult classes with 70–180 hours of classroom instruction. Here are three recommended ways in which various components in the *All-Star* program can be combined to meet student and teacher needs.

- **70–100 hours.** Teachers are encouraged to work through all of the Student Book materials. Teachers should also look to the Teacher's Edition for teaching suggestions and testing materials as necessary. Students are encouraged to "Plug in and practice" at home with the Work-Out CD-ROM for each unit. *Time per unit: 7–10 hours.*

- **100–140 hours.** In addition to working through all of the Student Book materials, teachers are encouraged to incorporate the Workbook and Work-Out CD-ROM activities for supplementary practice. Students are encouraged to "Plug in and practice" at home with the Work-Out CD-ROM for each unit. *Time per unit: 10–14 hours.*

- **140–180 hours.** Teachers and students working in an intensive instructional setting can take advantage of the wealth of expansion activities threaded through the Teacher's

Edition to supplement the Student Book, Workbook, and Work-Out CD-ROM materials. Students are encouraged to "Plug in and practice" at home with the Work-Out CD-ROM for each unit.
Time per unit: 14–18 hours.

ASSESSMENT

The *All-Star* program offers teachers, students and administrators the following wealth of resources for monitoring and assessing student progress and achievement:

- **Standardized testing formats.** *All-Star* is correlated to the CASAS competencies and many other national and state standards for adult learning. Students have the opportunity to practice answering CASAS-style listening questions in Lesson 7 of each unit. Students practice with the same item types and bubble-in answer sheets they encounter on CASAS and other standardized tests. Students also practice CASAS-style listening items in the Work-Out CD-ROM Listening and Practice Test sections.

- **Achievement tests.** The *All-Star Teacher's Edition* includes end-of-unit tests. These paper-and-pencil tests help students demonstrate how well they have learned the instructional content of the unit. Adult learners often show incremental increases in learning that are not always measured on the standardized tests. The achievement tests may demonstrate learning even in a short amount of instructional time. Twenty percent of each test includes questions that encourage students to apply more academic skills such as determining meaning from context, making inferences, and understanding main ideas. Practice with these question types will help prepare students who may want to enroll in academic classes.

- **EZ Test Online.** *All-Star's* online test generator provides a databank of assessment items from which instructors can create customized tests within minutes. The EZ Test Online assessment materials are available at www.eztestonline.com. For EZ Test tutorials, go to http://mpss.mhhe.com/eztest/eztotutorials.php.

- **Performance-based assessment.** *All-Star* provides several ways to measure students' performance on productive tasks, including the Spotlight: Writing located in the Workbook in the second edition. In addition, the Teacher's Edition suggests writing and speaking prompts that teachers can use for performance-based assessment. These prompts derive from the "big picture" scene in each unit, which provides rich visual input as the basis for the speaking and writing tasks asked of the students.

- **Portfolio assessment.** A portfolio is a collection of student work that can be used to show progress. Examples of work that the instructor or the student may submit in the portfolio include writing samples, audio and video recordings, or projects. Every Student Book unit includes several activities that require critical thinking and small-group project work. These can be included in a student's portfolio.

- **Self-assessment.** Self-assessment is an important part of the overall assessment picture, as it promotes student involvement and commitment to the learning process. When encouraged to assess themselves, students take more control of their learning and are better able to connect the instructional content with their own goals. The Student Book includes *Learning Logs* at the end of each unit, which allow students to check off the vocabulary they have learned and the skills they feel they have acquired. In the Workbook, students complete the Practice Test Performance Record on the inside back cover.

- **Other linguistic and nonlinguistic outcomes.** Traditional testing often does not account for the progress made by adult learners with limited educational experience or low literacy levels. Such learners tend to take longer to make smaller language gains, so the gains they make in other areas are often more significant. These gains may be in areas such as self-esteem, goal clarification, learning skills, access to employment, community involvement and further academic studies. The SCANS and EFF standards identify areas of student growth that are not necessarily language based. *All-Star* is correlated with both SCANS and EFF standards. Like the Student Book, the Workbook includes activities that provide documentation that can be added to a student portfolio.

About the Author and Series Consultants

Linda Lee is lead author on the *All-Star* series. Linda has taught ESL/ELT in the United States, Iran, and China, and has authored or co-authored a variety of successful textbook series for English learners. As a classroom instructor, Linda's most satisfying teaching experiences have been with adult ESL students at Roxbury Community College in Boston, Massachusetts.

Grace Tanaka is professor and coordinator of ESL at the Santa Ana College School of Continuing Education in Santa Ana, California, which serves more than 20,000 students per year. She is also a textbook co-author and series consultant. Grace has 25 years of teaching experience in both credit and non-credit ESL programs.

Shirley Velasco is principal at Miami Beach Adult and Community Education Center in Miami Beach, Florida. She has been a classroom instructor and administrator for the past 28 years. Shirley has created a large adult ESL program based on a curriculum she helped develop to implement state/national ESL standards.

Welcome to *All-Star*

Second Edition

All-Star is a four-level series featuring a "big picture" approach to meeting adult standards that systematically builds language and math skills around life-skill topics.

Complete Standards Coverage Using the "Big Picture" Approach

ACCESSIBLE, TWO-PAGE LESSON FORMAT follows an innovative layout with a list of activities labeled "Things to Do" on the left and picture-dictionary visuals on the right.

COMPREHENSIVE COVERAGE OF REVISED KEY standards, such as CASAS, Florida, Texas, LAUSD, and EFF, prepares students to master critical competencies.

PREDICTABLE UNIT STRUCTURE includes the same logical sequence of seven two-page lessons in each unit.

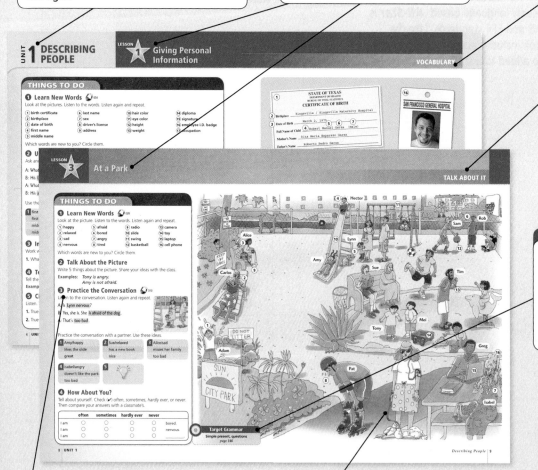

NEW

TARGET GRAMMAR point students to the Target Grammar Pages where they find manageable chunks of grammar with clear examples and plentiful follow up activities.

STRUCTURED SPEAKING ACTIVITIES invite students to discuss the picture dictionary scene, simulate real-life conversations, and express their thoughts and opinions.

"BIG PICTURE" SCENES are springboards to the lesson and to a wealth of all-skills expansion activities in the Teacher's Edition and *NEW* Work-Out CD-ROM.

NEW Comprehensive Grammar Program

 **DESCRIBING PEOPLE**

 **LESSON 1** Simple Present of *Be*, Statements pages 4–5

CAREFULLY SEQUENCED GRAMMAR covers grammar standards, and introduces, builds on, and practices grammar throughout the book and series.

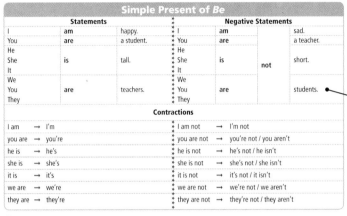

Simple Present of *Be*

Statements			Negative Statements			
I	am	happy.	I	am		sad.
You	are	a student.	You	are		a teacher.
He			He			
She	is	tall.	She	is	not	short.
It			It			
We			We			
You	are	teachers.	You	are		students.
They			They			

Contractions

I am	→	I'm	I am not	→	I'm not
you are	→	you're	you are not	→	you're not / you aren't
he is	→	he's	he is not	→	he's not / he isn't
she is	→	she's	she is not	→	she's not / she isn't
it is	→	it's	it is not	→	it's not / it isn't
we are	→	we're	we are not	→	we're not / we aren't
they are	→	they're	they are not	→	they're not / they aren't

GRAMMAR CHARTS with clear presentations and examples make it easy to learn the target grammar.

❶ Look at the driver's licenses. Complete the sentences with *is*, *isn't*, *are*, or *aren't*.

CONTEXTUALIZED GRAMMAR PRACTICE helps students internalize the grammar.

NEW YORK DRIVER LICENSE

EXPIRES: 03-31-13 7805067644 CLASS: 2

MAYRA HENDERSON
1359 OAK STREET
WHITE PLAINS, NY
10605

DOB: 03-31-72

HAIR: BLONDE EYES: BRN
HT: 5'6" WT: 135 LBS

Mayra Henderson

NEW YORK DRIVER LICENSE

EXPIRES: 08-26-13 7805067644 CLASS: 2

JANET M. GUAN
28 WHITEHALL DRIVE
BRONX, NY
10454

DOB: 08-26-80

HAIR: BRN EYES: BRN
HT: 5'4" WT: 120 LBS

Janet M. Guan

1. Janet ____is____ five feet two inches tall.
2. Janet's date of birth _____ 08-26-11.
6. Janet and Mayra _____ women.
7. Janet's last name _____ Guan.

NEW Work-Out CD-ROM with Interactive Activities and Complete Student Audio

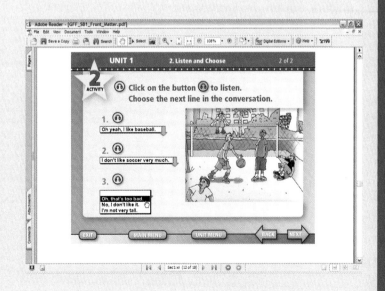

- Over 25 hours of listening, reading, writing, and grammar activities
- Voice record activities
- Entire student audio program MP3s for download

Integrated Skills with Enhanced Listening

REALIA-BASED READINGS AND NARRATIVE SELECTIONS such as maps, advertisements, descriptive paragraphs, and short stories provide the basis for developing reading skills.

NEW

LISTENING ACTIVITIES in every unit prepare students for a variety of situations and include the types of listening items found on the CASAS test.

ABUNDANT OPPORTUNITIES FOR WRITING prepare students for a variety of academic and real-world writing challenges, such as completing standard forms and writing complete sentences.

PRONUNCIATION INSTRUCTION AND PRACTICE helps students produce sounds in English and addresses issues of stress, rhythm, and intonation.

PRACTICE THE CONVERSATION ACTIVITIES invite students to engage in everyday conversations with their classmates, using the vocabulary and grammar they have learned.

LESSON 4 — Likes and Dislikes: Bio Poems

READING AND WRITING

THINGS TO DO

1 Learn New Words
Look at the pictures. Listen to the words. Listen again and repeat.
1. music
2. swimming
3. loud noises
4. soccer
5. baseball
6. housework
7. motorcycles
8. pets

2 Read and Take Notes
Listen to the poems. Then read the poems and take notes in the chart.

First name	Yuko	Paul	Abel
Description	brown hair, brown eyes, intelligent		
Likes	music, swimming, Japanese food		
Doesn't Like	pets, loud noises, the color yellow		
Languages	Japanese, English		
Occupation	student		
Last Name	Tanaka		

3 Write
Write a poem about someone you know. Read your poem to the class.

Yuko
my classmate
brown hair, brown eyes, intelligent
likes music, swimming, and Japanese food
doesn't like pets, loud noises, and the color yellow
speaks Japanese and English
a student
Tanaka

Paul
my friend
tall, slim, good-looking
likes cars, loud music, and soccer
doesn't like baseball, housework, and homework
speaks Chinese, French, and English
a student
Ho

LESSON 5 — Meeting People

CONVERSATIONS

1 Practice Pronunciation: Vowel Sounds in *Slip* and *Sleep*
We pronounce e, ea, and ee with a long vowel E sound when these sounds are in a stressed syllable. We usually pronounce i with a short vowel I sound.

A. Listen to the words. Listen again and repeat.
1. this
2. these
3. meet
4. live
5. fifth
6. leave
7. me
8. fit
9. feet
10. slim
11. slip
12. sleep
13. is
14. easy
15. he
16. his
Circle the words with the long vowel [E] sound.

B. Listen to the pairs of sentences. Listen again and repeat.
1. This is for you. / These are for you.
2. Did you slip yesterday? / Did you sleep yesterday?
3. I want to live. / I want to leave.
4. Is he shopping? / Easy shopping?

C. Listen as your partner says a sentence from each pair in Activity B. Circle the sentence you hear.
1. A. This is for you.
   B. These are for you.
2. A. Did you slip yesterday?
   B. Did you sleep yesterday?
3. A. I want to live.
   B. I want to leave.
4. A. Is he shopping?
   B. Easy shopping?

2 Practice the Conversation: Greeting a Friend
Listen to the conversation. Listen again and repeat.
A: Hi, David. How are you?
B: Fine, thanks. And you?
A: Not bad. How's your class?
B: Good. I like it.
Practice the conversation with a partner. Use these items.
1. How is it going? / Pretty good!
2. How are you doing? / Not too bad.
3. How are things? / Great, thanks.
4.

3 Practice the Conversation: Making Introductions
Listen to the conversation. Listen again and repeat.
A: Hello, Mr. Carter. How are you?
B: Fine, thanks. And you?
A: I'm very well, thank you. Mr. Carter, this is my friend Sally Smith.
B: How do you do, Ms. Smith?
C: How do you do, Mr. Carter? It's nice to meet you.
Practice the conversation with two partners. Use these items.
1. I'd like to introduce / It's a pleasure to
2. I want you to meet / I'm glad to
3. let me introduce / Nice to
4.

4 Practice the Conversation: Introducing Yourself
Listen to the conversation. Listen again and repeat.
A: Hi, my name is Paul. I live on the fifth floor.
B: Hi. Nice to meet you. I'm Cora. I live on the second floor.
A: Nice to meet you, Cora. Do you know Mary? She lives on the second floor, too.
B: Yes, I do. She's a good friend of mine.
Practice the conversation with a partner. Use these items.
1. Ted. I work on the second floor. / Meg. I work in the cafeteria. / Meg works in the cafeteria.
2. Sam. I'm in Mr. Reed's class. / Sara. I'm in Ms. Spender's class. / Sara is in Ms. Spender's class.
3. Carl. I'm from Mexico. / Mei. I'm from China. / Mei is from China.
4.

12 UNIT 1

Describing People 13

Real World Applications

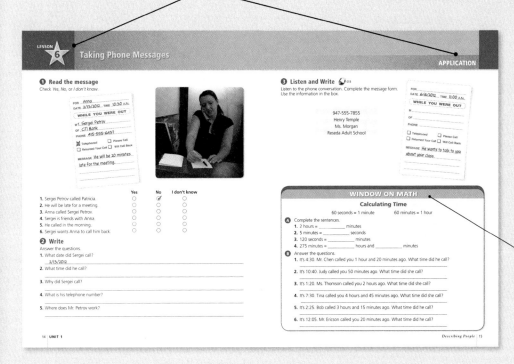

Multiple Opportunities for Assessment

CASAS LISTENING REVIEW helps teachers assess listening comprehension, while giving students practice with the item types and answer sheets they encounter on standardized tests.

GRAMMAR REVIEW provides an opportunity to assess and review the unit grammar point.

LISTENING DICTATION provides an opportunity to assess listening and writing.

LEARNING LOGS ask students to catalog the vocabulary, grammar, and life skills they have learned, and determine which areas they need to review.

WORKBOOK AND NEW WORK-OUT CD-ROM PRACTICE TESTS provide additional practice.

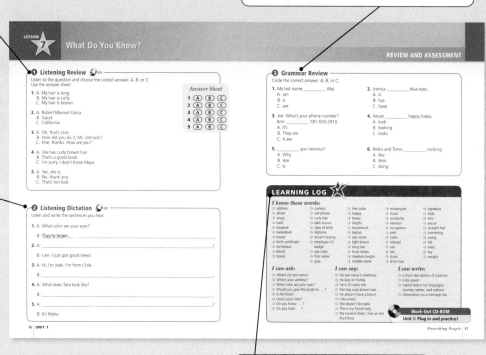

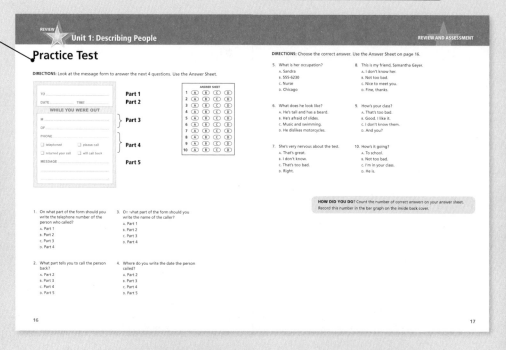

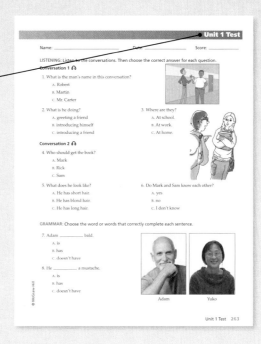

UNIT TEST in the Teacher's Edition rounds out the assessment program.

NEW Online Teacher Resource Center

- EZ Test Online bank of 500+ test questions for teachers to create customized tests.
- Study Guide reproducible worksheets support a portfolio-based approach to assessment.
- Persistence Kit includes reproducible worksheets that promote student goal setting and achievement.
- Interactive Correlations Chart allows teachers easy and immediate access to standards coverage in the *All-Star Second Edition* program.

❶ Practice the Conversation

Work with a partner. Practice the conversation. Tell about yourself.

A: Hi. My name is _____.

B: Hi. I'm _____.

A: Nice to meet you.

B: Nice to meet you, too.

Introduce yourself to 5 more classmates.

❷ Complete the Conversations 🎧 002

Use a question or sentence from the box to complete the conversations. Listen again and check your answers.

Useful Expressions

- Could you repeat that?
- How do you spell that? ✓
- What about you?
- What is _____ ?
- That's interesting!
- I'm sorry. I don't understand your question.

1. A: What's your name?

   B: Keiko.

   A: _____How do you spell that_____?

   B: K-e-i-k-o.

2. A: Where are you from?

   B: I'm from Mexico. _____?

   A: I'm from China.

3. A: What languages do you speak?

   B: Russian, French, and English.

   A: Really? _____!

4. A: Do you like to watch flicks?

   B: I'm not sure. _____ a flick?

   A: It is a movie.

   B: Then yes, I do.

5. A: Please turn to page 12.

   B: _____?

   A: Please turn to page 12.

6. A: Would you be interested in studying tomorrow?

   B: _____.

   A: Do you want to study with me tomorrow?

   B: Yes, thank you.

Work with a partner. Practice the conversations.

❸ Follow Instructions 003

Look at the pictures. Listen to the classroom instructions. Listen again and repeat.

1 Listen to the words.	**2** Say, "Hello."	**3** Write your name.	**4** Sign your name.

5 Check (✔) *True* or *False*.	**6** Take out a piece of paper.	**7** Practice the conversation.	**8** Raise your hand.

9 Underline the word.	**10** Circle the word.	**11** Hand in your homework.	**12** Listen and repeat.
	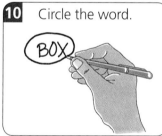		

Work with a partner. Take turns giving 5 instructions.

Example:

A: Raise your hand.

B: Write your name and then circle it.

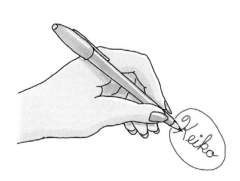

THINGS TO DO

❶ Learn New Words 004

Look at the pictures. Listen to the words. Listen again and repeat.

1. birth certificate
2. birthplace
3. date of birth
4. first name
5. middle name
6. last name
7. sex
8. driver's license
9. address
10. hair color
11. eye color
12. height
13. weight
14. diploma
15. signature
16. employee I.D. badge
17. occupation

Which words are new to you? Circle them.

❷ Use the Words

Ask and answer questions about Robert.

A: What's his last name ?

B: His last name is Garza .

A: What's his address ?

B: His address is 1521 Market Street .

Use these ideas.

1 first name	**2** date of birth	**3** height	**4** eye color
first name / ?	date of birth / ?	height / ?	eye color / ?
middle name	birthplace	weight	hair color
middle name / ?	birthplace / ?	weight / ?	hair color / ?

❸ Interview

Work with a partner. Ask the questions. Write your partner's answers.

1. What's your first name? **2.** What's your last name? **3.** What color are your eyes? **4.** What's your birthplace?

❹ Tell the Class

Tell the class about your partner. Use the information from Activity 3.

Example: *My partner's name is Gloria Ramirez. Her eyes are brown. Her birthplace is Mexico City.*

❺ Circle *True* or *False* 005

Listen. Then circle *True* or *False*.

1. True	False	**3.** True	False	**5.** True	False
2. True	False	**4.** True	False	**6.** True	False

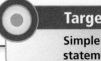

Target Grammar

Simple present of *be*, statements *page 144*

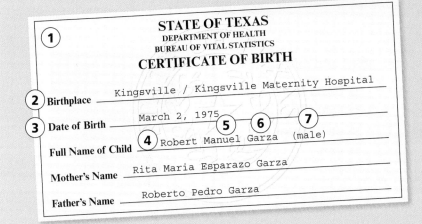

(1) STATE OF TEXAS
DEPARTMENT OF HEALTH
BUREAU OF VITAL STATISTICS
CERTIFICATE OF BIRTH

(2) Birthplace _Kingsville / Kingsville Maternity Hospital_

(3) Date of Birth _March 2, 1975_ **(5) (6) (7)**

Full Name of Child **(4)** _Robert Manuel Garza_ (male)

Mother's Name _Rita Maria Esparazo Garza_

Father's Name _Roberto Pedro Garza_

(16) SAN FRANCISCO GENERAL HOSPITAL

Robert Garza
(17) Nursing Assistant

(8) DMV CALIFORNIA DMV
DRIVER'S LICENSE
EXPIRES: 03-02-12   7805067644   CLASS: 2

ROBERT MANUEL GARZA
1521 MARKET STREET
SAN FRANCISCO, CA
94821   **(9)**

DOB: 03-02-75

(10)   **(11)**
HAIR: BRN   EYES: BRN
HT: 5'10"   WT: 160 LBS
(12)   **(13)**

Robert Garza

(14) Kingsville High School

Class of
1993
This diploma ia awarded to

Robert Manuel Garza

who has successfully completed the curriculum required by the
State of Texas Board of Education this 20th day of June, 1993.

(15)
Principal, Kingsville High School

💿 **Work-Out CD-ROM**
Unit 1: Plug in and practice!

Describing People | 5

Talking About People

THINGS TO DO

❶ Learn New Words 🎧 006

Look at the picture. Listen to the words. Listen again and repeat.

① long hair
② short hair
③ straight hair
④ curly hair
⑤ bald
⑥ beard
⑦ mustache
⑧ tall
⑨ medium height
⑩ short
⑪ slim
⑫ heavy
⑬ blond
⑭ light brown
⑮ dark brown
⑯ gray

Which words are new to you? Circle them.

❷ Listen and Write 🎧 007

Listen. Write the correct name under each picture.

1. Robert
2. Lisa
3. Estela
4. Rick
5. Dan
6. Paul
7. Sam

❸ Practice the Conversation 🎧 008

Listen to the conversation. Listen again and repeat.

A: Would you give this book to Robert ?

B: I'm sorry. I don't know Robert .

A: He has a mustache . You can't miss him.

B: A mustache ?

A: Right.

Practice the conversation with a partner. Ask about these people.

1 Dan	2 Rick	3 Sam	4 Paul
Dan	Rick	Sam	Paul
He's tall and heavy.	He's bald.	He has long hair.	He is very tall and slim.
Tall and heavy	Bald	Long hair	Tall and slim

❹ Write

Write a sentence about a classmate. Then read it to the class and ask, "Who is it?"

Example: *This person is tall. He has short, straight brown hair and brown eyes. Who is it?*

Target Grammar

Simple present of *have*, statements *page 145*

Robert

At a Park

THINGS TO DO

① Learn New Words 🎧 009

Look at the picture. Listen to the words. Listen again and repeat.

① happy	⑤ afraid	⑨ radio	⑬ camera
② relaxed	⑥ bored	⑩ slide	⑭ toy
③ sad	⑦ angry	⑪ swing	⑮ laptop
④ nervous	⑧ tired	⑫ basketball	⑯ cell phone

Which words are new to you? Circle them.

② Talk About the Picture

Write 5 things about the picture. Share your ideas with the class.

Examples: *Tony is angry.*
Amy is not afraid.

③ Practice the Conversation 🎧 010

Listen to the conversation. Listen again and repeat.

A: Is Lynn nervous?

B: Yes, she is. She is afraid of the dog.

A: That's too bad.

Practice the conversation with a partner. Use these ideas.

1 Amy/happy	**2** Sue/relaxed	**3** Alice/sad
likes the slide	has a new book	misses her family
great	nice	too bad

4 Isabel/angry	**5** 
doesn't like the park	
too bad	

④ How About You?

Tell about yourself. Check (✔) *often*, *sometimes*, *hardly ever*, or *never*.
Then compare your answers with a classmate's.

	often	sometimes	hardly ever	never	
I am	○	○	○	○	bored.
I am	○	○	○	○	nervous.
I am	○	○	○	○	_____.

Target Grammar

Simple present, questions
page 146

Likes and Dislikes: Bio Poems

THINGS TO DO

❶ Learn New Words 011

Look at the pictures. Listen to the words. Listen again and repeat.

① music
② swimming
③ loud noises
④ soccer
⑤ baseball
⑥ housework
⑦ motorcycles
⑧ pets

❷ Read and Take Notes 🎧 012

Listen to the poems. Then read the poems and take notes in the chart.

First name	Yuko	Paul	Abel
Description	brown hair, brown eyes, intelligent		
Likes	music, swimming, Japanese food		
Doesn't Like	pets, loud noises, the color yellow		
Languages	Japanese, English		
Occupation	student		
Last Name	Tanaka		

❸ Write

Write a poem about someone you know. Read your poem to the class.

Line 1—the person's first name or given name

Line 2—the person's relation to you

Line 3—three adjectives that describe the person

Line 4—three things the person likes

Line 5—three things the person doesn't like

Line 6—languages the person speaks

Line 7—the person's occupation

Line 8—the person's last name or family name

Target Grammar

Simple present, statements *page 148*

Yuko
my classmate
brown hair, brown eyes, intelligent
likes music, swimming, and Japanese food
doesn't like pets, loud noises, and the color yellow
speaks Japanese and English
a student
Tanaka

1

3

2

4

Paul
my friend
tall, slim, good-looking
likes cars, loud music, and soccer
doesn't like baseball, housework, and homework
speaks Chinese, French, and English
a student
Ho

5

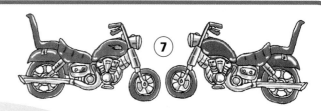

6

7

Abel
my husband
tall, dark, handsome
likes cameras, motorcycles, and good food
doesn't like American coffee, alarm clocks, and pets
speaks Spanish and English
a businessperson
Diaz

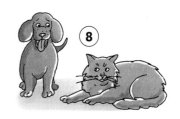

8

Meeting People

❶ Practice Pronunciation: Vowel Sounds in *Slip* and *Sleep* 013

We pronounce e, *ea*, and *ee* with a long vowel E sound when these sounds are in a stressed syllable. We usually pronounce *i* with a short vowel I sound.

A. Listen to the words. Listen again and repeat.

①	this	⑤	fifth	⑨	feet	⑬	is
②	these	⑥	leave	⑩	slim	⑭	easy
③	meet	⑦	me	⑪	slip	⑮	he
④	live	⑧	fit	⑫	sleep	⑯	his

Circle the words with the long vowel [E] sound.

B. Listen to the pairs of sentences. Listen again and repeat. 014

1. This is for you.   These are for you.
2. Did you slip yesterday?   Did you sleep yesterday?
3. I want to live.   I want to leave.
4. Is he shopping?   Easy shopping?

C. Listen as your partner says a sentence from each pair in Activity B. Circle the sentence you hear.

1. A. This is for you.
  B. These are for you.

2. A. Did you slip yesterday?
  B. Did you sleep yesterday?

3. A. I want to live.
  B. I want to leave.

4. A. Is he shopping?
  B. Easy shopping?

❷ Practice the Conversation: Greeting a Friend 015

Listen to the conversation. Listen again and repeat.

A: Hi, David. How are you ?

B: Fine, thanks . And you?

A: Not bad. How's your class?

B: Good. I like it.

Practice the conversation with a partner. Use these items.

1 How is it going?
  Pretty good!

2 How are you doing?
  Not too bad.

3 How are things?
  Great, thanks.

4

❸ Practice the Conversation: Making Introductions 016

Listen to the conversation. Listen again and repeat.

A: Hello, Mr. Carter. How are you?

B: Fine, thanks. And you?

A: I'm very well, thank you. Mr. Carter, this is my
friend Sally Smith.

B: How do you do, Ms. Smith?

C: How do you do, Mr. Carter? It's nice to meet you.

Practice the conversation with two partners. Use these items.

1 I'd like to introduce	**2** I want you to meet	**3** let me introduce	**4**
It's a pleasure to	I'm glad to	Nice to	

❹ Practice the Conversation: Introducing Yourself 017

Listen to the conversation. Listen again and repeat.

A: Hi, my name is Paul. I live on the fifth floor.

B: Hi. Nice to meet you. I'm Cora. I live on the second floor.

A: Nice to meet you, Cora. Do you know Mary?
She lives on the second floor, too.

B: Yes, I do. She's a good friend of mine.

Practice the conversation with a partner. Use these items.

1 Ted. I work on the second floor.	**2** Sam. I'm in Mr. Reed's class.	**3** Carl. I'm from Mexico.	**4**
Meg. I work in the cafeteria.	Sara. I'm in Ms. Spender's class.	Mei. I'm from China.	
Meg/works in the cafeteria	Sara/is in Ms. Spender's class	Mei/is from China	

❶ Read the message

Check *Yes*, *No*, or *I don't know*.

FOR __Anna__
DATE __2/13/2012__ TIME __10:30__ A.M.

WHILE YOU WERE OUT

Mr. __Sergei Petrov__
OF __CTI Bank__
PHONE __415-555-6437__

☒ Telephoned   ☐ Please Call
☐ Returned Your Call ☐ Will Call Back

MESSAGE __He will be 20 minutes__
__late for the meeting.__

	Yes	No	I don't know
1. Sergei Petrov called Patricia.	○	✓	○
2. He will be late for a meeting.	○	○	○
3. Anna called Sergei Petrov.	○	○	○
4. Sergei is friends with Anna.	○	○	○
5. He called in the morning.	○	○	○
6. Sergei wants Anna to call him back.	○	○	○

❷ Write

Answer the questions.

1. What date did Sergei call?

   __2/13/2012__

2. What time did he call?

_____

3. Why did Sergei call?

_____

4. What is his telephone number?

_____

5. Where does Mr. Petrov work?

_____

③ Listen and Write 🎧 018

Listen to the phone conversation. Complete the message form. Use the information in the box.

947-555-7855
Henry Temple
Ms. Morgan
Reseda Adult School

FOR _____

DATE _6/6/2012_ TIME _11:00_ A.M.

WHILE YOU WERE OUT

M _____

OF _____

PHONE _____

☐ Telephoned   ☐ Please Call

☐ Returned Your Call ☐ Will Call Back

MESSAGE _He wants to talk to you_
about your class.

WINDOW ON MATH

Calculating Time

60 seconds = 1 minute   60 minutes = 1 hour

A Complete the sentences.

1. 2 hours = _____ minutes

2. 5 minutes = _____ seconds

3. 120 seconds = _____ minutes

4. 275 minutes = _____ hours and _____ minutes

B Answer the questions.

1. It's 4:30. Mr. Chen called you 1 hour and 20 minutes ago. What time did he call?

_____

2. It's 10:40. Judy called you 50 minutes ago. What time did she call?

_____

3. It's 1:20. Ms. Thomson called you 2 hours ago. What time did she call?

_____

4. It's 7:30. Tina called you 4 hours and 45 minutes ago. What time did she call?

_____

5. It's 2:25. Bob called 3 hours and 15 minutes ago. What time did he call?

_____

6. It's 12:05. Mr. Ericson called you 20 minutes ago. What time did he call?

_____

What Do You Know?

❶ Listening Review 🎧 019

Listen to the question and choose the correct answer: *A, B,* or *C.*
Use the answer sheet.

1. A. My hair is long.
   B. My hair is curly.
   C. My hair is brown.

2. A. Robert Manuel Garza
   B. Garza
   C. California

3. A. Oh, that's nice.
   B. How did you do it, Ms. Johnson?
   C. Fine, thanks. How are you?

4. A. She has curly brown hair.
   B. That's a good book.
   C. I'm sorry. I don't know Maya.

5. A. Yes, she is.
   B. No, thank you.
   C. That's too bad.

Answer Sheet

1 Ⓐ Ⓑ Ⓒ
2 Ⓐ Ⓑ Ⓒ
3 Ⓐ Ⓑ Ⓒ
4 Ⓐ Ⓑ Ⓒ
5 Ⓐ Ⓑ Ⓒ

❷ Listening Dictation 🎧 020

Listen and write the sentences you hear.

1. A: What color are your eyes?

   B: They're brown. _____

2. A: _____ !

   B: I am. I just got good news!

3. A: Hi, I'm José. I'm from Chile.

   B: _____ .

4. A: What does Tara look like?

   B: _____ .

5. A: _____ ?

   B: It's Maria.

3 Grammar Review

Circle the correct answer: *A*, *B*, or *C*.

1. My last name _____ Abji.
  A. am
  B. is
  C. are

2. Joshua _____ blue eyes.
  A. is
  B. has
  C. have

3. Joe: What's your phone number?
  Ann: _____ 781-555-2910.
  A. It's
  B. They are
  C. It are

4. Aman _____ happy today.
  A. look
  B. looking
  C. looks

5. _____ you nervous?
  A. Why
  B. Are
  C. Is

6. Reiko and Tomo _____ cooking.
  A. like
  B. likes
  C. liking

LEARNING LOG

I know these words:

- address
- afraid
- angry
- bald
- baseball
- basketball
- beard
- birth certificate
- birthplace
- blond
- bored

- camera
- cell phone
- curly hair
- dark brown
- date of birth
- diploma
- driver's license
- employee I.D. badge
- eye color
- first name
- gray

- hair color
- happy
- heavy
- height
- housework
- laptop
- last name
- light brown
- long hair
- loud noises
- medium height
- middle name

- motorcycle
- music
- mustache
- nervous
- occupation
- pets
- radio
- relaxed
- sad
- sex
- short
- short hair

- signature
- slide
- slim
- soccer
- straight hair
- swimming
- swing
- tall
- tired
- toy
- weight

I can ask:

- What's his last name?
- What's your address?
- What color are your eyes?
- Would you give this book to . . . ?
- Is Pat tired?
- How's your class?
- Do you know . . . ?
- Do you have . . . ?

I can say:

- His last name is Martinez.
- He lives in Florida.
- He is 35 years old.
- She has curly brown hair.
- He doesn't have a beard.
- I like music.
- She doesn't like pets.
- This is my friend Sally.
- My name is Peter. I live on the third floor.

I can write:

- a short description of a person
- a bio poem
- capital letters for languages, country names, and cultures
- information on a message slip

Work-Out CD-ROM

Unit 1: Plug in and practice!

THINGS TO DO

1 Learn New Words 🎧 021

Look at the pictures. Listen to the words. Listen again and repeat. Which words are new to you? Circle them.

2 Listen and Write 🎧 022

Look at the pictures. Listen and write the names.

1. _____Pat_____ 4. _____ 7. _____
2. _____ 5. _____ 8. _____
3. _____ 6. _____ 9. _____

3 Practice the Conversation 🎧 023

Talk about the people in the pictures.

A: Where's Carlos ?

B: He's at the post office .

A: What's he doing?

B: He's buying stamps .

A: Where's Sue ?

B: She's at the bank .

A: What's she doing?

B: She's cashing a check .

Practice the conversation with a partner. Use the ideas below.

1 Sue	2 Ana	3 Tom
bank / cashing a check	drugstore / buying medicine	library / studying

4 Janet	5 Laura	6
library / checking out books	supermarket / buying groceries	💡

4 Interview

Ask a partner these questions. Record your partner's answers.

Example: *A: How often do you buy stamps?*
B: A few times a year.

How often do you _____?	Every day	Every week	Every month	A few times a year
buy stamps	○	○	○	○
buy groceries	○	○	○	○
cash a check	○	○	○	○
see a doctor	○	○	○	○

Tell the class about your partner.

① Library

Tom   Janet

② study   ③ check out book▶

⑪ Drugstore

PRESCRIPTION PICK UP   Ana

⑫ buy medicine

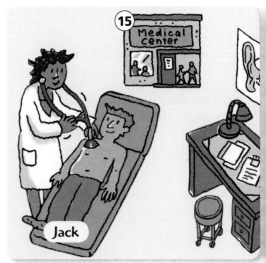

⑮ Medical Center

Jack

⑯ see a doctor

Target Grammar
Present continuous *page 150*

(7) mail packages

(4) Post Office

Barb

U.S.MAIL

Carlos

Maria

(5) buy stamps   (6) mail letters

(8) Bank

Lee

Sue

(9) get cash   (10) cash a check

(13) Supermarket

Laura

Sofia

(14) buy groceries

(17) Community Center

Emily

Luz

Greg

(18) socialize   (19) take classes

(20) Restaurant

Pat

Pamela

(21) get something to drink   (22) get something to eat

Work-Out CD-ROM

Unit 2: Plug in and practice!

Going Places | 19

THINGS TO DO

❶ Learn New Words 🎧 024

Listen to the words. Find the places on the map. Listen again and repeat.

On a map
1. avenue
2. boulevard
3. block
4. street

Describing location
5. on the corner of
6. between
7. next to
8. across from

Giving directions
9. go north
10. go east
11. go south
12. go west
13. take a right
14. take a left
15. go straight

Which words are new to you? Circle them.

❷ Circle *True* or *False* 🎧 025

Listen to the sentences. Look at the map. Circle *True* or *False*.

1. True False
2. True False
3. True False
4. True False
5. True False
6. True False
7. True False
8. True False

❸ Practice the Conversation 🎧 026

Listen to the conversation. Listen again and repeat.

A: Excuse me. Where's the fire station?

B: It's on Adams Boulevard between Diamond and Elm.

A: How do I get there from the Medical Center?

B: Just go north on Elm and take a left on Adams.

A: Thank you!

Practice the conversation with a partner. Ask about these places on the map.

1. community center
2. city bank
3. super-market
4. restaurant
5.

❹ Ask Questions

Work with a partner. Ask and answer questions about the map.

Examples:
A: Where's the library?
B: It's on River Street.
A: How do I get to the drugstore from the hotel?
B: Go west on Green Avenue and take a right on River Street.

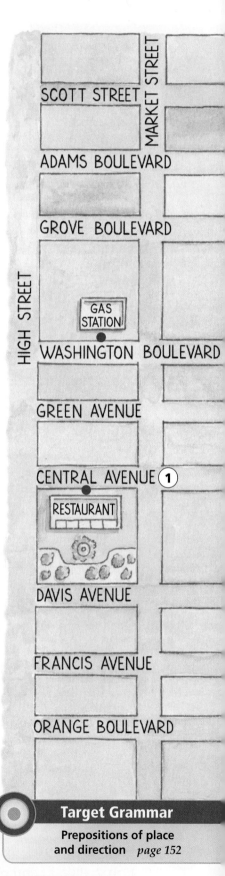

Target Grammar

Prepositions of place and direction *page 152*

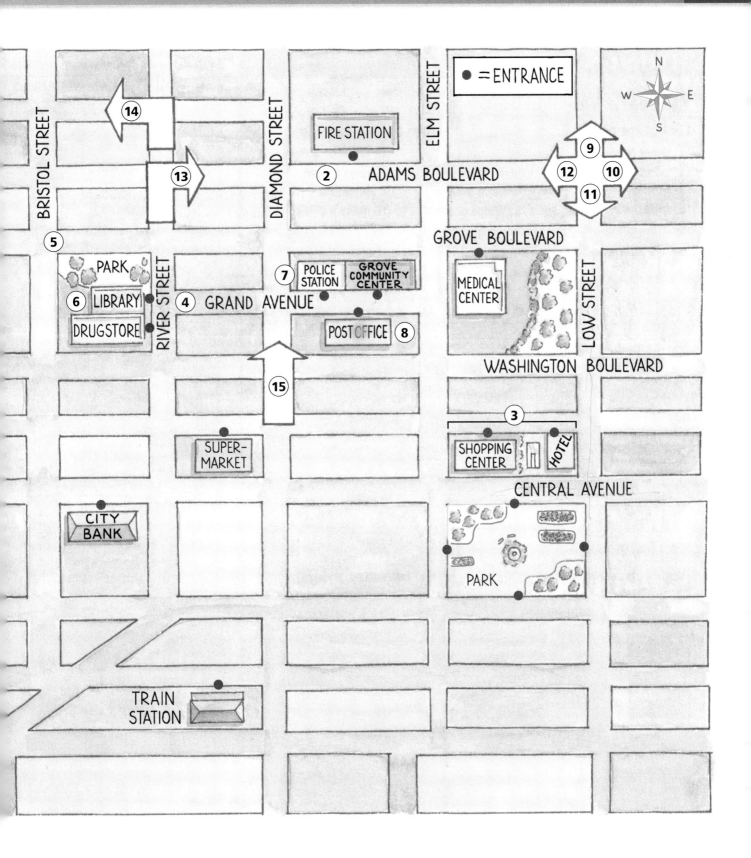

At a Train Station

TRAIN SCHEDULE

Washington ...... 10:30 ..... Track 3
Philadelphia ..... 10:42 ..... Track 8
New York .... 10:45 ..... Track 1
Boston .... 10:50 ..... Track

THINGS TO DO

① Learn New Words 027

Look at the picture. Listen to the words. Listen again and repeat.

- ① ticket machine
- ② ticket office
- ③ platform
- ④ track
- ⑤ snack bar
- ⑥ newsstand
- ⑦ information desk
- ⑧ waiting area
- ⑨ baggage check
- ⑩ buy a ticket
- ⑪ wait for a train
- ⑫ read a train schedule
- ⑬ make a phone call

Which words and phrases are new to you? Circle them.

❷ Talk About the Picture

Work with a partner. Look at the picture. Ask and answer questions.

Examples:

A: *Where is Mrs. Hassan?*
B: *She's at the information desk.*

A: *Who is at the snack bar?*
B: *David.*

❸ Practice the Conversation 028

Listen to the conversation. Listen again and repeat.

A: Excuse me. Where can I buy a ticket ?

B: At the ticket office .

A: Where's the ticket office ?

B: It's over there, next to the ticket machine .

Practice the conversation with a partner. Use the picture and the ideas below.

1 get a train schedule	**2** buy a newspaper	**3** get the train to Washington
At the information desk.	At the newsstand.	On Track 3.
the information desk ?	the newsstand ?	Track 3 ?

4 check my luggage	**5** get something to eat	**6**
At the baggage check.	At the snack bar.	
the baggage check ?	the snack bar ?	

Target Grammar

Wh- questions review   *page 154*

Train Maps and Schedules

THINGS TO DO

❶ Check *True* or *False*

Look at the rail map. Check (✔) *True* or *False*.
Read the statements.

	True	False
1. Irvine is south of L.A.*—Union Station.	○	○
2. Covina is west of L.A.—Union Station.	○	○
3. The San Bernardino Line runs north and south.	○	○
4. El Monte is directly east of Baldwin Park.	○	○
5. Irvine is far from Montalvo.	○	○
6. Sun Valley is near Downtown Burbank.	○	○

Work in a small group. Compare answers and correct the false statements.

*Note: L.A. = Los Angeles

A commuter train

❷ Read and Write

Read the train schedule. Answer the questions.

1. It's 7:00 in the morning, and Carl is waiting at Irvine station for a train to L.A. (Union Station). When is the next train?

_____

2. It's 7:30 in the morning, and Yun is sitting on train #683. Where is he now?_____

3. How long does it take to get from Irvine to Orange on train #601?

_____

4. How long does it take to get from Oceanside to L.A. (Union Station) on train #603?_____

5. Which train is faster, #603 or #605?_____

❸ Write

Write two true sentences and two false sentences about the map and schedule. Read your sentences to the class. Ask your classmates to identify and correct the false statements.

Examples: *The #683 train leaves Oceanside at 5:56.*   (false)
    L.A. County is north of Orange County.   (true)

WRITING TIP

We use a capital letter at the beginning of names of places.

■ Orange County ■ Burbank Airport ■ Los Angeles

Counties in Southern California

Target Grammar

Prepositions of time *page 155*

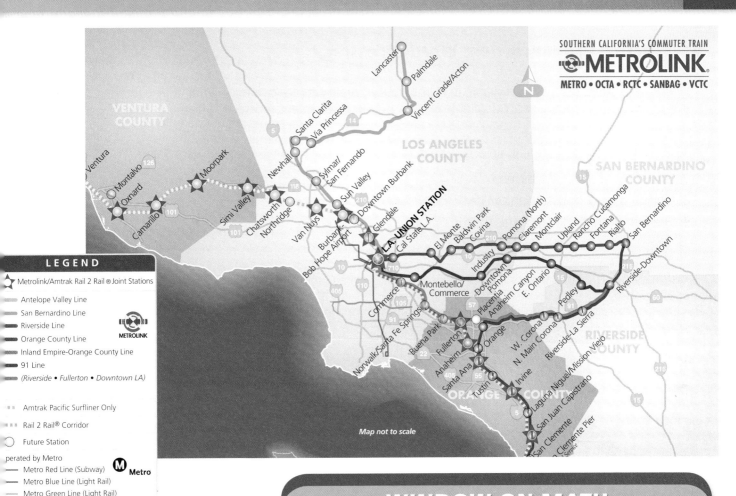

LEGEND

- ★ Metrolink/Amtrak Rail 2 Rail® Joint Stations
- Antelope Valley Line
- San Bernardino Line
- Riverside Line
- Orange County Line
- Inland Empire-Orange County Line
- 91 Line
- *(Riverside • Fullerton • Downtown LA)*
- ⋯ Amtrak Pacific Surfliner Only
- ⋯ Rail 2 Rail® Corridor
- ○ Future Station

Operated by Metro
- Metro Red Line (Subway)
- Metro Blue Line (Light Rail)
- Metro Green Line (Light Rail)
- Metro Gold Line (Light Rail)
- Metro Purple Line (Subway)

Southern California Regional Rail Authority

metrolinktrains.com

SOUTHERN CALIFORNIA'S COMMUTER TRAIN
METROLINK®
METRO • OCTA • RCTC • SANBAG • VCTC

Map not to scale

Train Schedule/Orange County

	601	603	605	683
Oceanside	4:47a	5:22a	5:56a	-
San Clemente	5:07a	5:43a	6:16a	-
San Juan Capistrano	5:16a	5:52a	6:25a	-
Laguna Niguel	5:23a	5:59a	6:30a	-
Irvine	5:33a	6:09a	6:40a	7:05a
Tustin	5:39a	6:15a	6:46a	7:12a
Santa Ana	5:46a	6:22a	6:53a	7:18a
Orange	5:51a	6:27a	6:57a	7:23a
Anaheim	5:55a	6:31a	7:01a	7:27a
Fullerton	6:02a	6:39a	7:09a	7:35a
Norwalk/S.F. Springs	L6:12a	L6:48a	L7:18a	L7:44a
Commerce	-	L6:58a	L7:28a	-
L.A. (Union Station)	6:40a	7:20a	7:50a	8:13a

Train may leave up to five minutes ahead of schedule.

WINDOW ON MATH

Talking About Distance

1 foot = 12 inches	1 inch = 2.54 centimeters	1 meter = 39.37 inches
1 yard = 3 feet	1 foot = 30.48 centimeters	1 meter = 1.09 yards
1 mile = 5280 feet	1 mile = 1.6 kilometers	1 kilometer = 0.62 miles

A Read the information. Then write the answers on the lines.

1. 24 inches = _____ feet
2. 36 inches = _____ yard
3. 25.4 centimeters = _____ inches
4. 100 miles = _____ kilometers

B Read the sentences. Answer the questions.

1. Chatsworth is 50 kilometers from Los Angeles. How many miles is it to Los Angeles? _____

2. Tony walks .8 miles to the Fontana train station every day. Then he takes the train for 8.7 miles to the San Bernadino station. When he gets to San Bernadino, he walks .5 miles to the school.

   How far is Tony's house from the school? _____ miles

   How many kilometers does he travel? _____

Getting Travel Information

❶ Practice Pronunciation: Word Stress 029

We put the stress on the first syllable in numbers that are multiples of ten (twenty, thirty, forty).
We put the stress on the second syllable in teen numbers (thirteen, fourteen, fifteen).

A. Listen to the words. Listen again and repeat.

1. thirty	thirteen	**5.** seventy	seventeen
2. forty	fourteen	**6.** eighty	eighteen
3. fifty	fifteen	**7.** ninety	nineteen
4. sixty	sixteen		

Listen as your partner says one of the words in each pair. Circle the word you hear. 030

B. Listen to the conversations. Circle the correct time or number.

1. a. 10:15	b. 10:50	**5.** a. 16	b. 60
2. a. 9:13	b. 9:30	**6.** a. 8:15	b. 8:50
3. a. 12:14	b. 12:40	**7.** a. 17	b. 70
4. a. 6:13	b. 6:30	**8.** a. 14	b. 40

❷ Read and Write

Match the times with the clocks. Then practice saying the times.

a. 5:15
b. 6:10
c. 3:20
d. 9:30
e. 1:10
f. 11:45

It's 9:30.

1. _____9:30_____   **2.** _____   **3.** _____

4. _____   **5.** _____   **6.** _____

❸ Practice the Conversation: Buying a Ticket 031

Listen to the conversation. Listen again and repeat.

A: I'd like a one-way ticket to Irvine, please.

B: Did you say one-way?

A: Yes, that's right.

B: That's $12.50, please.

A: Okay. When's the next train?

B: 5:15.

A: 5:50?

B: No. 5:15.

A: Okay. Thanks.

One-way

Chicago
↓
Los Angeles

Round-trip

Chicago
⟳
Los Angeles

Practice the conversation with a partner. Use these items.

1 a round-trip ticket to Chicago	**2** a one-way ticket to San Diego	**3** a round-trip ticket to Houston	**4** 
round-trip / $14.50 / 3:13	one-way / $18.60 / 2:15	round-trip / $70.50 / 4:40	
3:30	2:50	4:14	
3:13	2:15	4:40	

❹ Practice the Conversation: Asking for Travel Information  032

Listen to the conversation. Listen again and repeat.

A: Is the 9:00 o'clock bus on time?

B: No, it's about 15 minutes late.

A: How late?

B: 15 minutes.

A: Okay. Which platform will it be on?

B: Number 5.

A: Okay, thanks.

B: You're welcome.

Bus Schedule

Departure Schedule for Saturday, February 7

Departs	Arrives	Duration	Transfers	Platform
01:00a	03:45a	2h, 45m	0	9
03:00a	05:30a	2h, 30m	0	8
05:15a	08:55a	3h, 40m	0	3
06:00a	08:30a	2h, 30m	0	7
06:40a	09:50a	3h, 10m	0	6
07:00a	09:30a	2h, 30m	0	
08:00a	10:30a	2h, 30m	0	2
09:00a	11:59a	2h, 59m	0	5
09:30a	12:10p	2h, 40m	0	4
11:00a	01:30p	2h, 30m	0	
12:00p	02:10p	2h, 10m	0	1

Practice the conversation with a partner. Use these items.

1 7:00 o'clock	**2** 12:00 o'clock	**3** 11 o'clock	**4** 5:15	**5** 
an hour / An hour / I don't know	/ 20 minutes / Number 1	/ 30 minutes / I don't know	/ 45 minutes / Number 3	

LESSON 6

Locating Community Agencies

① Answer the Questions

Read the questions below and look for the answers in the telephone directory on page 29.

1. You are new in town, and you want to get a library card. What is the address of the library?

_____

2. You want to know when the post office on Cross Blvd. closes today. What telephone number should you call?

_____

3. You want to know which bus stops near the medical center. What number should you call?

_____

4. You want to take the exam to get a driver's license. Where should you go?

_____

5. You see a fire in a trash can in the park. What number should you call?

_____

6. A dog bites you. What number should you call to report the dog?

_____

7. You want to find out the hours of the post office on S. Main St. What number should you call?

_____

8. People drive very fast on your street. You think it's dangerous. What number should you call?

_____

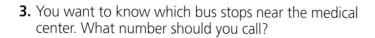
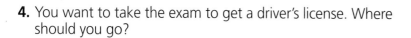
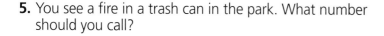
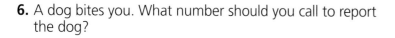
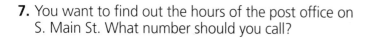

TELEPHONE DIRECTORY

ALTON-CITY OF

AMBULANCE
Emergency Only 911

FIRE DEPT.   17 City Plaza
To Report a Fire 911
Fire Chief 718-555-5940

LIBRARY   2258 N. Main St.
Hours 718-555-5849
Information Desk 718-555-3476

MEDICAL CENTER   140 Lincoln Ave.
General Information 718-555-9685

POLICE DEPT.   40 City Plaza
Emergency Only 911
Citizen Complaint Line 718-555-9685
Dog Officer 718-555-5746
Domestic Violence 718-555-6958
General Business 718-555-6954

PUBLIC WORKS DEPT.   594 S. Main St.
Parks and Recreation 718-555-5584

TRANSIT AUTHORITY   121 Hillside Rd.
Bus Travel 718-555-9887
Metrolink 718-555-4665

STATE GOVERNMENT
DEPT. OF MOTOR VEHICLES   601 Oak St.
Licensing Exam Office 718-555-7477

U.S. (FEDERAL) GOVERNMENT
SOCIAL SECURITY ADMINISTRATION
453 S. Main St.
Information 718-555-9329

U.S. POSTAL SERVICE
Washington Square 718-555-6845
459 S. Main St. 718-555-9445
1198 Cross Blvd. 718-555-9347

We often use abbreviations in the phone book.
- St. = Street
- Rd. = Road
- Ave. = Avenue
- Blvd. = Boulevard
- N. = North
- S. = South
- E. = East
- W. = West
- Dept. = Department

2 Write

Look in your telephone directory. Find the addresses and telephone numbers for these services in your town or city.

AMBULANCE _____

FIRE DEPARTMENT _____

LIBRARY _____

POLICE EMERGENCY _____

POST OFFICE _____

What Do You Know?

❶ Listening Review 🎧 033

Look at the pictures and listen. Choose the correct answer: *A, B,* or *C*.
Use the Answer Sheet.

1. A   B   C

2. A   B   C

3. A 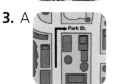 B   C

4. A   B   C

5. A   B   C

Answer Sheet

1	Ⓐ	Ⓑ	Ⓒ
2	Ⓐ	Ⓑ	Ⓒ
3	Ⓐ	Ⓑ	Ⓒ
4	Ⓐ	Ⓑ	Ⓒ
5	Ⓐ	Ⓑ	Ⓒ

❷ Listening Dictation 🎧 034

Listen. Write the words you hear.

1. A: Excuse me, where's the bank?

B: It's on Main St. .

2. A: Where's Tina? the

B: she is at the library she is studing .

3. A: What time does the train arrive in New York?

B: it arrives 4:50 .

4. A: Can I help you?

B: yes I'd like a one way ticket to sendueg a place .

5. A: How do I get to the drack a sfoor ?

B: Just go south on Elm Street and take a left on Center Street.

❸ Grammar Review

Circle the correct answer: *A*, *B*, or *C*.

1. Jenna _____ groceries.

A. buying
B. is buy
C. is buying

2. _____ is the police station?

A. When
B. Where
C. Who

3. Joe: _____ is he doing?
Ann: He's buying stamps.

A. What
B. Where
C. When

4. The restaurant is _____ the bank.

A. next to
B. between
C. on the corner of

5. Just go north on Oak Street
and _____ on River Street.

A. take right
B. take a right
C. right turn

6. The train leaves _____ 4:00.

A. in
B. on
C. at

LEARNING LOG

I know these words:

- across from
- avenue
- baggage check
- bank
- between
- block
- boulevard
- buy a ticket
- buy groceries
- buy medicine
- buy stamps
- cash a check
- check out books
- community center
- drugstore
- get cash
- get something to drink
- get something to eat
- go east
- go north
- go south
- go straight
- go west
- information desk
- library
- mail letters
- mail packages
- make a phone call
- medical center
- newsstand
- next to
- on the corner of
- one way
- platform
- post office
- read a train schedule
- restaurant
- round trip
- see a doctor
- snack bar
- socialize
- street
- study
- supermarket
- take a left
- take a right
- take classes
- ticket machine
- ticket office
- track
- wait for a train
- waiting area

I can ask:

- Where's Jack?
- What is she doing?
- How often do you buy groceries?
- Where can I buy a train ticket?
- Where's the library?
- How do I get there?
- Who is at the snack bar?
- When's the next train?
- Is the bus on time?
- Which platform will it be on?

I can say:

- He is studying at the library now.
- The fire station is on Adams Boulevard.
- Go north on Main and take your first right.
- Take a left on Grove Street.
- He's at the information desk.
- I'd like a one-way ticket, please.

I can write:

- schedule information
- capital letters for names of places
- an emergency telephone list

Work-Out CD-ROM

Unit 2: Plug in and practice!

THINGS TO DO

1 Learn New Words 035

Look at the pictures. Listen to the words. Listen again and repeat.

1. groceries
2. recreation
3. toiletries
4. bus fare
5. car repairs
6. car payments
7. rent
8. utilities
9. gas
10. electricity
11. cash
12. credit card
13. personal check
14. money order
15. electronic debit

Which words are new to you? Circle them.

2 Listen and Write 036

Listen. How much did Lei spend last month? Fill in the chart.

How much did Lei spend on ____ last month?	$$$ a lot	$$ an average amount	$ not very much
groceries	○	○	○
recreation	○	○	○
toiletries	○	○	○
bus fare	○	○	○
rent	○	○	○

3 Interview

Work with a partner. Ask the questions. Tell the class about your partner.

Example: *My partner spent a lot on groceries last month, but he didn't spend very much on recreation.*

How much did you spend on ____ last month?	$$$ a lot	$$ an average amount	$ not very much
groceries	○	○	○
recreation	○	○	○
toiletries	○	○	○
bus fare	○	○	○
rent	○	○	○

Target Grammar

Simple past, statements *page 156*

Personal Expenses

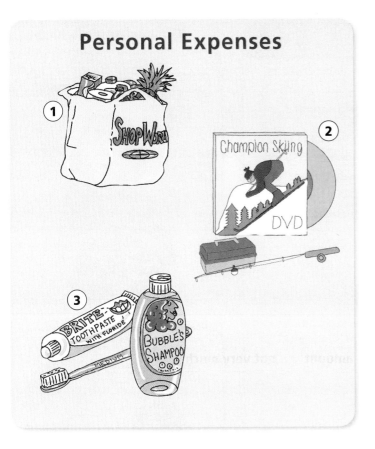

Transportation Expenses

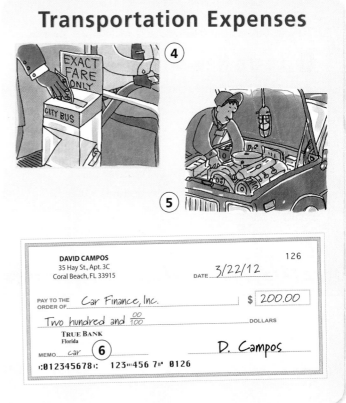

DAVID CAMPOS
35 Hay St., Apt. 3C
Coral Beach, FL 33915
DATE 3/22/12
126

PAY TO THE
ORDER OF Car Finance, Inc. $ 200.00

Two hundred and 00/100 DOLLARS

TRUE BANK
Florida

MEMO car (6) D. Campos
⑈012345678⑈ 123⑈456 7⑈ 0126

Housing Expenses

DAVID CAMPOS
35 Hay St., Apt. 3C
Coral Beach, FL 33915
DATE 3/22/12
127

PAY TO THE
ORDER OF Ace Management Co. $ 600.00

Six hundred and 00/100 DOLLARS

TRUE BANK
Florida

MEMO rent (7) D. Campos
⑈012345678⑈ 123⑈456 7⑈ 0127

Ways to Pay

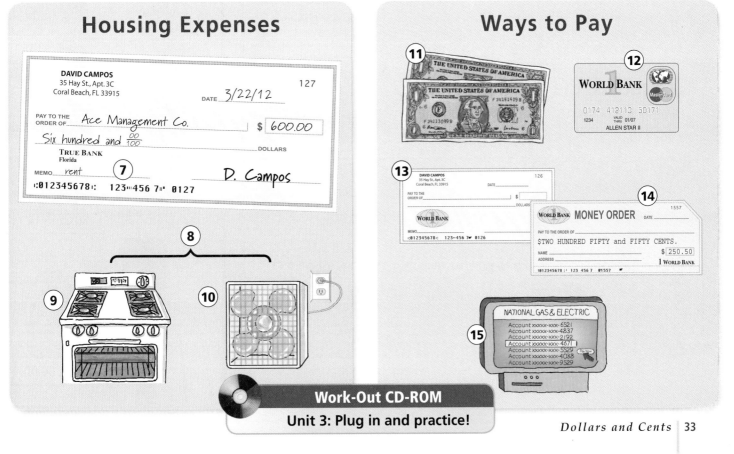

THE UNITED STATES OF AMERICA
THE UNITED STATES OF AMERICA

WORLD BANK 1
MasterCard
0174 412113 50171
1234 VALID THRU 01/07
ALLEN STAR II

DAVID CAMPOS
35 Hay St., Apt. 3C
Coral Beach, FL 33915
DATE
126
PAY TO THE
ORDER OF $
DOLLARS
WORLD BANK
MEMO
⑈012345678⑈ 123⑈456 7⑈ 0126

WORLD BANK MONEY ORDER DATE
1557
PAY TO THE ORDER OF
$TWO HUNDRED FIFTY and FIFTY CENTS.
NAME $ 250.50
ADDRESS
⑈012345678 ⑈ 123 456 7 ⑈1557 1 WORLD BANK

NATIONAL GAS & ELECTRIC
Account xxxxx-xxx-6521
Account xxxxx-xxx-4837
Account xxxxx-xxx-2192
Account xxxxx-xxx-4671
Account xxxxx-xxx-5529
Account xxxxx-xxx-4038
Account xxxxx-xxx-9529

Work-Out CD-ROM
Unit 3: Plug in and practice!

THINGS TO DO

The customer bought...

❶ Learn New Words 🎧 037

Look at the pictures. Listen to the words. Listen again and repeat.

① toothbrush
② razor
③ shaving cream
④ shampoo
⑤ toothpaste

⑥ penny (1¢)
⑦ nickel (5¢)
⑧ dime (10¢)
⑨ quarter (25¢)
⑩ dollar ($1.00)

⑪ five dollars ($5.00)
⑫ ten dollars ($10.00)
⑬ twenty dollars ($20.00)
⑭ fifty dollars ($50.00)

Which words are new to you? Circle them.

❷ Check *True* or *False* 🎧 038

Listen to the sentences. Look at the pictures. Check (✔) *True* or *False*.

	True	False		True	False		True	False
1.	○	○	**3.**	○	○	**5.**	○	○
2.	○	○	**4.**	○	○	**6.**	○	○

❸ Talk About the Picture

Work with a partner. Make statements about the people in the pictures. Your partner says who you are describing.

Examples: *A: This person bought shaving cream.*
B: Sam.

A: This person's change was $6.41.
B: Dana.

❹ Practice the Conversation 🎧 039

Listen to the conversation in a store. Listen again and repeat.

A: The total is $1.25 .

B: Can you change a twenty ?

A: Sure. Your change is $17.75 .

B: I thought it was $18.75 .

A: Oh, sorry. You're right.

Practice the conversation with a partner. Ask about this money.

1 $5.15	**2** $10.50	**3** $41.14	**4**
a ten	a fifty	a fifty	
$4.75	$38.50	$8.56	
$4.85	$39.50	$8.86	

The customer gave the cashier...   **The customer's change was...**

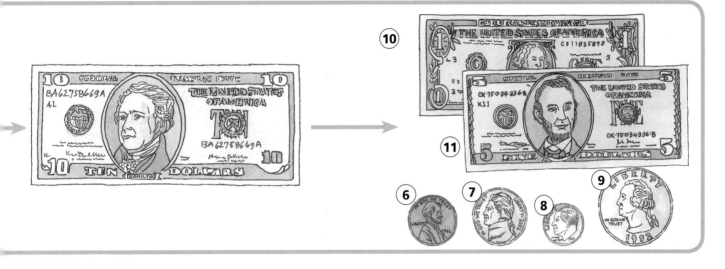

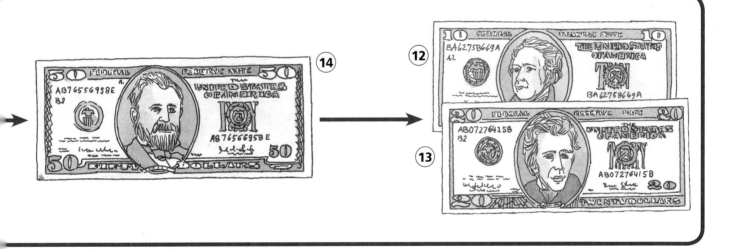

Target Grammar

Simple past of *be*,
statements   *page 158*

THINGS TO DO

❶ Learn New Words 🎧 040

Look at the picture. Listen to the words. Listen again and repeat.
Which words are new to you? Circle them.

1. bank officer
2. bank teller
3. safe-deposit box
4. ATM
5. check register
6. checkbook
7. deposit slip
8. withdrawal slip
9. savings account
10. debit card
11. monthly statement
12. paycheck
13. endorse a check
14. make a deposit
15. make a withdrawal
16. open a checking account

❷ Talk About the Picture

Write 5 things about the picture. Share your ideas with the class.

Examples: *There are two bank tellers working now.*
The ATM is near the front door.

❸ Practice the Conversation 🎧 041

Listen to the conversation. Listen again and repeat.

A: I'd like to make a deposit.

B: Did you fill out a deposit slip?

A: A deposit slip?

B: Yes. You can get one by the front door.

Practice the conversation with a partner. Use these ideas.

1 open a checking account

bring a photo I.D.

A photo I.D.

You can use your driver's license or passport.

2 make a withdrawal

fill out a withdrawal slip

A withdrawal slip

You can get one by the front door.

3 use the ATM

bring your debit card

Debit card

You apply for one with the bank officer.

4 cash a check

endorse it

Endorse it

You need to sign your name on the back.

Marie

EMPLOYEES ONLY

Target Grammar

Simple past, *yes/no* questions   *page 159*

TODAY'S RATES

Super Savings......3.00%

6-Month CD..........3.10%

1-Year CD.............4.10%

Money Market.......3.14%

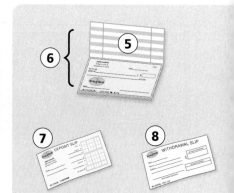

Completing a Check Register

THINGS TO DO

❶ Learn New Words 042

Look at the pictures. Listen to the words. Listen again and repeat.

① check register ② transaction amount ③ balance ④ check number

BankTwo//

1234567890123456 7

AL MOORE
CKG ACCT 1234567890

ATM

❷ Answer the Questions

Answer the questions. Then compare answers with the class.

1. What is the name of Al's Bank? _____ Bank Two _____

2. When did Al write a check to Jon's Garage?_____

3. Who did Al write a check to on 9/16?_____

4. How many deposits did Al make in September?_____

5. How much money did Al have in his checking account on August 30? _____

❸ Read and Take Notes 043

Read the personal checks and deposit slips and complete Al's check register on page 39.
Listen again and check your work.

❹ Write

Complete Al's check #325. Use the information in the check register.

Target Grammar

Simple past, *wh-*
questions *page 161*

WRITING TIP

When we write a check, we write the amount two ways. We write it all in
numbers in the box on the right. Then on the next line, we use words for the
dollars and numbers for the cents.

499.99   *Four hundred ninety-nine and 99/100*

AL MOORE
8721 Vista Terrace
Miami, FL 33109   325

DATE_____

PAY TO THE
ORDER OF_____ $ [   ]

_____ DOLLARS

BankTwo
Florida

MEMO_____ *Al Moore*

⑆012345678⑆: 123⑈456 7⑇ 0325

① CHECK REGISTER

CHECK NO. or ATM	DATE	DESCRIPTION	② TRANSACTION AMOUNT	DEPOSIT AMOUNT	③ BALANCE
ATM	8/30	Cash Withdrawal	$60.00		$385.89
325	9/4	Jon's Garage	$114.75		$271.14
326	9/16	Veritas Tel. Co.	$42.76		
ATM		deposit		$312.00	
	9/18	Bank Two			
ATM	9/26				
	9/30	deposit			

AL MOORE
8721 Vista Terrace
Miami, FL 33109

326 ④

DATE 9-16-12

PAY TO THE ORDER OF Veritas Tel. Co. $ 42.76

Forty-two and 76/100 DOLLARS

BankTwo
Florida

MEMO

Al Moore

⑆012345678⑆ 123ⵏ456 7⑋ 0326

AL MOORE
8721 Vista Terrace
Miami, FL 33109

DEPOSIT TICKET

1122 CASH
CHECKS → 3 1 2 0 0

Date 9-17-12

OR TOTAL FROM OTHER SIDE

SUBTOTAL →

*LESS CASH RECEIVED →

BankTwo

NET DEPOSIT $ 3 1 2 0 0

⑆012345678⑆ 123ⵏ456 7⑋

AL MOORE
8721 Vista Terrace
Miami, FL 33109

327

DATE 9-18-12

PAY TO THE ORDER OF Bank Two $ 356.76

Three hundred fifty-six and 76/100 DOLLARS

BankTwo
Florida

MEMO

Al Moore

⑆012345678⑆ 123ⵏ456 7⑋ 0327

AL MOORE
8721 Vista Terrace
Miami, FL 33109

DEPOSIT TICKET

1584 CASH
CHECKS → 8 5 0 0 0

Date 9-30-12

OR TOTAL FROM OTHER SIDE

SUBTOTAL →

*LESS CASH RECEIVED →

BankTwo

NET DEPOSIT $ 8 5 0 0 0

⑆012345678⑆ 123ⵏ456 7⑋

BankTwo

DATE: 08-30-12
TIME: 15:22
ACCT: 1234567

WITHDRAWAL: $60.00

THANK YOU
BANK/TWO

AI

SEPT 17

BankTwo

DATE: 09-26-12
TIME: 10:57
ACCT: 1234567

WITHDRAWAL: $50.00

THANK YOU
BANK/TWO

Talking About Money

❶ Practice Pronunciation: *Ng* versus *Nk* 044

> We pronounce the *g* in *ng* and the *k* in *nk* very quietly.
> You should be able to hear the final *k* in the *nk* sound.

A. Listen to the words. Listen again and repeat.

bank	thing	long	think
thank	drink	sink	checking
ink	saving	nothing	young
bang	sing	wondering	

B. Listen to the questions and answers. Listen again and repeat. 045

Questions	Answers
1. What is that bank?	**a.** First National Bank.
What is that bang?	**b.** Something fell in the kitchen.
2. Do you have a sink?	**a.** Yes, in the bathroom.
Do you have to sing?	**b.** No, I can tell a story.
3. Now think. What do you want?	**a.** I can't. I'm too tired.
Nothing. What do you want?	**b.** I don't want anything either.

C. Now listen again. You will hear one question from each pair in Activity B. Circle the correct answer. 046

❷ Listen and Write: Listening to an Automated Phone System 047

Listen and write the missing words. Listen again and check your answers.

_____Thank_____ you for calling
Horizon _____. For existing account
information, press _____. For all other
services, press _____.
To speak to a customer service specialist at any time,
press _____.
For checking accounts, press _____.
For _____, press _____.
For credit cards, press _____.

Please enter your _____
account number followed by the pound (#) sign. For
personal accounts, please enter the last four digits of your
Social Security number followed by the pound (#) sign. Your
available _____ is _____.

❸ Practice the Conversation: Buying a Money Order 048

Listen to the conversation. Listen again and repeat.

A: Welcome to Horizon Bank.

B: Thank you.

A: How can I help you?

B: I'd like to buy a money order.

A: How much do you want it for?

B: Two hundred dollars .

A: Anything else?

B: No, that's all.

A: Okay. Your total is $205.00 .

Practice the conversation with a partner. Use these amounts.

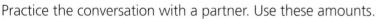

1 $100.00	**2** $75.00	**3** $90.00	**4** $65.55	**5**
$105.00	$80.00	$95.00	$70.55	

❹ Practice the Conversation: Asking for Change 049

Listen to the conversation. Listen again and repeat.

A: Do you have change for a twenty ?

B: I think so. How do you want it?

A: Do you have 2 tens ?

B: Sure. Here you are— ten, twenty .

A: Thanks.

Practice the conversation with a partner. Use these items.

1 fifty /
  2 twenties and a ten
  twenty, forty, fifty

2 twenty /
  a ten and 2 fives
  ten, fifteen, twenty

3 fifty /
  4 tens and 2 fives
  ten, twenty, thirty, forty,
  forty-five, fifty

4

Understanding a Pay Stub

❶ Learn New Words

Guess the meanings of the underlined words. Circle the best answer or definition.

1. Andy is an <u>employee</u> at Bank Two. He works as a bank teller. An employee is a _____.

   A. customer   **B.** worker   **C.** student

2. Andy's <u>salary</u> from Bank Two is $800 a week. His salary is his _____.

   A. rent   **B.** utilities   **C.** pay

3. Andy earns $800 a week, but Bank Two <u>deducts</u> $120 for federal taxes. Another word for *deducts* is

   A. adds   **B.** subtracts   **C.** equals

❷ Answer the Questions

Read the pay stub below. Answer the questions.

PAY STUB

BankTwo

Employee name: **Andy Kalish**

Period beginning: 02/01/12
Period ending: 02/15/12

SOCIAL SECURITY NUMBER: **928-62-5555**

Earnings	Hours Worked This Pay Period	This Pay Period	Year to Date
$20.00/hour	80	$1,600.00	$4,800.00
Federal taxes deducted		– $ 240.00	– $ 720.00
State taxes deducted		– $ 80.00	– $ 240.00
FICA		– $ 112.00	– $ 336.00
Health insurance		– $ 40.00	– $ 120.00
Check amount		$1,128.00	$3,384.00

1. What is Andy's pay per hour? <u>His pay is $20 per hour.</u> _____.

2. How many hours did he work in this pay period? _____

3. How long is this pay period? _____

4. What was the amount of his paycheck this pay period? _____

5. How much was deducted from this check for health insurance? _____

> FICA is a tax that is used to pay for retirement benefits, or Social Security.

❸ Write

Complete the story and the deposit slip below. Use information from the pay stub in Activity 2.

Andy Kalish works _____40_____ hours per week. He earns _____an hour, or $ _____ a week. Every _____ weeks he gets a paycheck. In the last pay period, his earnings were $ _____, but he got a paycheck for $ _____. That's because the company _____ some money for taxes and health insurance. Andy deposited his $1,128 paycheck in his checking account. He took out $200 in cash. Complete his deposit slip.

DEPOSIT TICKET	
ANDY KALISH 4832 Main Street Houston, TX 77001	CASH →
	CHECKS →
Date ____2/17/12____ *(deposits may not be available for immediate withdrawal)*	→
	OR TOTAL FROM OTHER SIDE →
_____ *(sign here if cash received from deposit) **	SUBTOTAL →
	*LESS CASH RECEIVED →
BankTwo	NET DEPOSIT $
⑈012345678⑈ 123⑈456 7⑈	

WINDOW ON MATH

Computing Deductions

Ⓐ Read the information below.

Employers deduct money for taxes and health insurance. The deduction for taxes depends on how much you earn and where you live. The deduction for health insurance depends on your insurance and your employer.

Example: *Sally Ying earns $10 an hour. Her employer deducts 20% for taxes and $25 from each paycheck for health insurance. If she works 40 hours, she will earn $400, but her take-home pay will be $295:*

- $10 x 40 = $400
- $400 – 20% ($80) = $320
- $320 – $25 = $295

> Take-home pay (also net pay) = the amount of money you actually receive after deductions.

Ⓑ Answer the word problems.

1. Jan earns $20 an hour. She pays 30% in taxes and $40 for insurance. How much does she take home in a 40-hour week?
2. Juan earns $15 an hour. He pays 25% in taxes and $35 for insurance. How much does he take home in a 40-hour week?

❶ Listening Review 050

You will hear a question. Listen to the conversation. You will hear the question again. Choose the correct answer: *A, B,* or *C*. Use the Answer Sheet.

1. A. the electric bill
   B. with a check
   C. with a money order

2. A. A lot.
   B. An average amount.
   C. Not much.

3. A. $12.15
   B. $12.25
   C. $12.50

4. A. a withdrawal slip
   B. from a teller
   C. from an ATM

5. A. $215
   B. $250
   C. $255

Answer Sheet

1 (A) (B) (C)
2 (A) (B) (C)
3 (A) (B) (C)
4 (A) (B) (C)
5 (A) (B) (C)

❷ Listening Dictation 051

Listen and write the sentences you hear.

1. A: How much did you spend on recreation last month?

   B: ___I didn't spend very much.___

2. A: How did you pay the gas bill last month?

   B: _____

3. A: The total is $8.95.

   B: _____

   A: Sure. Your change is $41.05.

4. A: _____

   B: Did you fill out a withdrawal slip?

   A: Yes, I did.

5. A: I'd like to buy a money order.

   B: How much do you want it for?

   A: _____

❸ Grammar Review

Circle the correct answer: A, B, or C.

1. I _____ the rent with cash last month.
   A. am paying
   B. pay
   C. paid

2. I _____ a lot on bus fare last month.
   A. didn't spend
   B. not spend
   C. didn't spent

3. Did you _____ a photo I.D.?
   A. bringing
   B. brought
   C. bring

4. Was _____ at the bank yesterday?
   A. Marie
   B. you
   C. Tom and Marie

5. I _____ tired yesterday.
   A. am
   B. was
   C. were

6. Joe: _____ did you go yesterday?
   Ann: I went to the grocery store.
   A. Who
   B. When
   C. Where

LEARNING LOG

I know these words:

- ○ ATM
- ○ balance
- ○ bank officer
- ○ bank teller
- ○ bus fare
- ○ car payments
- ○ car repairs
- ○ cash
- ○ checkbook
- ○ check register
- ○ credit card

- ○ debit card
- ○ deduct
- ○ deposit slip
- ○ dime (10¢)
- ○ dollar ($1.00)
- ○ electricity
- ○ employee
- ○ endorse a check
- ○ fifty dollars ($50.00)
- ○ five dollars ($5.00)
- ○ gas

- ○ groceries
- ○ make a deposit
- ○ make a withdrawal
- ○ money order
- ○ monthly statement
- ○ nickel (5¢)
- ○ open a checking account
- ○ paycheck
- ○ penny (1¢)
- ○ personal check

- ○ quarter (25¢)
- ○ razor
- ○ recreation
- ○ rent
- ○ safe-deposit box
- ○ salary
- ○ savings account
- ○ shampoo
- ○ shaving cream
- ○ ten dollars ($10.00)

- ○ toiletries
- ○ toothbrush
- ○ toothpaste
- ○ transaction amount
- ○ twenty dollars ($20.00)
- ○ utilities
- ○ withdrawal slip

I can ask:

- ○ How much did you spend on groceries?
- ○ Can you change a twenty?
- ○ Shouldn't that be …?
- ○ Do you have change for a twenty?
- ○ Did you fill out a deposit slip?
- ○ How much do you want it for?
- ○ How do you want it?

I can say:

- ○ I'm paying the electric bill.
- ○ I paid with cash.
- ○ I spent a lot on car repairs.
- ○ Bob bought a razor.
- ○ John's change was $1.25.
- ○ I'd like to make a deposit.
- ○ He earns $20 an hour.

I can write:

- ○ information in a check register
- ○ information in a personal check
- ○ information on a deposit slip

Work-Out CD-ROM

Unit 3: Plug in and practice!

THINGS TO DO

❶ Learn New Words 🎧 052

Look at the pictures. Listen to the words. Listen again and repeat.

Which phrases are new to you? Circle them.

❷ Listen and Write 🎧 053

Listen to people talk about goals. Look at the pictures. Write the correct number.

a. __8__   b. _____   c. _____   d. _____   e. _____   f. _____

❸ Write

List your goals in a chart like this.

Personal Goals	1. be a good parent 2.
Educational Goals	1. 2.
Work Goals	1. 2.

Tell a partner about three of your goals.

Example: *A: What is your personal goal?*
              B: I would like to be a good parent.

❹ Find Someone Who

Talk to your classmates. Find classmates who have the same goals listed in the chart. Write their names in the chart.

Find someone who would like to _____.	Person's Name
1. buy a house	_____
2. become a U.S. citizen	_____
3. get a job	_____
4. get a GED	_____
5. get married	_____
6. start a business	_____

Personal Goals

① become a U.S. citizen

② get married

③ buy a house

④ be a good parent

⑤ be a good citizen

Target Grammar

Want to, like to, would like to
page 162

Educational Goals

6 get good grades

7 get vocational training

8 graduate from a university

9 get a GED

10 learn something new

Work Goals

11 get a job

12 get a raise

13 get a promotion

14 start a business

15 win an award

Work-Out CD-ROM

Unit 4: Plug in and practice!

THINGS TO DO

❶ Learn New Words 054

Look at the pictures. Listen to the words. Listen again and repeat.

① go back to school
② take a business course
③ save money
④ learn to use a computer

⑤ take a writing course
⑥ learn more English
⑦ vote
⑧ do volunteer work

⑨ read to your children
⑩ spend time with your children

Which words or phrases are new to you? Circle them.

❷ Practice the Conversation 055

Listen to the conversation. Listen again and repeat.

A: What is your goal?

B: My goal is to start my own business, so I'm going to take a writing course. How about you?

A: My goal is to get a raise, so I'm going to learn to use a computer.

B: That's great. Good luck!

Practice the conversation with a partner. Use these ideas.

1 get a good job / study English

buy a house / save money

2 start a business / take a business course

get a promotion / go back to school

3 be a good parent / read to my children

be a good citizen / do volunteer work

4 be a good citizen / vote

graduate from a university / learn to use a computer

5 become a U.S. citizen / learn more English

be a good parent / spend time with my children

6

❸ Write

Choose a goal. List three or more things you should do to reach the goal. Write your ideas in a cluster diagram like this one.

take a class

meet new people

Now talk about your goal with a partner. Use your diagram to help you.

Goal: to open my own clothing store

Goal: to be a good citizen

Goal: to be a good parent

Target Grammar

Future with *be going to* *page 163*

THINGS TO DO

❶ Learn New Words 056

Look at the picture. Listen to the words. Listen again and repeat.

1. office manager
2. office worker
3. designer
4. bookkeeper
5. salesperson
6. supervisor
7. mechanic
8. late
9. on time
10. organized
11. disorganized
12. good with people
13. hardworking
14. lazy
15. bad attitude
16. good attitude

Which words are new to you? Circle them.

❷ Talk About the Picture

Work with a partner. Describe the people in the picture. Your partner says who you are describing.

A: He's angry because someone is late.

B: It's the office manager.

A: Right!

❸ Practice the Conversation 057

Listen to the conversation. Listen again and repeat.

A: Who will get the job as the new bookkeeper?

B: I think Jon will get the job. He's organized.

A: Yes, and he is always on time.

Practice the conversation with a partner. Use these ideas.

1 sales manager	2 supervisor	3 salesperson
Ben / hardworking	Tim / never late	Ken / good with people
has a good attitude	is good with people	is very organized

❹ Find Someone Who

Talk to your classmates. Find someone who answers *yes* to your question. Write the person's name in the chart.

Are you _____?	Person's Name
1. very organized	_____
2. hardworking	_____
3. good with people	_____
4. sometimes disorganized	_____

Target Grammar

Future with *will*   *page 165*

A Success Story

THINGS TO DO

❶ Learn New Words 058

Look at the pictures and photos. Listen to the words. Listen again and repeat.

❷ Preview

Look at the picture and the title of the reading. What do you think the story is about? Check (✔) one or more ideas.

○ a gymnast ○ an important place
○ a doctor ○ an important person

❸ Read and Underline

Read the story and underline the important events and years. Then answer the questions.

1. When was Nadia Comaneci born? _____

2. How old was she when she started learning gymnastics? _____

3. When did she win the Olympic gold medal in Montreal? _____

4. When did she leave Romania? _____

5. When did she get married? _____

6. When did she give birth to her son? _____

Add the missing information to the timeline of Nadia's life on page 53.

❹ Write

List five important events in your life.

⭐ **WRITING TIP**

Make a List Before you start writing, make a list of the important details you want to write about.

EVENT	YEAR
I was born in Haiti.	1987

Make a timeline of the events in your life.

① gymnastics

1968
Nadia began
studying gymnastics

1961
_____
_____

UKRAINE
HUNGARY
MOLDOVA
Prut
Onesti ★
ROMANIA
Bucharest ●
Danube
BLACK SEA
SERBIA   BULGARIA

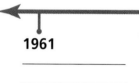

Target Grammar

Because and *to* for reasons
page 166

Biography: Former Olympic Gymnast Nadia Comaneci

Nadia Comaneci was born in Romania on November 12, 1961. When she was six years old, gymnastics coach Bela Karolyi saw her doing gymnastics in her schoolyard. He invited her to join his gymnastics school because she was a good gymnast. From age 7 to age 13, Nadia lived with her family in Onesti, Romania, and learned gymnastics at Karolyi's school.

Nadia soon became a world-famous gymnast. When she was 13 years old, she won four gold medals at the 1975 European championships. After that, she won many more gold medals and even got a score of a perfect 10. She was the first gymnast that ever got a perfect 10 in a competition. When Nadia was 14 years old, she won six medals in the 1976 Olympic Games in Montreal, Canada, including the all-around gold medal. In the 1980 Olympics in Moscow, Russia, she won the silver medal. She retired from gymnastics in 1981.

After Nadia retired, she began coaching gymnastics in Romania. In 1989, she left Romania because she wanted to live in the United States. First she moved to Canada. Later she moved to Oklahoma to be near her boyfriend, Bart Conner. They got engaged in 1994 and married in 1996. In 2001, Nadia became a U.S. citizen. In 2006, she gave birth to their son, Dylan. Today, the family continues to live in Oklahoma.

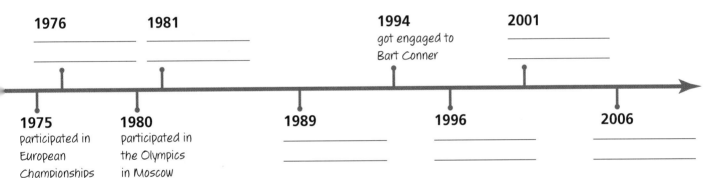

1976
_____
_____

1981
_____
_____

1994
got engaged to
Bart Conner

2001
_____
_____

1975
participated in
European
Championships

1980
participated in
the Olympics
in Moscow

1989
_____
_____

1996
_____
_____

2006
_____
_____

② gold medal

Nadia receiving the gold medal in the 1976 Olympic Games

③ coach

Nadia coaching gymnastics

Nadia with husband Bart Conner

Plans and Goals 53

Asking for and Giving Advice

❶ Practice Pronunciation: Past Endings 🎧 059

> We pronounce the –ed in regular verbs in the past in three different ways:
>
> **1.** If the word ends in a voiceless consonant sound (*ck, k, f, p, ch, sh, s, x*), the past tense ending (*ed*) sounds like /t/, as in *trap → trapped*.
>
> **2.** If the word ends in a voiced consonant sound (*b, g, j, m, n, r, z*) or a vowel sound, the past tense ending (*ed*) sounds like /d/, as in *jog → jogged*.
>
> **3.** If the word ends in a *t* or *d* sound, the past tense ending (*ed*) sounds like /id/, as in *want → wanted*.

A. Listen to the words. Listen again and repeat.

1. married	**4.** relaxed	**7.** cashed	**10.** studied	**13.** practiced
2. wanted	**5.** liked	**8.** voted	**11.** graduated	**14.** saved
3. volunteered	**6.** helped	**9.** immigrated	**12.** learned	**15.** promoted

B. Write the words from the list above in the correct place in the chart.

Ending sounds like *t*	Ending sounds like *d*	Ending sounds like *id*
1. relaxed	**1.** married	**1.** wanted
2.	**2.**	**2.**
3.	**3.**	**3.**
4.	**4.**	**4.**
5.	**5.**	**5.**

C. Work with a partner. Ask and answer the questions. Use complete sentences.

1. What did you like to do when you were a child?

2. What kind of job did you want when you were young?

3. What was the best thing you learned in school as a child?

❷ Listen and Write: Listening to a Recorded Message 🎧 060

Listen and write the missing words. Listen again and check your answers.

Welcome to Westville Adult School. Sorry we _____

your call. For information about adult ESL classes, press 1. For information

about _____, press 2. For information

about _____, press 3. To register for

_____, press 4. To hear this message again,

press _____.

❸ Practice the Conversation: Asking for Advice  061

Listen to the conversation. Listen again and repeat.

A: You look happy. What's up?

B: I just got a raise.

A: That's great. I want to get a raise, too. How did you do it?

B: I worked hard and was always on time.

A: That's good advice.

Practice the conversation with a partner. Use these ideas.

1 got a promotion	**2** retired	**3** bought a house	**4** started my own business	**5**
get a promotion	retire	buy a house	start my own business	
graduated from a good university	worked hard and saved money	saved money for ten years	took some business classes	

❹ Practice the Conversation: Giving Advice  062

Listen to the conversation. Listen again and repeat.

A: Are you going to take a writing course next term?

B: No, I'm not going to take one.

A: I think you should.

B: Really? Why?

A: Because it will help you meet your goal of getting a GED.

B: Maybe you're right. I think I will take one.

Practice the conversation with a partner. Use these items.

1 vote in the next election	**2** organize your office soon
vote	organize it
being a good citizen	getting a promotion
vote	organize it

3 work more hours	**4** go back to school	**5** do volunteer work
work more	go back	do volunteer work
getting a raise	getting a job	winning an award
work more	go back	do some

Help Your Child Succeed in School!

① Before You Read

Check the circle if you agree.

○ Parents need to read to their children.

○ Parents should talk to their child's teacher if he or she is having problems in school.

○ Learning is important for everyone in the family.

○ Parents need to help with homework.

○ All adult family members need to be involved in their children's school.

○ Children don't need limits on TV and video games.

Discuss your opinions with a partner.

② Read

Read the information. In your opinion, what are the three best tips for parents?

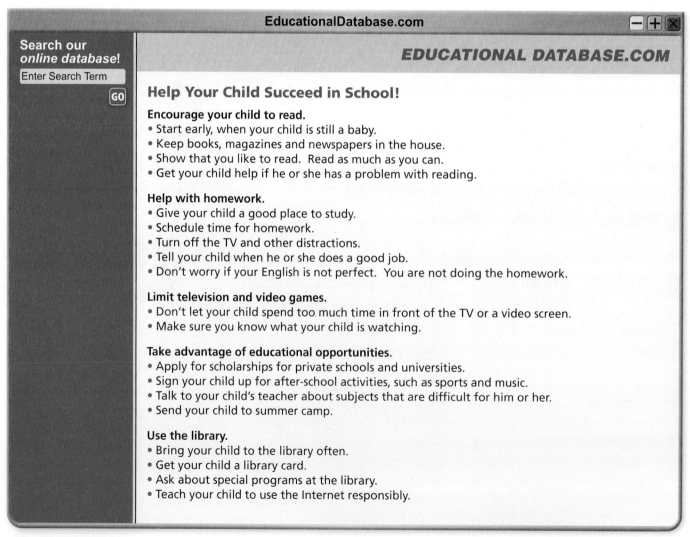

EducationalDatabase.com   ⊖ ⊕ ☒

Search our online database!

Enter Search Term
GO

EDUCATIONAL DATABASE.COM

Help Your Child Succeed in School!

Encourage your child to read.
- Start early, when your child is still a baby.
- Keep books, magazines and newspapers in the house.
- Show that you like to read. Read as much as you can.
- Get your child help if he or she has a problem with reading.

Help with homework.
- Give your child a good place to study.
- Schedule time for homework.
- Turn off the TV and other distractions.
- Tell your child when he or she does a good job.
- Don't worry if your English is not perfect. You are not doing the homework.

Limit television and video games.
- Don't let your child spend too much time in front of the TV or a video screen.
- Make sure you know what your child is watching.

Take advantage of educational opportunities.
- Apply for scholarships for private schools and universities.
- Sign your child up for after-school activities, such as sports and music.
- Talk to your child's teacher about subjects that are difficult for him or her.
- Send your child to summer camp.

Use the library.
- Bring your child to the library often.
- Get your child a library card.
- Ask about special programs at the library.
- Teach your child to use the Internet responsibly.

❸ Check *True* or *False*

Read the information from the website again. Check *True* or *False*.

	True	False
1. You don't need to read to babies because they are too young to understand.	○	○
2. Don't let your children watch too much TV. When they do watch, know what they are watching.	○	○
3. Get your child his or her own library card.	○	○
4. If your children don't understand their homework, do it for them.	○	○
5. Limit activities such as sports and music so that your children can spend more time doing homework.	○	○
6. If your English isn't very good, you can't help with homework.	○	○

❹ Interview

Work with a partner who has children. Ask the questions. Write your partner's answers.

1. How many children do you have?	
2. What are three things you have in your house to read?	
3. How do you help your child with reading?	
4. How do you help your child with homework?	

WINDOW ON MATH

Calculating a Grade Point Average

Ⓐ Read the information below.

Most secondary schools and universities give students a grade for each class they take. Then the schools find the average of all the grades to give students a Grade Point Average (GPA). The GPA tells students and their parents how they are doing in general. To calculate a GPA, most schools give students 4 points for an A, 3 points for a B, 2 points for a C, 1 point for a D, and 0 points for an F. Then the schools find the average for these numbers.

EXAMPLE: *This year, Lily got a B in math, a B in English, a C in science, a B in history, and an A in art.*

Math	English	Science	History	Art	Total	Average
3	3	2	3	4	3 + 3 + 2 + 3 + 4 = 15	15 ÷ 5 = **3.0**

Her GPA is 3.0.

Ⓑ Answer these word problems.

1. This year, Patrick got an A in math, a B in English, an A in science, a C in history, and a B in art. What was his GPA? _____

2. This year, Juanita got an A in math, an A in English, a C in science, a B in history, and an A in art. What was her GPA? _____

What Do You Know?

① Listening Review 🎧 063

Look at the pictures and listen. Choose the correct answer: *A*, *B*, or *C*. Use the Answer Sheet.

1. A B C

2. A  B C

3. A B  C

4. A B  C

5. A B C

Answer Sheet

1	Ⓐ	Ⓑ	Ⓒ
2	Ⓐ	Ⓑ	Ⓒ
3	Ⓐ	Ⓑ	Ⓒ
4	Ⓐ	Ⓑ	Ⓒ
5	Ⓐ	Ⓑ	Ⓒ

② Listening Dictation 🎧 064

Listen. Write the words you hear.

1. A: What are your goals?
B: _____.

2. A: What is your goal?
B: _____.

3. A: What is your goal?
B: _____.

4. A: _____?
B: I think Sara will get it. She's hardworking.

5. A: You look happy. What's up?
B: _____.

❸ Grammar Review

Circle the correct answer: *A*, *B*, or *C*.

1. Joe wants to _____ good grades.
A. get
B. gets
C. to get

2. I am going _____ this year.
A. vote
B. to votes
C. to vote

3. I _____ to buy a house, so I am going to save money.
A. wants
B. want
C. like

4. I _____ do volunteer work at the youth center.
A. am going
B. am going to
C. is going to

5. Laura went to Chicago _____ her friend.
A. visit
B. to visit
C. because visit

6. I think Joshua _____ soon.
A. calls
B. will call
C. will calls

LEARNING LOG

I know these words:

○ bad attitude
○ be a good citizen
○ be a good parent
○ become a U.S. citizen
○ bookkeeper
○ buy a house
○ coach
○ designer
○ disorganized
○ do volunteer work
○ get a GED
○ get a job

○ get a promotion
○ get a raise
○ get good grades
○ get married
○ get vocational training
○ go back to school
○ gold medal
○ good attitude
○ good with people
○ graduate from a university
○ gymnast

○ hardworking
○ late
○ lazy
○ learn more English
○ learn something new
○ learn to use a computer
○ mechanic
○ office manager
○ office worker
○ on time
○ organized
○ read to your children

○ salesperson
○ save money
○ senator
○ spend time with your children
○ start a business
○ supervisor
○ take a business course
○ take a writing course
○ vote

I can ask:

○ What's up?
○ How did you do it?
○ Do you think I will get the job?
○ Who is going to get the job?

I can say:

○ I would like to get a raise.
○ I am going to take a writing course next year.
○ You will have to work hard to get a promotion.
○ I moved to the U.S. because I wanted a better life.

I can write:

○ a list of goals
○ information on a timeline
○ information from a recorded message
○ about a sequence of events

Work-Out CD-ROM

Unit 4: Plug in and practice!

THINGS TO DO

❶ Learn New Words 🎧 065

Look at the picture. Listen to the words. Listen again and repeat.
Which words or phrases are new to you? Circle them.

❷ Practice the Conversation 🎧 066

Listen to the conversation. Listen again and repeat.

A: Where are you going?

B: I'm going shopping. I need to get a heavy coat.

A: Can I come with you? I want to get a coffeemaker.

B: Sure. Let's go!

Practice the conversation with a partner. Use the information below.

1 a refrigerator	**2** a pair of boots	**3** some dish soap	**4**
a dishwasher	a blender	a bucket	

❸ Listen and Take Notes 🎧 067

Amanda is moving into a new apartment. Listen to her talk about what she has and what she wants to buy. Complete the chart.

	has it	doesn't have it	wants to buy it
1. refrigerator	○	○	○
2. washing machine	○	○	○
3. toaster	○	○	○
4. coffeemaker	○	○	○
5. blender	○	○	○

❹ Interview

Work with a partner. Ask about the items below. Complete the chart.

Do you have a ____?	has it	doesn't have it	wants to buy it
1. heavy coat	○	○	○
2. vacuum cleaner	○	○	○
3. blender	○	○	○
4. can opener	○	○	○
5. _____	○	○	○

Clothing

2 jacke

1 pair of athletic shoes

Cleaning Supplies

14 vacuum cleaner

Target Grammar

Go + verb-ing page 168

(3) heavy coat

(4) pair of boots

Appliances

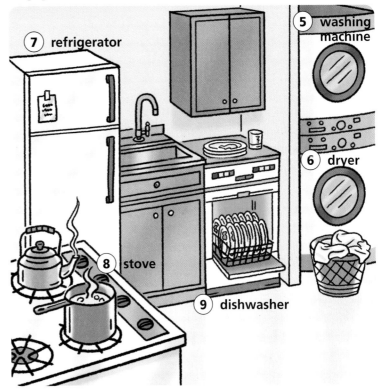

(7) refrigerator

(5) washing machine

(6) dryer

(8) stove

(9) dishwasher

Kitchen Equipment

(10) dish soap

(12) mop

(13) bucket

(11) broom

(15) coffemaker

(16) blender

(20) cutting board

(19) peeler

(18) can opener

(17) toaster

Work-Out CD-ROM

Unit 5: Plug in and practice!

Activities at a Mall

THINGS TO DO

❶ Learn New Words 068

Look at the pictures. Listen to the words. Listen again and repeat.

① carry
② take a break
③ go out of business
④ jewelry store
⑤ go into
⑥ toy store
⑦ push a stroller
⑧ furniture store
⑨ sale
⑩ demonstrate
⑪ mall directory
⑫ appliance store

Which words or phrases are new to you? Circle them.

❷ Check *True* or *False* 069

Listen to the sentences about the mall. Look at the picture.
Check (✔) *True* or *False*.

	True	False		True	False		True	False
1.	○	○	3.	○	○	5.	○	○
2.	○	○	4.	○	○	6.	○	○

❸ Talk About the Picture

Write 3 true and 3 false statements about the picture. Read your
sentences to the class. Ask your classmates to identify the true or false
statements.

Example: *A: Gina bought something at the shoe store.*
        B: That's true.

❹ Practice the Conversation 070

Listen to the conversation. Listen again and repeat.

A: Where do you buy shoes ?

B: I like May's Department Store.

A: Is May's better than Arches ?

B: I think so. It has a bigger selection .

Practice the conversation with a partner. Ask about these things.

1 appliances /	**2** toys /	**3** jewelry /
Sam's	Jingle's	Gemma's
is cheaper	has a bigger selection	has better sales

4 furniture /	**5** kitchen items /	**6**
Ben's	Kitchens Galore	
has nicer furniture	has more helpful salespeople	

Target Grammar

Comparative adjectives   *page 169*

THINGS TO DO

❶ Learn New Words 🎧 071

Look at the picture. Listen to the words. Listen again and repeat.

1. refund
2. exchange
3. receipt
4. regular price
5. marked down 50 percent
6. half price
7. 20 percent off
8. clearance sale

❷ Compare

Read the sale ads and figure out the savings for each item.

Al's Superstore

Item	Regular Price	Sale Price	Savings
coffeemakers	_____	_____	_____
vacuum cleaners	_____	_____	_____
blenders	_____	_____	_____

Barb's Discount House

Item	Regular Price	Sale Price	Savings
coffeemakers	_____	_____	_____
vacuum cleaners	_____	_____	_____
blenders	_____	_____	_____

Talk with a partner. Where would you buy each item? Why?

❸ Practice the Conversation 🎧 072

Listen to the conversation. Listen again and repeat.

A: There was a big sale at Al's yesterday.

B: Really? Was there a sale on toasters ?

A: No, but there were great prices on blenders . I got one for only $29.99 !

B: That's a good deal. How much did you save?

A: I saved $10.00 .

Practice the conversation with a partner. Use the chart in Activity 2.

③ Al's Superstore

Whirly Vacuum Cleaner	$34.99
High Mtn. Jacket	$37.50
5% TAX	$3.62
TOTAL	**$76.11**

Thank You!

1 Barb's	**2** Al's	**3** Barb's	**4** Al's
brooms	can openers	heavy coats	dishwashers
vacuum cleaners / $31.48	coffeemakers / ?	jackets / ?	stoves / ?
$58.50	?	?	?

Target Grammar

There was** and **there were
page 171

Cut's Blenders   Reg. $39.99
$10 off   Sale $29.99

Athletic Shoes—all brands   30% off

High Mountain Jackets   Regular $125
50% off   Now $37.50

Sierra Stoves ⑥ ½ price!!!
Reg. $899   Sale $449.50

AL'S
SUPERSTORE
STOREWIDE SALE!!!
OPEN EVERY DAY 8 A.M.–10 P.M.

Karol Coffeemakers

Reg. $24.99 ④
Sale $17.99

ENTIRE STOCK MARKED DOWN 50% ⑤

Whirly Bagless Upright Vacuum Cleaner

Reg. $69.98
Sale $34.99

All sales final. No refund or exchanges.

BARB'S DISCOUNT HOUSE

Ovay Coffeemakers
Now **20% off!**
Reg. $28.99 ⑦
Sale price $23.19

Hadley Vacuum Cleaners—Now **Reduced 65%**
Were $89.98   Now $31.48

Westford Blenders—On sale!
Now **20% off!**
Reg. $33.94   Sale $27.15

All Nilke Athletic Shoes—½ price!

40% off Memory Brand Jackets
Were $79   Now $47.40

All Stoves—$200 off
Reg. $699.95   Sale $499.95

Exchanges with a receipt for 7 days

⑧

A Shopper's Calendar

THINGS TO DO

❶ Preview

Scan the article. Which of the things below can you learn from it?
Check (✔) your answers.

○ the best time to get sales   ○ what you should buy in the winter
○ finding the cheapest stores   ○ how much appliances cost

❷ Read and Take Notes

Read the article. Take notes in the chart below.

Item	The Best Time to Buy
summer clothes	in August
outdoor furniture	
fall clothes	
a DVD player	
spring clothes	
sheets and towels	
a laptop computer	

❸ Talk

Write your answers. Then share them with a partner.

1. What stores in your area have the best sales? _____

2. What is something you bought on sale? What was the sale price?
How much did you save? _____

_____

❹ Write

Look in a newspaper for information about sales in your area.
Then write about the sales that interest you.

WRITING TIP
We use the simple present when we write a description.

Example: *It's February now, and a lot of things are on sale.
At Leblanc's Hardware store, everything
is 10–70 percent off. At Fortunes, winter clothes
are on sale. On February 19, you can get an extra
20 percent off at the Presidents' Day sale.*

In September, it's time for back-to-school shopping. Parents take their children to the mall to buy new clothes for school. But what are the smartest shoppers buying? They are buying summer clothes. Smart shoppers know that "off season" clothes are 60–80% less than the original price. As the seasons change, so do the items on sale. Here's what's for sale at different times during the year:

Target Grammar
Superlative adjectives   *page 172*

A Shopper's Calendar:
Save Money All Year

JANUARY

Go shopping in January for the last of the fall clothing. Leftovers from the December holidays are also marked down now. There are also sales on sheets and towels.

JUNE AND JULY

Father's Day is a good time to shop for consumer electronics.

On sale are:

- DVD players
- portable speakers
- home computers
- smartphones
- MP3 players
- digital cameras

OCTOBER

The first big sales of fall clothing begin in October. But don't get too excited. Prices will get a lot cheaper in January.

APRIL

Spring clothes first go on sale in April. However, final markdowns are months away.

AUGUST

This is the time for final markdowns on spring and summer clothes.

SEPTEMBER

At the end of the summer, garden supplies go on sale. This is a good time to buy plants and outdoor furniture.

NOVEMBER

The Friday after Thanksgiving is called Black Friday. It is the start of the holiday shopping season, and many stores have big sales, often as early as 5 A.M.! The following Monday is called Cyber Monday. On this day, many stores have Internet-only sales so that people can buy gifts in time for the holidays. These are good days to get the best prices on electronics, video games, and dolls.

5 Making Exchanges, Returns, and Purchases

❶ Practice Pronunciation: Stress 073

When we talk, we stress the most important words or phrases.

A. Listen to the stress in these conversations. Listen again and repeat.

1. A: What's wrong with it?
    B: It's too (tight.)

2. A: Is it tight enough?
    B: It's too tight.

3. A: How is that one?
    B: It's much softer.

4. A: Is it softer?
    B: Yes, it's much softer.

Listen to the conversations again. Circle the stressed words.

B. Work with a partner. Practice the conversations. Stress the important words. Circle the stressed word in each conversation.

1. A: What's wrong with it?
    B: It's too (small)

2. A: Is it a heavy coat?
    B: Yes, it's too heavy

3. A: Is this one quieter?
    B: It's much quieter.

4. A: Why do you like that one?
    B: It's much cheaper.

❷ Practice the Conversation: Exchanging Something 074

Listen to the conversation. Listen again and repeat.

A: Can I help you?

B: Yes. I want to return this jacket .

A: Okay. Was there something wrong with it?

B: Yes. It's too tight .

A: Do you want to exchange it for a bigger one?

B: Yes, I do.

A: Okay. I'll be right with you.

Practice the conversation with a partner. Use these ideas.

1 vacuum cleaner / heavy	**2** coat / long	**3** toaster / small	**4** stove / big	**5**
lighter	shorter	bigger	smaller	

❸ Practice the Conversation: Asking for a Refund  075

Listen to the conversation. Listen again and repeat.

A: Can I help you?

B: Yes, I want to return these toys . They're just too noisy .

A: Do you want some quieter ones?

B: No, thank you. I just want a refund.

A: Do you have your receipt?

B: Yes, I have it right here.

Practice the conversation with a partner. Use these ideas.

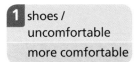 **1** shoes / uncomfortable
more comfortable

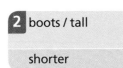 **2** boots / tall
shorter

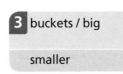 **3** buckets / big
smaller

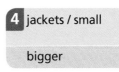 **4** jackets / small
bigger

 **5**

❹ Practice the Conversation: Comparing Price and Quality 076

Listen to the conversation. Listen again and repeat.

A: Which coat do you like better?

B: This one. It's much softer .

A: Yes, but it's a lot more expensive, too.

B: How much more expensive?

A: Fifty dollars .

B: It's a little nicer, but fifty dollars is a lot more expensive.
I'll get the other one.

Practice the conversation with a partner. Use these ideas.
Read the price tags to compare the prices.

 **1** toaster oven
bigger

 **2** vacuum cleaner
easier to use

 **3** jacket
more attractive

LESSON 6

Shopping Tips

❶ Check *True* or *False*

Read the shopping tips on page 71. Then look at the statements below and check (✔) *True* or *False*.

	True	False
1. You can find store coupons in the newspaper.	○	○
2. To use a store coupon, you should mail it to the store.	○	○
3. You can use a store coupon when you make your purchase.	○	○
4. Comparison shopping websites give you prices for online stores.	○	○
5. All of the stores on the comparison shopping websites are good businesses.	○	○
6. A warranty tells how much you paid for something.	○	○
7. If you bought something with a warranty and it needs repair, call the store where you bought it.	○	○

❷ Answer the Questions

Answer the questions. Use the information on page 71. Then talk with your classmates.

1. Sara wants to buy the Caron Camera model X665. Look at the Nextag.com ratings of online stores that sell it. Which online store do you think she should buy it from? Why?

_____

2. Tim bought a new Shark washing machine for $600. After six months, the machine stopped working. What should Tim do?

_____

3. Dana is looking for a new coat and an electric coffeemaker. From the newspaper, she cut out a bonus coupon for May's department store. The coupon gives $10 off a purchase of $50 or more. At May's, she found an $80 coat marked down to $50. She also found a coffeemaker on sale for $30. With the coupon, how much will she pay for the coat and the coffeemaker?

_____

❸ Write

Think about something you do to save money when you are shopping. Then write your shopping tip and share it with your classmates.

WINDOW ON MATH

Percentages

Ⓐ Read the sentences.

   1. 10% (ten percent) = 10/100 (ten over one hundred) = .10 (point ten)
   2. Ten percent of fifty dollars equals five dollars.
   3. 50% (fifty percent) = 50/100 (fifty over one hundred) = .50 (point fifty)
   4. Fifty percent of fifty dollars equals twenty-five dollars.

Ⓑ Answer the questions.

   1. A $200 coat is marked down 50 percent. How much does it cost?
   2. A $50 coffeemaker is 10 percent off. How much does it cost?
   3. A $100 vacuum is 70 percent off. How much does it cost?

Tips from Smart Shoppers

Tip #1: Use Store Coupons

You can save money by cutting coupons from newspapers and store flyers. Just give the coupons to the cashier when you make your purchase, and you'll get a discount. Keep these things in mind when you use coupons:

- Check the expiration date on the coupon. Most coupons are valid, or good, for a short period of time.

- Some stores use coupons to get you to buy something you don't really need.

STOREWIDE BONUS COUPON

EXTRA **15%** OFF

VALID FRIDAY AND SATURDAY

JUNE 6 & 7

MAY'S DEPARTMENT STORE

NO DISCOUNT on jewelry or cosmetics.

Tip #2: Compare Prices Online

When you are shopping online, you can compare prices before you buy. Use a comparison shopping website, such as Nextag (www.nextag.com). These websites can help you find the lowest prices for products such as computers, baby furniture, and kitchen appliances.

- Type in the name of the item you are looking for, and the site will tell you how much it is at different online stores.

- Be sure to check the store ratings and buy from a good store only.

- Most of the comparison shopping sites are free to use.

Caron Camera X665

store	store ratings	description	price
cameraworld	★☆☆☆☆	in stock	$149
camera.com	★★★★★	in stock	$179
elecusa.com	★★★★☆	in stock	$199
greatbuy.com	★★★★★	in stock free shipping	$209

Tip #3: Read the Warranty

A warranty or guarantee tells what a company will do if you have a problem with something you buy. It's especially important to read the warranty before you buy something expensive. You should save the warranty and any packaging your purchase came in.

SHARK® Washing Machine Warranty

Full One-Year Warranty

For one (1) year from the date of original retail purchase, any part that fails in normal home use will be repaired or replaced free of charge.

To Receive Warranty Service

Call Shark Customer Service toll-free at 1-800-555-4566. You will need the model and serial numbers of your appliance, the name and address of the dealer, and the date of purchase.

What Do You Know?

❶ Listening Review 077

You will hear a question. Listen to the conversation. You will hear the question again. Choose the correct answer: *A*, *B*, or *C*. Use the Answer Sheet.

1. A. She's going shopping.
   B. A washing machine
   C. A dishwasher

2. A. 15% off
   B. 50% off
   C. half price

3. A. Athletic shoes
   B. They are too small.
   C. They are too big.

4. A. to buy a jacket
   B. to exchange a jacket
   C. to get a refund for a jacket

5. A. furniture
   B. Ben's
   C. May's

Answer Sheet

1 Ⓐ Ⓑ Ⓒ
2 Ⓐ Ⓑ Ⓒ
3 Ⓐ Ⓑ Ⓒ
4 Ⓐ Ⓑ Ⓒ
5 Ⓐ Ⓑ Ⓒ

❷ Listening Dictation 078

Listen. Write the sentences you hear.

1. A: Where are you going?

   B: I'm going shopping. I want to get a new heavy coat.

2. A: _____ ?

   B: At May's department store. There was a sale.

3. A: Were they having a sale at Jingle's?

   B: _____ !

4. A: Is CompWorld better than ElecUSA?

   B: _____ .

5. A: Why do you always shop at May's?

   B: _____

   _____ .

❸ Grammar Review

Choose the correct answer: *A, B,* or *C.* Circle the correct answer.

1. I go _____ on weekends. I like to walk in the mountains.

A. hike
B. hiking
C. to hike

2. There _____ a lot of shoes on sale.

A. is
B. was
C. were

3. _____ a cooking demonstration at Kitchens Galore.

A. There has
B. There was
C. There were

4. I think Tom's has _____ prices than Gemma's.

A. good
B. better
C. best

5. Do you think Le Chic has _____ May's?

A. bigger sales than
B. more bigger sales than
C. big sales than

6. _____ shoppers wait for sales.

A. Most smartest
B. The most smart
C. The smartest

LEARNING LOG ✓

I know these words:

○ 20 percent off
○ appliance store
○ blender
○ broom
○ bucket
○ can opener
○ carry
○ clearance sale
○ coffeemaker

○ cutting board
○ demonstrate
○ dish soap
○ dishwasher
○ dryer
○ exchange
○ furniture store
○ go into
○ go out of business

○ half price
○ heavy coat
○ jacket
○ jewelry store
○ mall directory
○ marked down
○ mop
○ pair of athletic shoes

○ pair of boots
○ peeler
○ push a stroller
○ receipt
○ refrigerator
○ refund
○ regular price
○ sale
○ stove

○ take a break
○ toaster
○ toy store
○ vacuum cleaner
○ washing machine

I can ask:

○ Where did you buy it?
○ Where do you buy shoes?
○ Which store is better?
○ Which store has better sales?
○ Did you get a good deal?

I can say:

○ I got it on sale.
○ I saved seven dollars.
○ It's marked down 50 percent.
○ The best time to buy sheets is in January.
○ I want to return this jacket.
○ I just want a refund.

I can write:

○ sentences comparing two things
○ a price comparison chart
○ notes about a reading
○ shopping tips

Work-Out CD-ROM

Unit 5: Plug in and practice!

UNIT 6 FOOD

LESSON 1 Identifying Foods

THINGS TO DO

❶ Learn New Words 🎧 079

Look at the pictures. Listen to the words. Listen again and repeat.
Which words are new to you? Circle them.

❷ Read and Write

Read the bar graph on pages 74–75. Complete the sentences.

1. Americans eat about 175 pounds of _____*flour*_____ each year.
2. Americans drink about 50 pounds of _____ each year.
3. Americans eat about 75 pounds of _____ and _____ each year.
4. Americans eat more _____ than fruit each year.
5. Americans eat the same amount of fish and _____ each year.

> **Target Grammar**
>
> Count and noncount
> nouns   *page 174*

❸ Talk About the Picture

Work with a partner. Make statements about the bar graph.
Your partner says if the statements are true or false.

Examples:

> *A: Americans eat about*
> *300 pounds of sugar a year.*
> *B: That's false.*

> *A: Americans drink more*
> *milk than coffee.*
> *B: That's true.*

❹ Interview

Work with a partner. Ask your partner the questions. Check (✔) your
partner's answers in the chart.

A: Did you eat any fish yesterday?   A: Did you eat any eggs yesterday?

B: Yes, I did . I had fish for dinner .   B: No, I didn't .

Did you eat any _____ yesterday?	Yes, I did. I had _____ for _____.				No, I didn't.
	breakfast	**lunch**	**dinner**	**a snack**	
fish	○	○	○	○	○
red meat	○	○	○	○	○
fruit	○	○	○	○	○
vegetables	○	○	○	○	○
_____	○	○	○	○	○

Work-Out CD-ROM
Unit 6: Plug in and practice!

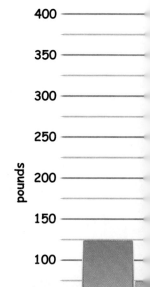

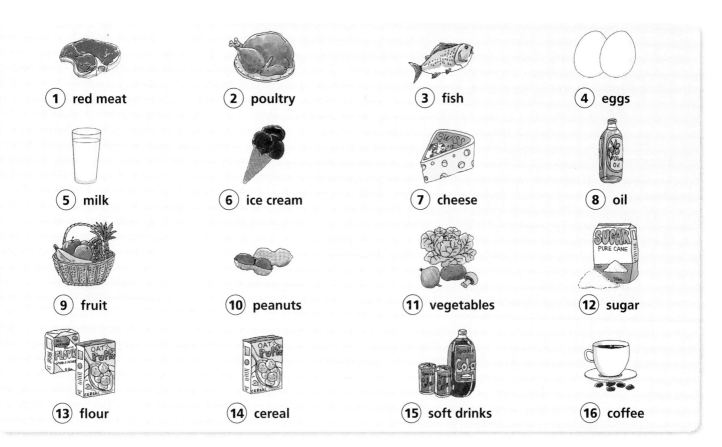

1. red meat
2. poultry
3. fish
4. eggs
5. milk
6. ice cream
7. cheese
8. oil
9. fruit
10. peanuts
11. vegetables
12. sugar
13. flour
14. cereal
15. soft drinks
16. coffee

How much does the average person in the United States eat each year?

Source: U.S. Department of Agriculture

Activities at a Restaurant

THINGS TO DO

❶ Learn New Words 080

Look at the picture. Listen to the words. Listen again and repeat.

(1) counter	(7) tray	(13) pour
(2) menu	(8) plate	(14) trip over
(3) waiter	(9) bowl	(15) fall off
(4) check	(10) napkin	(16) set the table
(5) booth	(11) serve food	(17) clear the table
(6) hostess	(12) take an order	(18) spill

Which words are new to you? Circle them.

❷ Write the Names 081

Listen to the sentences about the picture. Write the person's name.

1. _____   3. _____   5. _____

2. _____   4. _____   6. _____

❸ Talk About the Picture

Write 5 questions about the picture. Ask your classmates the questions.

Examples: *How many people are in the restaurant?*
What is the person behind Dot doing?

❹ Practice the Conversation 082

Listen to the conversation. Listen again and repeat.

A: Excuse me.

B: Yes. Can I help you?

A: Yes. Can you bring me a menu , please?

B: Sure. I'll get one right away.

Practice the conversation with a partner. Ask about these things.

1 some sugar	**2** some water	**3** a napkin
some	some	one

4 another cup of coffee	**5** the check	**6** some tea
another one	it	some

Lucy

Janet

Target Grammar

One, each, some, another, and the other(s) page 176

THINGS TO DO

1 Learn New Words 083

Look at the menu. Listen to the words. Listen again and repeat. Which words are new to you? Circle them.

2 Complete the Chart 084

Listen to the people ordering at the Casa Alberto Restaurant. Check (✔) the types of food they order.

	appetizer	soup	salad	main dish	dessert	beverage
1	○	○	✔	✔	○	✔
2	○	○	○	○	○	○
3	○	○	○	○	○	○
4	○	○	○	○	○	○
5	○	○	○	○	○	○

3 Practice the Conversation 085

Listen to the conversation. Listen again and repeat.

A: Are you ready to order?

B: Yes. I'd like a small onion soup and a chicken sandwich.

A: Do you want something to drink with your sandwich?

B: Yes. I'd like some tea, please.

A: Large or small?

B: Small, please.

Practice the conversation with a partner. Ask about these things.

1 the fish stew and a side order of fries

stew

a cup of tea / Large

2 the hamburger special and a small garden salad

hamburger

an orange soda / Small

3 the stuffed mushrooms and a large vegetable soup

soup

a root beer / Large

4

Casa Albert

1 appetizers

STUFFED MUSHROOMS	5.25
SHRIMP COCKTAIL	4.75

2 soups

	Small	Large
ONION	2.50	3.50
CHICKEN	1.75	2.50
BLACK BEAN	1.75	2.50
VEGETABLE	1.75	2.50

3 salads

	Small	Large
FRUIT SALAD	2.50	4.50
GARDEN SALAD	2.00	4.00

Target Grammar

Quantifiers   page 177

4 main dishes

FISH STEW	10.75
CHICKEN IN A BASKET	8.50
HAMBURGER SPECIAL	7.50
SPAGHETTI AND MEATBALLS	6.50

5 sandwiches

CHICKEN	4.50
STEAK	6.00
GRILLED CHEESE	3.00

6 side orders

MASHED POTATOES	2.25
FRENCH FRIES	2.75
WHITE RICE	2.25
GREEN BEANS	2.50
MIXED VEGETABLES	2.50

7 desserts

RICE PUDDING	2.25
CAKE	2.75
ICE CREAM	2.25

8 beverages

	Small	Large
TEA	1.50	2.25
COFFEE	1.50	2.25
MILK	1.25	2.00
COLA, GINGER ALE, ORANGE, ROOT BEER	1.75	2.50

Enjoy! CA

WINDOW ON MATH

Computing a Tip

A Read the meal receipt and explanation.

In many states, you pay a tax on food in a restaurant. It is often 5–8%. People usually pay a tip for service. It is often 20%. To compute a 20% tip, change 20% to a decimal number, .20. Then multiply the total food cost, before tax, by .20.

EXAMPLE: $7.00 × .20 = $1.40

B Complete the chart below.

Total food cost:	$16.00	$24.00	$32.00
5% tax:	_____	_____	_____
20% tip:	_____	_____	_____
Total cost of meal:	_____	_____	_____

Casa Alberto

total food:	$7.00
tax:	$0.35
tip:	$1.40
Total:	**$8.75**

Thank you!

Cooking at Home: Thanksgiving

THINGS TO DO

❶ Learn New Words 🎧 086

Look at the pictures. Listen to the words. Listen again and repeat. Which words are new to you? Circle them.

❷ Preview

Scan the story. Circle the correct answers.

1. Where do people celebrate Thanksgiving?

   A. in the United States only   **B.** in the United States and Canada

2. Why do people celebrate Thanksgiving?

   A. to give thanks for food   **B.** to celebrate their freedom

3. When was the first Thanksgiving?

   A. in 1921   **B.** in 1621

❸ Check *True* or *False*

Read the story and check (✔) *True* or *False*.

	True	False
1. People celebrate Thanksgiving on different days in Canada and in the United States.	○	○
2. The first Thanksgiving meal was held in Massachusetts.	○	○
3. The Pilgrims lived in Canada before they came to the United States.	○	○
4. Today, people don't celebrate Thanksgiving.	○	○
5. Turkey is the main dish on Thanksgiving.	○	○

❹ Write

A. Look at the recipe for mashed potatoes and answer the questions.

1. How many ingredients are in the recipe? _____

2. How many steps are there in the instructions for making mashed potatoes? _____

3. How much milk do you use? _____

4. What do you boil? _____

5. What do you mash? _____

B. Write the recipe for a dish you like. Then share it with the class.

① fry

② bake

③ boil

④ cut up

⑤ slice

⑥ mix

⑦ peel

⑧ mash

⑨ heat

Thanksgiving

Thanksgiving is a national holiday in the United States and Canada. In Canada, it is celebrated on the second Monday in October, and in the United States, it is celebrated on the fourth Thursday of November. The main message of Thanksgiving is to give thanks for the food we have and to share with people who don't have as much.

The first official Thanksgiving dinner in the United States was in 1621 in Plymouth, Massachusetts. The Native American people who lived there celebrated it with the Pilgrims. The Pilgrims were one of the first groups of European people who came to live in the United States. The Pilgrims and the Native Americans made a big dinner together to celebrate the food they grew.

Today, people usually celebrate Thanksgiving with family and close friends. They eat a big meal together like the Native Americans and Pilgrims did. The traditional menu is turkey with bread stuffing, mashed potatoes, vegetables, and cranberry sauce. Families spend the day cooking, eating, watching football, and in the United States, watching the Macy's Thanksgiving Day Parade on TV.

1621: the Native Americans and the Pilgrims

Mashed Potatoes

Ingredients

- 2 pounds of potatoes, peeled and cut up into small pieces
- 1/4 cup of butter, cut up into small pieces
- 1/2 cup of milk, heated
- salt and black pepper to taste

Instructions

1. Fill a large pot with water and heat until it boils.
2. Put potatoes into boiling water and cook them until they are soft.
3. Pour the water out of the pot.
4. Add the milk and butter to the potatoes. Mash them until they are soft and fluffy.
5. Mix in salt and pepper.

Target Grammar

Adjective + noun   *page 179*

LESSON 5 — Ordering at a Deli

❶ Practice Pronunciation: Intonation Patterns in Sentences and Questions 🎧 087

A. Listen to the sentences. Listen again and repeat.

1. We use falling intonation for statements.   I'd like a small coffee.

2. We use rising intonation for *yes / no* questions.   Would you like something to drink?

3. We use falling intonation for information questions.   What size salad?

B. Write the intonation marks over the questions and responses. Listen to check your answers. 🎧 088

1. Waiter: Would you like dessert tonight?
   Customer: No, thank you.

2. Waiter: What kind of soup would you like?
   Customer: I'll have the chicken soup.

3. Waiter: Are you ready to order?
   Customer: Yes. I'll have a hamburger.

4. Waiter: What can I get for you?
   Customer: I'll have a salad.

C. Work with a partner. Take turns asking and answering the questions from Activity B.

❷ Listen and Write 🎧 089

Listen to three people ordering at a deli. Check (✔) what each person orders. Then write the total you hear for each order.

	Customer 1	Customer 2	Customer 3
Sandwiches			
Steak	✔	○	○
Chicken	○	○	○
Veggie	○	○	○
Salads			
Garden	○	○	○
Fruit	○	○	○
Beverages			
Coffee	○	○	○
Tea	○	○	○
Orange soda	○	○	○
Root beer	○	○	○
Total	$ _____	$ _____	$ _____

❸ Practice the Conversation: Placing a Food Order 090

Listen to the conversation. Listen again and repeat.

A: What can I get for you?

B: I'd like a turkey sandwich .

A: Would you like something to drink with that?

B: Sure. I'll have a root beer .

A: What size root beer ?

B: Large , please.

Practice the conversation with a partner. Use these ideas.

1 roast beef sandwich	**2** large salad	**3** large onion soup	**4** turkey sub and some chips	**5**
some soup	something to drink	a salad	a side dish	
vegetable soup	some tea	a chicken salad	some french fries	
soup	tea	salad	french fries	
Small	Large	Small	Large	

❹ Practice the Conversation: Computing the Cost of a Meal  091

Listen to the conversation. Listen again and repeat.

A: Can I help you?

B: Yes. I'd like a veggie sandwich .

A: Do you want some chips with that?

B: No, thank you.

A: Will that be all for you?

B: Let's see ... I'll have a small coffee , too.

A: That will be $5.50 .

Sandwiches			Soups 2.50 (Small)/4.00 (Large)	
Turkey Sandwich		5.00	Chicken Soup	
Roast Beef Sandwich		6.00	Vegetable Soup	
Veggie Sandwich		4.50	Chili	

Salads	Small	Large	Side Orders	
Garden Salad	2.50	4.50	Potato Chips	1.00
Tuna Fish Salad	3.00	5.00	Fresh Fruit	1.25

Beverages
Lemonade **2.00** (Small)/**2.50** (Large)
Soft Drinks **1.50** (Small)/**2.00** (Large)
Root Beer, Cola, Diet Cola, Orange, Ginger Ale
Coffee & Tea **1.00** (Small)/**1.75** (Large)

Practice the conversation with a partner.
Use these ideas. Read the menu to find the prices.

1 a large chicken soup	**2** a large garden salad	**3** a turkey sandwich	**4** a small chili	**5**
something to drink	some soup	fresh fruit	something to drink	
some potato chips	a small diet cola	a large lemonade	a small garden salad	
$5.00	?	?	?	

Food | 83

Food Groups

❶ Check True or False

Read the information on food groups on page 85. Look at the statements. Check (✔) *True* or *False*.

	True	False
1. The six food groups are grains, vegetables, fruits, oils, milk & dairy, and meat & beans.	○	○
2. Every day you should eat an equal amount of foods from each food group.	○	○
3. At least 80 percent of the grains you eat should be whole grains.	○	○
4. Canned vegetables are not part of the vegetable food group.	○	○
5. Many fruit juices have added sugar in them.	○	○
6. Only about 5 percent of your diet should be from the oil food group.	○	○
7. Milk is an important part of our diet because it keeps our bones healthy and strong.	○	○
8. Nuts are part of the vegetable food group.	○	○

❷ Think About It

Look at the food that each person ate today and decide what the best choice is for dinner. Use the information on page 85.

Name	Food she / he ate today	The best choice for dinner
Joshua	Breakfast: oat cereal, milk, and orange juice Lunch: a sandwich with cheese, tomatoes, cucumbers, and lettuce on whole wheat bread; potato chips, and an apple	a. baked fish, broccoli, and potatoes b. salad, bread, and ice cream
Elle	Breakfast: eggs with spinach, mushrooms, and cheese Lunch: a salad with lettuce, cheese, nuts, and grilled chicken Snack: yogurt	a. pasta with tomato sauce, bread, and grapes b. roast beef, zucchini, and carrots
Shawn	Breakfast: bananas, blueberries, strawberries, yogurt, granola made from whole oats; orange juice, and tea with milk Lunch: fried fish sandwich on white bread, an apple, and french fries	a. spinach salad with carrots, peppers, cucumbers, tomatoes, and nuts b. fried chicken, mashed potatoes with gravy, and white bread

❸ Your Diet in a Day

Write down everything that you eat in a day. Then write the food group each food belongs to. How does your diet compare to the information in the article? What foods do you need to eat more of? What foods should you eat less of? Share your answers with a partner.

Eating from All Six Food Groups

Eating right and exercising are two of the most important ways that you can live a long and healthy life. Eating right involves having a healthful balance of the six food groups in your diet every day.

Grains
Any food made from wheat, oats, cornmeal, and other grains is considered part of the grain food group. Grains should make up about 20% of your diet.

Examples: bread, cereal, rice, and pasta

Tip: At least half of the grains you eat every day should be whole grains. Look for the word "whole" in the name.

Vegetables
All vegetables are part of the vegetable food group. They can be raw, cooked, fresh, frozen or canned. Vegetables should make up about 25% of your diet.

Examples: broccoli, carrots, celery, corn, lettuce, spinach

Tip: There are different types of vegetables. Try to eat a lot of dark green and orange vegetables.

Fruits
Any fruit or 100% fruit juice is part of the fruit food group. The fruit can be fresh, canned, frozen, or cooked. Fruits should make up about 15% of your diet.

Examples: apples, bananas, blueberries, grapes, oranges, strawberries

Tip: Be careful when choosing fruit juices. Many of them have a lot of added sugar in them.

Oils
Oils are fats that are liquids. They come from many different plants and animals, like avocados, fish, nuts, and olives. You should not eat too much oil. Oils should only be about 5% or less of your diet.

Examples: canola oil, olive oil, sesame oil

Tip: Read food labels. Try to avoid eating foods that have a lot of trans fat or saturated fat.

Milk & Dairy
Milk and any food made from it are part of the milk food group. Milk foods help our bones stay strong and healthy. Milk foods should make up about 25% of your diet.

Examples: cheese, ice cream, milk, yogurt

Tip: Buy milk and milk foods that are made from low-fat or nonfat (skim) milk.

Meat and Beans
Foods made from meat, poultry, fish, nuts, and beans are part of the meat and beans food group, and have protein. Foods in this group should make up about 10% of your diet.

Examples: almonds, black beans, beef, chicken, eggs, salmon, tofu

Tip: Choose meat and poultry that are lean or low fat. Try to bake, grill, or broil meat instead of frying it.

What Do You Know?

❶ Listening Review 092

Listen to the conversation. To finish the conversation, listen and choose the correct answer: *A, B,* or *C.* Use the Answer Sheet.

1. A. No, thank you.
   B. Yes, I'd like some eggs.
   C. Yes, I did. I had some for breakfast.

2. A. Yes, I'll get one right away.
   B. Yes, you can have one.
   C. Yes, you are.

3. A. For here, please.
   B. Yes.I'd like a small chicken soup and a salad.
   C. Yes, it is.

4. A. Yes, I'd like some french fries please.
   B. Yes, I'd like some ice cream.
   C. No, thank you.

5. A. Large, please.
   B. No, thank you.
   C. Yes, it is.

Answer Sheet

	A	B	C
1	Ⓐ	Ⓑ	Ⓒ
2	Ⓐ	Ⓑ	Ⓒ
3	Ⓐ	Ⓑ	Ⓒ
4	Ⓐ	Ⓑ	Ⓒ
5	Ⓐ	Ⓑ	Ⓒ

❷ Listening Dictation 093

Listen and write the sentences you hear.

1. A: _____ ?
   B: Yes, I'd like a turkey sandwich and a small coffee.

2. A: Can you bring me a glass of water, please?
   B: _____ ?

3. A: _____ ?
   B: Yes. I'd like the baked fish dinner and an orange juice.

4. A: Do you want something to drink with your green salad?
   B: _____ .

5. A: What size soup would you like?
   B: _____ ?

3 Grammar Review

Circle the correct answer: *A, B,* or *C.*

1. I need _____ for my coffee.
- A. some sugars
- B. some sugar
- C. a sugar

2. Can you bring me _____ menu?
- A. another
- B. each
- C. some

3. Did you eat any _____ yesterday?
- A. fish
- B. fishes
- C. fishs

4. I'd like _____ soup, please.
- A. any
- B. some
- C. many

5. Some juice has _____ sugar added to it.
- A. many
- B. much
- C. a lot of

6. Eat lots of _____ every day.
- A. vegetables green
- B. green vegetables
- C. green

LEARNING LOG

I know these words:

- appetizer
- bake
- beverage
- boil
- booth
- bowl
- cereal
- check
- cheese
- clear the table
- coffee
- counter
- cut up

- dessert
- eggs
- fall off
- fish
- flour
- fruit
- fry
- heat
- hostess
- ice cream
- main dish
- mash
- menu

- milk
- mix
- napkin
- oil
- peanuts
- peel
- plate
- poultry
- pour
- red meat
- salad
- sandwich
- serve food

- set the table
- side order
- slice
- soft drink
- soup
- spill
- sugar
- take an order
- tip
- tray
- trip over
- vegetable
- waiter

I can ask:

- How much flour do you need?
- How many eggs do you want?
- Can you bring me a menu, please?
- What's your favorite dessert?
- How much was the tax?

I can say:

- I had fruit for breakfast yesterday.
- I'd like a small soup, please.
- I'd like a chicken sandwich.

I can write:

- a list of food
- a menu
- a recipe

Work-Out CD-ROM

Unit 6: Plug in and practice!

Manuel

THINGS TO DO

❶ Learn New Words 🎧 094

Look at the pictures. Listen to the words. Listen again and repeat.

① grandparents
② parents
③ aunt
④ uncle
⑤ cousin
⑥ brother-in-law
⑦ nephew
⑧ niece
⑨ fiancée
⑩ co-worker
⑪ boss
⑫ friend
⑬ neighbors
⑭ landlady

Which words are new to you? Circle them.

④ Richard

③ Lupe

❷ Listen and Circle *True* or *False* 🎧 095

Listen to Juan describe his family relationships. Circle *True* or *False*.

1. True	False	**3.** True	False	**5.** True	False
2. True	False	**4.** True	False	**6.** True	False

❸ Practice the Conversation 🎧 096

Listen to the conversation. Listen again and repeat.

A: Is this your coat ?

B: No, it's not mine. It's Maria's .

A: Who is Maria ?

B: She's Juan's grandmother .

⑤ Marco

⑥ Paul

Practice the conversation with a partner. Use these ideas.

1 plate	**2** jacket	**3** cup of coffee	**4**
Tom's	Lupe's	Marco's	💡
Tom	Lupe	Marco	
He's Juan's __?__	She's Juan's __?__	He's Juan's __?__	

❹ Write

Make a family tree with information about your family. Use Juan's diagram as an example. Tell a classmate about your family.

Example:

This is my sister.
Her name is Wen Yin.
She likes cooking.

This is my brother-in-law.
His name is Lee.
He likes cars.

Target Grammar

It's, *its*, and *'s*   *page 180*

⑦ Nick

Maria

1

9

Lisa

Tom

10

11

Mr. Li

Tito

Rosa

12

Joe

13

Mr. and Mrs. Nath

Marta

Me!(Juan)

Mrs. Chen

14

8

Sofia

Work-Out CD-ROM
Unit 7: Plug in and practice!

Relationships 89

Activities at a Wedding

THINGS TO DO

① Learn New Words 097

Look at the picture. Listen to the words. Listen again and repeat.

- ① bride
- ② groom
- ③ kiss
- ④ musicians
- ⑤ in a bad mood
- ⑥ make a toast
- ⑦ gifts
- ⑧ photographer
- ⑨ in a good mood
- ⑩ dance
- ⑪ hug
- ⑫ shake hands

Which words are new to you? Circle them.

② Listen and Circle 098

Listen and circle the correct name.

1. Ted   Frank
2. Sylvia   Sara
3. Lisa   Sofia
4. Juan   Nick
5. Tito   Thomas
6. Joe   Bill
7. Mr. Nath   Mr. Li
8. Richard   Ron

③ Talk About the Picture

Write 5 things about the picture. Share your ideas with the class.

Example: *The groom is standing next to the bride.*

④ Practice the Conversation 099

Listen to the conversation. Listen again and repeat.

A: Look at Tito !

B: Who's dancing with him ?

A: That's the mother of the bride .

B: Do you know her ?

A: Yes, I do. She's very friendly .

Practice the conversation with a partner. Ask about these people.

1 Marta	**2** Joe	**3** Mr. Li	**4**
kissing her	hugging him	standing with him	
one of her friends	one of Lisa's friends	the photographer	
him	her	him	
He's a nice guy	She's always in a good mood	He's talented	

John

Lucy

⑤ Frank

⑦

Sofia

Target Grammar

Possessive pronouns and object pronouns   *page 181*

Communicating in Social Situations

THINGS TO DO

❶ Learn New Words 🎧 100

Look at the pictures. Listen to the words. Listen again and repeat.
Which words are new to you? Circle them.

❷ Listen and Write 🎧 101

Listen to the conversations. Number the words and phrases from 1–5.

_____ compliment _____ apologize _____ disagree

_____ criticize ____1____ talk back

❸ Practice the Conversation 🎧 102

Listen to the conversation. Listen again and repeat.

A: How was your day?   A: That's too bad. What did he say?

B: Not so good.   B: He said I was careless.

A: What happened?

B: My boss criticized me.

Practice the conversation with a partner. Ask about these things.

1 Great / My boss complimented my writing	**2** Terrible / A man yelled at me	**3** Awful / My son talked back to me
That's wonderful!	Really?	Really?
it was very nice	I should slow down	he didn't want to study

❹ Interview

Work in a group. Take turns asking the questions.

Did you _____ yesterday?	Yes	No	Who?
ask anyone* for advice	○	○	_____
take care of anyone	○	○	_____
compliment anyone	○	○	_____
apologize to anyone	○	○	_____
interrupt anyone	○	○	_____

* Note: *Anyone* means "any person."

Target Grammar
Indefinite pronouns *page 183*

What do you think I should do?

① **ask for advice**

Sorry I'm late.

④ **apologize**

You are so careless.

⑦ **criticize**

② take care of

③ compliment

⑤ disagree

⑥ yell at

⑧ talk back

⑨ interrupt

Family Traditions

THINGS TO DO

❶ Predict

Look at the pictures and the title of the reading on page 95. Read the sentences. Check (✔) *I think so* or *I don't think so*.

	I think so.	I don't think so.
1. The Four Brothers are family members.	○	○
2. The Four Brothers may be brothers and sisters.	○	○
3. The Four Brothers are musicians.	○	○
4. The family is originally from the U.S.	○	○
5. This reading is about a group of doctors.	○	○
6. This reading is about real people.	○	○

Read the interview and check your predictions.

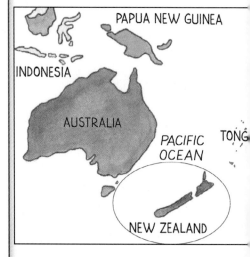

❷ Read and Take Notes

Read the interview and complete the sentences.

1. Paul said Marcel could ask him some _____.

2. Paul has _____ brothers and sisters.

3. He was born in _____.

4. His last name is _____.

5. Paul can speak English and _____.

6. Respecting your elders is an Italian _____.

❸ Write

Add 2 more interview questions about families to the list. Interview a classmate. Write your classmate's answers in the chart.

Interview Question	Answer
1. How many sisters and brothers do you have?	
2. Are small or large families traditional in your culture? Why do you think this is so?	
3. Can anyone in your family speak more than one language? If so, who?	
4. _____	
5. _____	

Example: *You: How many sisters and brothers do you have?*
Your Partner: I have 2 sisters and 2 brothers.

Target Grammar

Can, could, would, and *may* for requests and offers *page 184*

The Four Brothers: All in the Family

To The Four Brothers, music is a family affair. In fact, four of the five members of this music group are the children of Maria and Antonio Conti from New Zealand. Paul Conti is the oldest of The Four Brothers.

Interviewer:	Hi Paul. I'm Marcel Bettles from Snare magazine. Could I ask you a few questions?
Paul:	Hi Marcel. Sure, I'd be happy to answer your questions.
Interviewer:	There are 12 children in your family, 7 boys and 5 girls. Are large families common in New Zealand?
Paul:	No, they aren't very common.
Interviewer:	Can you tell me where you were born? Did you all grow up in New Zealand?
Paul:	I was born in Australia, but we all grew up in New Zealand. Our parents are from Italy. So we learned those customs.
Interviewer:	What are some of the customs?
Paul:	Respecting your elders. Not talking back. Listening to your parents.
Interviewer:	With such a large family, how do you take care of the little problems that come up?
Paul:	We have family meetings. We talk about anything that makes us unhappy. Like borrowing things without asking or taking too long in the bathroom.
Interviewer:	What languages do you speak at home?
Paul:	We all speak English and Italian.
Interviewer:	One more thing. Could you tell me the name of your most popular song?
Paul:	Sure! It's "Tell Me Again."

WINDOW ON MATH

Calculating Time Changes

There are different time zones around the world. To find out what time it is in a different country, add or subtract the difference from the time where you are. Remember that the clock starts over at 12 P.M. and 12 A.M.

Example: *New Zealand is 18 hours ahead of New York City. It is 1 P.M. in New York City. What time is it in New Zealand?*

1 P.M. + 18 hours = **7 A.M. (the next day)**

A Calculate the times.

1. Mexico City is 1 hour behind New York City. It is 12 P.M. in New York City. What time is it in Mexico City?_____

2. Beijing is 16 hours ahead of Los Angeles It is 6 A.M. in Los Angeles. What time is it in Beijing?
_____

3. Cape Verde is 4 hours ahead of Boston. It is 9 A.M. in Boston. What time is it in Cape Verde?
_____

Disagreeing Politely and Offering Help

❶ Practice Pronunciation: Suffixes and Syllable Stress 103

A suffix is a short syllable that we add to the end of a word to change the part of speech. When we add some suffixes to words, we need to change the syllable stress. When we add other suffixes, it stays the same.

A. Listen to the words and underline the syllable that receives the most stress. Listen again and repeat.

Base word	+ suffix		Base word	+ suffix
1. problem	problematic		**5.** invite	invitation
2. tradition	traditional		**6.** marry	marital
3. apology	apologize		**7.** music	musician
4. critic	criticize		**8.** photograph	photographic

B. Write the words in the correct place in the chart.

-ic suffix	-ize suffix	-al suffix	-ion / -ian suffix
problematic			

Which suffixes change the syllable stress? _____

❷ Practice the Conversation: Disagreeing Politely 104

Listen to the conversation. Listen again and repeat.

A: This is a great movie .

B: Do you really think so?

A: Yes, I love it . Don't you?

B: No, not really. I think it's kind of boring .

A: Okay. Let's watch the other movie .

B: Okay!

Practice the conversation with a partner. Use these ideas.

1 terrific pizza /
think it's delicious

too salty

order from the other restaurant

2 wonderful house /
think it's beautiful

too traditional

buy the other house

3 nice car /
think it's sporty

kind of small

rent the other car

4

❸ Practice the Conversation: Offering to Help 105

Listen to the conversation. Listen again and repeat.

A: Can I help you with the dishes?

B: Thanks for offering, but I'm all set.

A: Is there something else I can do?

B: Well, you could clear the kitchen table.

A: Sure. I'd be happy to clear it!

Practice the conversation with a partner. Use these ideas.

1 Could I help you carry that box	**2** Can I help you write the invitations	**3** Would you like help with dinner	**4**
I can get it	I'm almost finished	I'm almost finished	
I can do	I can do for the wedding	I can do to help	
open the door	help decorate	put away these groceries	
open it	help with that	put them away	

❹ Practice the Conversation: Asking for Clarification 106

Listen to the conversation. Listen again and repeat.

A: Could you mail this invitation for me?

B: Sure. No problem.

A: It needs to get there by tomorrow.

B: So should I send it by Express Mail?

A: Yes, that would be great.

B: Okay. I'll go to the post office now to send it.

Practice the conversation with a partner. Use these ideas.

1 set the table	**2** make the mashed potatoes	**3** download this music	**4**
I'd be happy to	No problem	I'd be happy to	
The Murphys are eating with us tonight	I need to leave for work so I don't have time to make them	I love this musician	
set it for six people / set the table now	peel the potatoes first / peel and chop the potatoes now	download a few songs / download them now	

Getting Along with Others

❶ Preview and Check *True* or *False*

Look at the title of the article and the photo on page 99. Then look at the statements and check (✔) *True* or *False*.

	True	False
1. I think you would find this article in a newspaper or magazine.	○	○
2. I think this article is for people who work alone.	○	○
3. I think this article is about how to find a job.	○	○
4. I think this article has advice in it.	○	○

❷ Read and Match

Read the article on page 99. Match the sentences.

1. __d__ If you don't understand something …   **a.** you should not take it personally.

2. _____ If someone says something that upsets you …   **b.** you should compliment him or her.

3. _____ If you have a question …   **c.** you shouldn't stand too close.

4. _____ When your co-worker does a good job …   **d.** you should ask a question.

5. _____ When someone is sick …   **e.** you should offer to help out.

6. _____ If someone criticizes you …   **f.** you should ask it in a clear and positive way.

7. _____ When you talk to people …   **g.** you should finish it on time.

8. _____ When you are doing a project …   **h.** you should ask how you can do a better job.

❸ Interview

Work with a partner. Ask the questions below and fill out the chart.

At work or school, how often do you _____ ?	Never	Sometimes	Always
ask questions when you don't understand something	○	○	○
get upset when someone says something negative	○	○	○
compliment others on good work	○	○	○
ask for more information when you are criticized	○	○	○
offer to help others	○	○	○
finish assignments on time	○	○	○

Tell the class about your partner.

Getting Along with Others at Work

If you want to succeed in your job, you need to get along, or have good relationships, with your co-workers. Here are a few suggestions:

- Watch your co-workers and supervisor. See how they do things. Ask questions if you don't understand something.

- Don't take things personally. A co-worker may say something that upsets you. Remember that he or she may just be in a bad mood.

- Ask questions in a clear and positive way. (For example: "Thank you for showing me how to operate the machine. Could you show me how to use this, too?")

- Be a team player. Give ideas and suggestions to others. Offer to help out when someone is sick.

- Be upbeat. Compliment co-workers on their good work.

- Be open to new ideas. If someone criticizes you, ask how you can do a better job.

- Use professional body language. Stand at least two feet away from people when you talk to them. Also, be sure that you look and smell clean when you are at work.

- Be on time. Time is very important in the United States, especially at work. Arrive to work and meetings on time and finish projects when they are due.

❶ Listening Review 🎧 107

Look at the pictures and listen. Choose the correct answer: *A*, *B*, or *C*.
Use the Answer Sheet.

1. A  B  C

2. A B C

3. A B C

4. A B  C

5. A  Sorry I'm late. B We're having chicken for dinner. I hate chicken. C The chicken is delicious. Thank you.

Answer Sheet

1 (A) (B) (C)
2 (A) (B) (C)
3 (A) (B) (C)
4 (A) (B) (C)
5 (A) (B) (C)

❷ Listening Dictation 🎧 108

Listen and write the sentences you hear.

1. A: _____?
B: Twelve.

2. A: _____?
B: That's Ron.

3. A: _____?
B: Yes, I do. He's a nice guy.

4. A: How was your day?
B: _____.

5. A: Can I help you clean the house?
B: _____.

❸ Grammar Review

Circle the correct answer: *A*, *B*, or *C*.

1. This is my nephew. _____ name is Pat.

   A. My
   B. Her
   C. His

2. Sue: Excuse me. Is this your jacket?
   Joe: No, it's not _____ . My jacket is blue.

   A. my
   B. mine
   C. yours

3. Who's hugging _____ ?

   A. she
   B. her
   C. hers

4. Do you know _____ ?

   A. they
   B. them
   C. their

5. Did you compliment _____ yesterday?

   A. anyone
   B. she
   C. I

6. _____ you go to the store for me?

   A. May
   B. Could
   C. When

LEARNING LOG

I know these words:

- ○ apologize
- ○ ask for advice
- ○ aunt
- ○ boss
- ○ bride
- ○ brother-in-law
- ○ compliment
- ○ cousin

- ○ co-worker
- ○ criticize
- ○ dance
- ○ disagree
- ○ fiancée
- ○ friend
- ○ gifts
- ○ grandparents

- ○ groom
- ○ hug
- ○ in a bad mood
- ○ in a good mood
- ○ interrupt
- ○ kiss
- ○ landlady
- ○ make a toast

- ○ musicians
- ○ neighbors
- ○ nephew
- ○ niece
- ○ parents
- ○ photographer
- ○ shake hands
- ○ take care of

- ○ talk back
- ○ tradition
- ○ uncle
- ○ yell at

I can ask:

- ○ Where do your grandparents live?
- ○ What are your parents' first names?
- ○ Who's dancing with . . . ?
- ○ Do you know her?
- ○ What did he say?
- ○ How was your day?
- ○ Can I help with the dishes?
- ○ Is there anything else I can do?
- ○ Do you really think so?

I can say:

- ○ The groom is standing next to the bride.
- ○ That's the mother of the bride.
- ○ My boss criticized me.
- ○ That's too bad.
- ○ Thanks for offering, but I'm all set.
- ○ That would be great.

I can write:

- ○ information in a family diagram
- ○ a description of your family
- ○ interview questions and answers

Work-Out CD-ROM

Unit 7: Plug in and practice!

THINGS TO DO

❶ Learn New Words 109

Look at the pictures. Listen to the words. Listen again and repeat. Which words are new to you? Circle them.

❷ Write

Complete the chart with parts of the body for each category below. Then compare lists with a partner.

I have muscles in my _____ .	I have bones in my _____ .	My _____ is a joint.
1. arm	1. finger	1. shoulder
2. _____	2. _____	2. _____
3. _____	3. _____	3. _____
4. _____	4. _____	
5. _____	5. _____	

❸ Check *True, False,* or *I Don't Know*

Read the statements. Check (✔) *True, False,* or *I don't know.* Correct the false statements.

	True	False	I don't know.
1. You breathe with your lungs.	○	○	○
2. An ankle is a joint.	○	○	○
3. You can move your arm at the joints.	○	○	○
4. You have hair on your teeth.	○	○	○
5. Your muscles move your blood around.	○	○	○
6. You have more bones than teeth.	○	○	○
7. People cannot live without a brain.	○	○	○
8. In the past, doctors could not help people with heart problems, but now they can.	○	○	○

❹ Work Together

Work with a partner. Take turns. Name a body part. Your partner points to it.

Examples: *Point to your left ear.*
Point to your right ankle.

Target Grammar

Can and *could* for ability
page 186

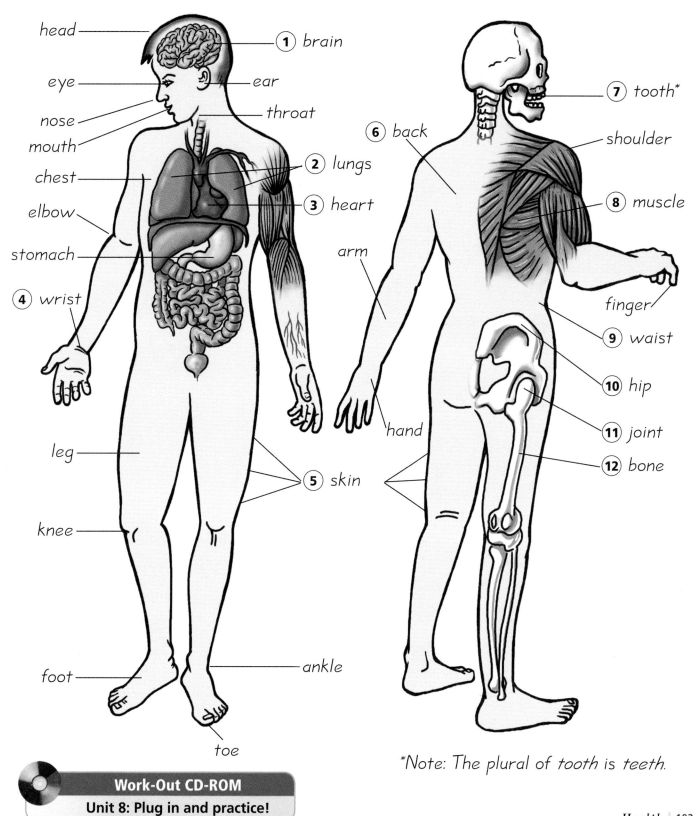

head

eye

nose

mouth

chest

elbow

stomach

(4) wrist

leg

knee

foot

toe

(1) brain

ear

throat

(2) lungs

(3) heart

(5) skin

ankle

(6) back

arm

hand

(7) tooth*

shoulder

(8) muscle

finger

(9) waist

(10) hip

(11) joint

(12) bone

*Note: The plural of *tooth* is *teeth*.

Work-Out CD-ROM

Unit 8: Plug in and practice!

Describing Illnesses and Injuries

THINGS TO DO

❶ Learn New Words 110

Look at the pictures. Listen to the words. Listen again and repeat. Which words are new to you? Circle them.

❷ Listen and Write 111

Listen and look at the pictures. Write the name of the person that has the illness or injury.

① _____   ③ _____   ⑤ _____

② _____   ④ _____   ⑥ _____

❸ Practice the Conversation 112

Listen to the conversation. Listen again and repeat.

A: Is your fever getting any better?

B: No, I don't think so. Do you think I should see a doctor?

A: Yes. And I think you should drink more liquids.

B: Maybe you're right.

Practice the conversation with a partner. Ask about these things.

1 sprain	**2** cold
put ice on it	take some medicine
shouldn't go to soccer practice today	should stay home from work today

3 cut	**4**
put a bandage on it	
should go to the doctor	

❹ Find Someone Who

Talk to your classmates. Find someone who answers *yes*. Write the person's name in the chart.

Find someone who at least once _____.	Person's Name
1. had a cold	_____
2. had a burn	_____
3. had a cut	_____
4. had a bruise	_____
5. had an infection	_____
6. had a blister	_____

Injuries

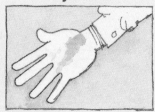

① burn

Chad

② cut

③ fracture

④ sprain

Matt

⑤ bruise

Shawn

⑥ shock

Symptoms and Illnesses

7 rash

8 fever

9 cold

10 flu

11 infection

12 feel dizzy

13 blister

14 feel nauseous

15 bleed

Target Grammar

Should and *shouldn't* *page 188*

THINGS TO DO

❶ Learn New Words 🎧 113

Look at the picture. Listen to the words. Listen again and repeat.

① emergency room   ⑥ sling   ⑪ waiting area
② examining room   ⑦ ice pack   ⑫ crutches
③ X-ray   ⑧ admissions desk   ⑬ cast
④ radiology   ⑨ splint   ⑭ bandage
⑤ stitches   ⑩ wheelchair

Which words are new to you? Circle them.

❷ Listen and Circle *True* or *False* 🎧 114

Listen to the sentences and look at the picture. Circle *True* or *False*.

① True   False   ③ True   False   ⑤ True   False
② True   False   ④ True   False   ⑥ True   False

❸ Talk About the Picture

Write 5 questions about the picture. Ask your classmates the questions.

Example: *What is wrong with Fred?*

❹ Practice the Conversation 🎧 115

Listen to the conversation. Listen again and repeat.

A: What happened to your leg ? It looks very painful.

B: I sprained my knee . I had to go to the emergency room.

A: Did they take an X-ray ?

B: Yes, and then they put this splint on my knee .

Practice the conversation with a partner. Ask about these things.

1 leg	**2** arm	**3** elbow	**4**
broke it	burned it	sprained it	
put you in a wheelchair	put burn cream on it	put ice on it	
put this cast on it	put this bandage on it	put it in this sling	

Nina

Ann

14

13

12

Fred

Lupe

Alice

Target Grammar

Adverbs of degree   *page 189*

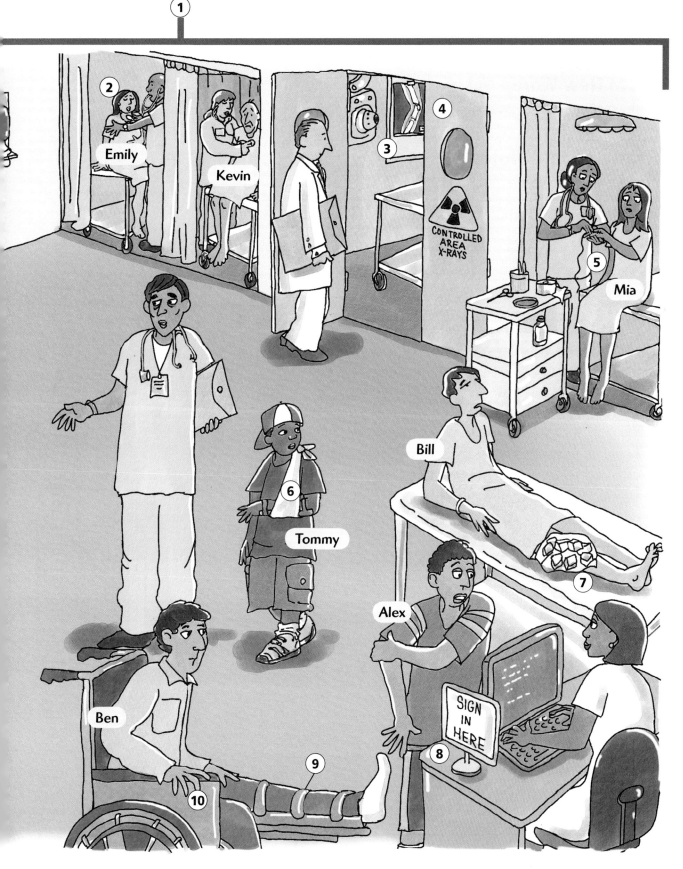

Reading Medicine Labels

THINGS TO DO

❶ Learn New Words 🎧 116

Look at the medicine labels. Listen to the words. Listen again and repeat.

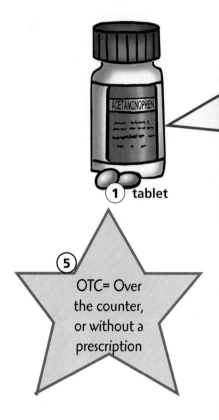

① tablet

❷ Read and Take Notes

Read the labels and complete the chart.

Name of Medicine	Form	How Much?	How Often?
A. acetaminophen	tablet		every 4–6 hours
B.	liquid		
C. hydrocortisone			
D.		1	

⑤ OTC= Over the counter, or without a prescription

❸ Check *True* or *False*

Read the statements. Check (✔) *True* or *False*. Correct the false statements.

	True	False
1. Children older than six can take acetaminophen.	○	○
2. You should never swallow hydrocortisone cream.	○	○
3. Ampicillin and Max-Relief are available OTC.	○	○
4. People sometimes take acetaminophen for a toothache.	○	○
5. People usually take ampicillin when they have a rash.	○	○
6. You can't use the ampicillin after 2013.	○	○

❹ Write

Make a chart like this. List medicines you or your family use. Write the health problem or symptom next to the name of the medicine.

⑥ caps

> **WRITING TIP**
> We use a lowercase letter to write medicine names unless they are brand names.

Name of Medicine	Use the Medicine for These Problems
ⓐcetaminophen	headache, backache
Ⓜax-Ⓡelief lowercase letter	
hydrocortisone cream	

capital letter

Target Grammar
Adverbs of frequency   *page 190*

A Acetaminophen

100 tablets 325 mg

For pain due to:

headache   toothache

backache   muscle aches

a cold

Directions: Do not take more than directed. Adults and children 12 years or older : take 2 tablets every 4 to 6 hours.

Keep out of reach of children.

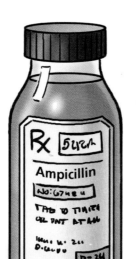

B Ampicillin

Best Drug

Rx# 6885150   Date 08/21/2012

Colin James

Shake well. Take one teaspoon three times a day for seven days for ear infection.
Ampicillin 150 mg #21
Discard after 8/21/2013

Dr. R. Jackson

② teaspoon

C Hydrocortisone cream

Drug Fair

RX# 74432   Date 12/03/2012

Claire Donnalley

Wash skin. Apply to affected area 3 to 4 times a day to relieve pain, swelling, and itching due to rashes.

Pr. by A. Dickinson, MD

Warnings: For external use only. Do not swallow. Do not use near eyes. KEEP THIS AND ALL DRUGS OUT OF THE REACH OF CHILDREN. If swallowed, call a Poison Control Center immediately.

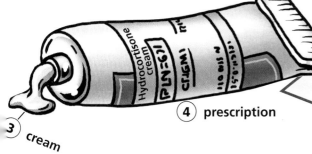

③ cream

④ prescription

D Max-Relief Cold and Flu

The strongest medicine available over the counter. For fever, headache, body aches, runny nose, and sneezing associated with a cold or flu.

12 capsules   Take 1 capsule every 12 hours.

Warnings:

Ask a doctor before use if you have breathing problems, lung, or heart disease.

Do not give to children under 12 years of age.

WINDOW ON MATH

Ounces, Tablespoons, and Teaspoons

1 tablespoon (tbsp.) = 3 teaspoons (tsp.)

2 tablespoons (tbsp.) = 1 fluid ounce (fl. oz.)

Complete the sentences.

1. 2 tbsp. = _____ tsp.

2. 1 tbsp. = _____ fl. oz.

3. 6 tsp. = _____ fl. oz.

4. 1.5 tsp. = _____ tbsp.

5. ½ fl. oz. = _____ tsp.

Talking to Health Professionals

❶ Practice Pronunciation: *can* and *can't* 117

We pronounce the *a* in *can* and *can't* differently in sentences. We use the schwa sound (*uh*) for the *a* in *can*. The *a* in *can't* sounds more like a short *a*, as in *cat*.

A. Listen to the sentences. Listen again and repeat.

1. Children can take some medicines.
2. Children can't take aspirin.
3. You can fill this prescription at the drugstore.

4. You can't take the medicine after the expiration date.
5. Can I play soccer?
6. Can't I play soccer?

B. Listen to the sentences. Underline the word you hear. 118

1. He can / <u>can't</u> come to school today.
2. She can / can't go back to work.
3. Bob can / can't play soccer today.

4. She can / can't walk without crutches.
5. I can / can't exercise today.
6. Tara can / can't take off her bandage.

C. Work with a partner. Take turns reading the sentences in Activity B. Respond with *Oh, good* or *That's too bad.*

Example: *A: He can come to school today.*
   B: Oh, good.

❷ Practice the Conversation: Describing an Illness 119

Listen to the conversation. Listen again and repeat.

A: I'd like to make an appointment as soon as possible.
B: What's the problem?
A: I have a high fever .
B: Do your joints hurt ?
A: Yes. Can the doctor see me today?
B: I have an opening this afternoon .
A: Great. I'll take it.

Practice the conversation with a partner. Use these ideas.

1 an ear infection	**2** a toothache	**3** the flu	**4** a rash	**5**
you have a fever / later today	you have any bleeding / tomorrow morning	you feel nauseous / this morning	you have a fever / this afternoon	

❸ Practice the Conversation: Following Instructions 120

Listen to the conversation. Listen again and repeat.

A: What happened?

B: I fell down in a soccer game and hurt my elbow .

A: It looks like you have a sprain . Use this sling until the next appointment.

B: Okay.

A: Also, here's a prescription for some pain medication.

B: How often do I take it?

A: Take one tablet two times a day . Don't take more than that.

B: Can I play soccer ?

A: No. Not until I see you again.

Practice the conversation with a partner. Use these ideas.

1 fell down the stairs / foot	**2** had an accident at work / hip	**3** slipped on some ice / ankle	**4** 
fracture We'll put on a cast / 2 tablets 3 times a day	bruise Use this ice pack as needed / 2 capsules 4 times a day	sprain Wear this bandage / 1 tablet 4 times a day	
drive my car	go back to work	exercise	

❹ Listen and Write 121

Listen to two people making doctor's appointments. Fill out the appointment cards.

①

Family Practice Physicians
Appointment

Name: _____

Date: _____   Time: _____ A.M / P.M.

Appointment: ❏ first time ❏ routine checkup ❏ follow-up

②

Family Practice Physicians
Appointment

Name: _____

Date: _____   Time: _____ A.M / P.M.

Appointment: ❏ first time ❏ routine checkup ❏ follow-up

Reading a Medical Advertisement

❶ Read and Check *True* or *False*

Read the information in the flyer on page 113. Check (✔) *True* or *False*. Correct the false statements.

	True	False
1. The flyer is for flu vaccinations.	○	○
2. They are giving flu shots on one day only.	○	○
3. The flu shots are free for everyone.	○	○
4. They are giving the flu shots at the Newton Senior Center.	○	○
5. People over the age of 65 should get a flu shot.	○	○
6. A flu shot can give you the flu.	○	○

❷ Read and Take Notes

Read the flyer and write the answers in the chart.

1. Where can you get a flu shot?	
2. When can you get a flu shot?	
3. Why should you get a flu shot?	
4. Who should get a flu shot?	
5. How much does a flu shot cost?	
6. What is one risk of getting a flu shot?	

❸ Interview

Work with a partner. Ask the questions. Write your partner's answers.

1. Did you ever get a vaccination? If yes, which one?

_____

2. Did you ever get a flu shot?

_____

3. Do you think flu shots work? Why or why not?

_____

4. Do you think small children should get vaccinations? Why or why not?

_____

5. Do you think schools should make all children get vaccinations before they can come to school? Why or why not?

_____

The Newton Recreation Center & The Newton Senior Center will be offering:

Flu Vaccinations*

Friday, October 5
9:00 A.M. to 11:30 A.M.
Tuesday, October 23
4:00 P.M. to 6:00 P.M.

at the
Newton Recreation Center
2nd Floor, Community Room
55 Oak Street
Newton, TX 75966

No appointments are necessary.
The vaccinations will be *FREE* to seniors 65 years and older.

Flu Vaccination: $30.00

For further information, you can contact the Newton Senior Center at (598) 555-2583 or the Newton Recreation Department at (598) 555-7444, or find us on the web: www.newtonrec.org

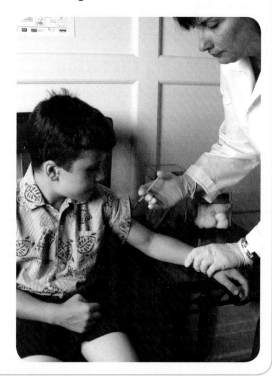

Q: Why should I get a flu shot?

A: The Centers for Disease Control recommend getting a flu shot every year. A flu shot helps protect you from the flu. People who might have more serious problems from the flu should be sure to get a flu shot. This includes children, pregnant women, people with heart and lung disease, and people 65 and older.

Q: What are the risks of getting a flu shot?

A: You cannot get the flu from a flu shot. The risk of a flu shot causing serious problems or death is extremely small. Allergic reactions could include breathing problems, rash, muscle weakness, or feeling dizzy.

*A *vaccination* protects people from some diseases.

❶ Listening Review  122

Look at the pictures and listen. Choose the correct answer: *A*, *B*, or *C*.
Use the Answer Sheet.

1. A   B   C

2. A   B   C

3. A   B   C

4. A   B   C

5. A   B    C

Answer Sheet

1 Ⓐ	Ⓑ	Ⓒ
2 Ⓐ	Ⓑ	Ⓒ
3 Ⓐ	Ⓑ	Ⓒ
4 Ⓐ	Ⓑ	Ⓒ
5 Ⓐ	Ⓑ	Ⓒ

❷ Listening Dictation 123

Listen and write the words you hear.

1. A: _____?

   B: No, I don't think so.

2. A: What happened to your hand?

   B: _____.

3. A: Did they put an ice pack on it?

   B: _____.

4. A: What happened?

   B: _____.

5. A: How often do I take it?

   B: _____.

❸ Grammar Review

Circle the correct answer: *A, B,* or *C.*

1. My sprained ankle is better, so now I _____ run again.

A. can
B. couldn't
C. should

2. You _____ to the doctor if you are sick.

A. should
B. should go
C. shouldn't go

3. You _____ today if you have a fever.

A. shouldn't
B. shouldn't work
C. should work

4. It looks _____.

A. very painful
B. very
C. painful very

5. How _____ should I take it?

A. sometimes
B. usually
C. often

6. When I was young, I _____ ski well.

A. can
B. can't
C. could

LEARNING LOG

I know these words:

- ○ admissions desk
- ○ back
- ○ bandage
- ○ bleed
- ○ blister
- ○ bone
- ○ brain
- ○ bruise
- ○ burn
- ○ capsule
- ○ cast
- ○ cold

- ○ cream
- ○ crutches
- ○ cut
- ○ emergency room
- ○ examining room
- ○ feel dizzy
- ○ feel nauseous
- ○ fever
- ○ flu
- ○ fracture
- ○ heart
- ○ hip

- ○ ice pack
- ○ infection
- ○ joint
- ○ lungs
- ○ muscle
- ○ OTC
- ○ prescription
- ○ radiology
- ○ rash
- ○ shock
- ○ skin
- ○ sling

- ○ splint
- ○ sprain
- ○ stitches
- ○ tablet
- ○ teaspoon
- ○ tooth
- ○ waist
- ○ waiting area
- ○ wrist
- ○ wheelchair
- ○ X-ray

I can ask:

- ○ Is your rash getting any better?
- ○ What happened to your leg?
- ○ What's wrong with Lupe's child?
- ○ Did you have to go to the emergency room?
- ○ How often do I take it?
- ○ Can I play soccer?

I can say:

- ○ Maybe you should see a doctor.
- ○ I sprained my knee.
- ○ I'd like to make an appointment.
- ○ You shouldn't go to work.
- ○ You should always read a medicine label.
- ○ You can't take medicine after the expiration date.

I can write:

- ○ a description of illnesses and medications
- ○ medicine names using lowercase and capital letters
- ○ information on an appointment card

Work-Out CD-ROM

Unit 8: Plug in and practice!

THINGS TO DO

❶ Learn New Words 124

Look at the pictures. Listen to the words. Listen again and repeat.

❷ Write

Make a chart like this. Write 3 things you see in each room.

BEDROOM	KITCHEN	LIVING ROOM
a lamp	a refrigerator	

❸ Listen and Write 125

Listen to the instructions. Write the number of the picture.

First, _____   Second, _____   Third, _____

Fourth, _____   After that, _____   Finally, _____

Compare your answers with a classmate's.

❹ Practice the Conversation 126

Listen to the conversation. Listen again and repeat.

A: Oh, no. We'd better hurry, or we'll be late.

B: Did you unplug the coffeepot ?

A: Yes, and I put away the milk .

B: Good. I turned off the TV .

A: Thanks. Let's go!

Practice the conversation with a partner. Use these ideas.

1 turn down the thermostat	**2** turn off the radio	**3** put back the milk
shut off the stove	locked the back door	took out the trash
put away the cereal	shut off the water	turned off the CD player

Target Grammar

Simple past review *page 192*

① shut off

⑤ take out

⑨ turn down

(2) plug in

(3) pick up

(4) put away

(6) turn on

(7) turn off

(8) put back

(10) lock

(11) unlock

(12) unplug

Work-Out CD-ROM

Unit 9: Plug in and practice!

Identifying Problems at Home

THINGS TO DO

❶ Learn New Words 🎧 127

Look at the pictures. Listen to the words. Listen again and repeat.

❷ Practice the Conversation 🎧 128

Listen to the conversation. Listen again and repeat.

A: Hi. This is your tenant in apartment 101.

B: Hi. What can I do for you?

A: Could you please take a look at my refrigerator?

B: Is the door stuck again?

A: No. This time it's leaking.

B: Okay. I'll be over as soon as I can.

Practice the conversation with a partner. Use these ideas.

1 dryer	**2** sliding door	**3** sink	**4** toilet
Is it overheating	Is it sticking	Is it leaking	Is it clogged
the door is stuck	I can't lock it	it's clogged	it's leaking

❸ Listen and Write 🎧 129

Listen to the telephone messages. Write the problem.

Apartment	Problem
103	
210	
507	
401	

❹ Write

Choose a problem from Activity 3. Complete the form below.

MAINTENANCE REQUEST FORM	
Date:	
Apartment Number:	
Problem:	
Signature:	

Things that leak

1 valve

Things that overheat

5 toaster oven

Things that clog

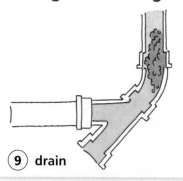

9 drain

Things that stick

13 window

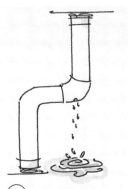

2 faucet

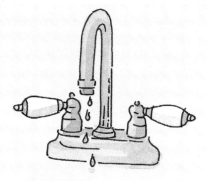

3 pipe

4 roof

6 space heater

7 clothes dryer

8 hair dryer

10 sink

11 toilet

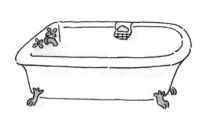

12 bathtub

14 key

15 drawer

16 sliding door

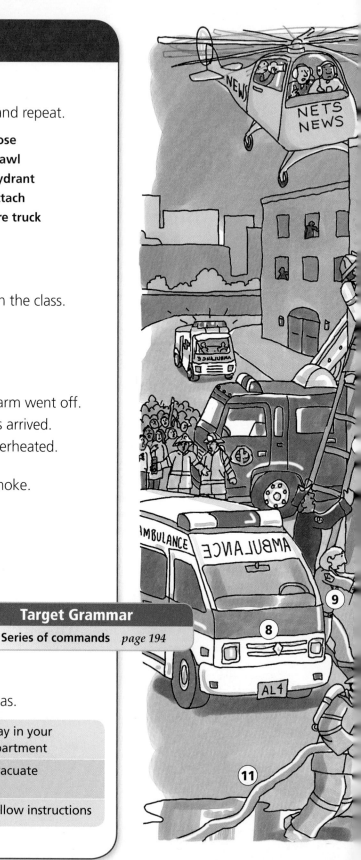

THINGS TO DO

❶ Learn New Words 130

Look at the picture. Listen to the words. Listen again and repeat.

① smoke
② spray
③ fire escape
④ rescue
⑤ climb

⑥ evacuate
⑦ ladder
⑧ ambulance
⑨ cover
⑩ firefighter

⑪ hose
⑫ crawl
⑬ hydrant
⑭ attach
⑮ fire truck

Which words are new to you? Circle them.

❷ Talk About the Picture

Write 5 things about the picture. Share your ideas with the class.

Example: *One firefighter is climbing up a ladder.*

❸ Put in Order

Put the events in order from first (1) to last (8).

_____ He went to bed.

_____ He called 911.

__1__ Sam turned on the space heater.

_____ He woke up.

_____ The smoke alarm went off.

_____ The fire trucks arrived.

_____ The heater overheated.

_____ He smelled smoke.

❹ Practice the Conversation 131

Listen to the conversation. Listen again and repeat.

A: What should we do if there is a fire?

B: Call 911. Don't take the elevator .

A: Should we go down the stairs ?

B: Yes, if possible. Or go down the fire escape .

A: Okay.

> ◎ **Target Grammar**
> Series of commands   *page 194*

Practice the conversation with a partner. Use these ideas.

1 jump out the window	**2** open the door to the hall	**3** stay in your apartment
go down the fire escape	crawl under the smoke	evacuate
use a ladder	wait by the window	follow instructions

APARTMENT FIRE LEAVES 17 HOMELESS

A fire last night at 1420 South Main St. damaged six apartments, forcing residents to find new homes for the night. Firefighters think the fire started when a space heater

THINGS TO DO

❶ Learn New Words 132

Listen to the words. Listen again and repeat.

① overload
② overheat
③ overflow
④ temperature
⑤ Celsius
⑥ Fahrenheit

❷ Think About the Topic

Look at the picture on page 123. What problems do you see? Share your ideas with your classmates.

❸ Read and Take Notes

Make a chart like this. Read the article. Write things you should do and things you shouldn't do to prevent a fire.

Do	Don't
keep materials away from stove	leave food on the stove unattended

❹ Write

> **WRITING TIP**
> When you tell a story, tell the events in order.

Write a story about a fire or other emergency at home that you know about.

Example: *My brother had a fire in his house a year ago. It was very cold outside—only 15°F. He turned on a space heater in his bedroom. He put the heater too close to the curtains. Then he went to bed. Later, the space heater overheated. The curtains were on fire. Fortunately, he got out of the house quickly.*

DANGER ZONE

KITCHEN

LIVING ROOM

BEDROOM

BATHROOM

BASEMENT, ATTIC, OR GARAGE

Target Grammar

Adverbs of point in time *page 19*

FIRE SAFETY TIPS

Keep loose materials, such as dish towels and pot holders, away from the stove. Lock up matches and lighters so children cannot play with them. Never leave food on the stove, in the oven, or in the microwave unattended. Keep kids at least three feet away from a hot stove.

Keep space heaters at least three feet away from rugs, walls, furniture, curtains, and other flammable materials. Never run electrical cords under rugs—the wires could fray and set the rug on fire. Also, don't overload electrical sockets with plugs.

Don't fold electric blankets while they are plugged in. Never leave a lit candle unattended, and never smoke in bed.

If an appliance is smoking or smells odd, unplug it immediately. Store flammable materials like nail polish, aerosol cans, towels, and magazines away from heated appliances like hair dryers.

Keep flammable liquids, clothes, and papers away from the furnace, chemicals, and heat sources. Throw out oily rags, or store them in sealed containers.

WINDOW ON MATH

Converting Temperatures

A Read the information below.
To convert Fahrenheit (F) to Celsius (C), subtract 32, multiply by 5, and divide the result by 9.

Example: *It's 50 degrees F. What is the temperature in Celsius?*
$50 - 32 = 18$; $18 \times 5 = 90$; $90/9 = 10$

To convert Celsius to Fahrenheit, multiply by 9, divide by 5, and add 32.

Example: *It's 10 degrees C. What is the temperature in Fahrenheit?*
$10 \times 9 = 90$; $90/5 = 18$; $18 + 32 = 50$

B Convert these temperatures.

1. 32° F = _____ ° C

2. 86° F = _____ ° C

3. 40° C = _____ ° F

4. 15° C = _____ ° F

LESSON 5

Talking About Emergencies

❶ Practice Pronunciation: *L* versus *R* Sounds 🎧 133

We make the *l* sound by curling the tongue against the roof of the mouth.
When we make the *r* sound, the tongue doesn't touch the roof of the mouth.

A. Listen to the pairs of words. Listen again and repeat.

1. file   fire   **4.** lamp   ramp
2. while   wire   **5.** list   wrist
3. call   car   **6.** light   right

B. Listen to the pairs of sentences. Listen again and repeat. 🎧 134

1. It will be a while.   It will be a wire.
2. There's a file in the supply closet.   There's a fire in the supply closet.
3. Take a light.   Take a right.

C. Work with a partner. Take turns reading each sentence and choosing a response.

Example: *You: It will be a wire.*   *Your partner: It will be a while.*
               Your partner: What color?   *You: How long?*

1. It will be a wire. OR   It will be a while.
   A. What color?   **B.** How long?

2. There's a file in the supply closet. OR   There's a fire in the supply closet.
   A. Should I get it?   **B.** Did you call the fire department?

3. Take a light. OR   Take a right.
   A. Is it dark outside?   **B.** Before or after I cross Main Street?

❷ Practice the Conversation: Reporting Emergencies 🎧 135

Listen to the conversation. Listen again and repeat.

A: Is this 911?

B: Yes. What's your emergency?

A: I'm calling to report a fire .

B: What is the location?

A: 1524 South Main Street .

B: A fire truck is on the way.

Practice the conversation with a partner. Use these ideas.

1 Someone is breaking into a house / 315 Market Street	**2** There's been a car accident / The intersection of Park and Trade Streets	**3** Electrical wires fell on a car / The 1200 block of Center Street	**4** Someone's bleeding / Joe's Restaurant on South Boulevard
A police car	A police car	A fire truck	An ambulance

❸ Practice the Conversation: Talking About Safety Problems 136

Listen to the conversation. Listen again and repeat.

A: Oh, no. We've got a problem.

B: What's the matter?

A: The dryer overheated and the wires melted .

B: We'd better call an electrician right away.

A: Good idea. I'm worried about a fire .

Practice the conversation with a partner. Use these ideas.

1 The toilet overflowed	**2** The ceiling is leaking and someone slipped in the hall	**3** There's smoke in the hallway	**4** The electrical outlet is overloaded
the landlord	an ambulance	911	the maintenance department
the apartment below us	an injury	a fire	electrical problems

❹ Listen and Write 137

Listen to the news report. Write the missing words. Listen again and check your answers.

This is Channel 5 news at _____.

We have breaking news of a major _____

in the 2000 block of _____, at the

Landview Apartments. We don't have many details

yet, but we do know that _____

families had to leave their homes at _____

this morning. _____

and other emergency personnel are on the scene. We'll bring you more news as the story develops.

Drivers should take _____ Street instead.

Home Emergency Plans

❶ Talk About It

Work with a partner. List 8 emergencies that could happen in your home.

1. _____   5. _____

2. _____   6. _____

3. _____   7. _____

4. _____   8. _____

❷ Read and Match

Read the article on page 127. Match the situation with a plan.

To Prepare for a Situation When _____.	Plan
_b_ **1.** you can't return home.	**a.** Have escape routes
____ **2.** you can't reach your family members by phone or in person.	**b.** Agree on a meeting place
____ **3.** there's a fire in the living room.	**c.** Post the phone numbers of the utility companies
____ **4.** there's a power outage.	**d.** Have a contact person outside of your city
____ **5.** there's an emergency at school.	**e.** Take first aid classes
____ **6.** someone has a medical emergency.	**f.** Keep your contact information current (up-to-date) at your child's school

❸ Make a Plan

Look at the article again. Check (✔) the things you did in the past year. Write 3 things you plan to do in the next year.

1. _____

2. _____

3. _____

Share your ideas with the class.

A FAMILY EMERGENCY PLAN

With your family, create a home emergency plan. Put it on the refrigerator or on a bulletin board where everyone can see it. Think about these things as you develop your plan:

- Discuss the dangers of fire, severe weather, floods, and other emergencies. Talk about what you would do in each situation.

- Discuss power outages and medical emergencies. Teach children how and when to call 9-1-1. Know the number to call if the power goes out.

- Draw a floor plan of your home. Think about at least two ways you can leave each room. Mark two escape routes from each room on your floor plan.

- Agree on two meeting places—one near your home in case of fire, and another that is outside your neighborhood, in case you cannot return home after a disaster.

- Learn how to turn off the water, gas, and electricity at their main switches.

- Post emergency numbers near each telephone in your home.

- Listen to the radio for emergency information.

- Take a basic first aid class and a CPR (cardiopulmonary resuscitation) class.

- Keep important records, such as passports or birth certificates, in a waterproof and fireproof container. Make extra copies to keep in another place.

Create an emergency communications plan.

Choose someone who lives in a different town to be your family's contact person. Everyone in your family can call or email the contact person to check on each other if a disaster occurs. Make sure everyone in your family has the contact person's email addresses and telephone numbers (home, work, pager, and cell). Leave these contact numbers at your children's schools, if you have children, and at your workplace.

Check on school emergency plans at your child's school.

Find out if school personnel will keep children at school until a parent can pick them up, or if the school sends children home on their own when there is an emergency. Be sure that the school has updated contact information for parents and other caregivers. During times of emergency, the school telephones may be very busy with calls.

LESSON 7

What Do You Know?

❶ Listening Review 138

You will hear part of a conversation. To finish the conversation, listen and choose the correct answer: *A*, *B*, or *C*. Use the Answer Sheet.

1. A. What's the matter?
   B. I don't know.
   C. Yes, I can.

2. A. There's a fire.
   B. 564 9th Street.
   C. Thank you.

3. A. In an hour.
   B. Apartment 13A.
   C. No. This time it's clogged.

4. A. Someone had a car accident.
   B. At the corner of Main and Pine Streets.
   C. I don't think so.

5. A. Is it the window again?
   B. Okay. I'll be right over.
   C. Thank you.

Answer Sheet

1	Ⓐ	Ⓑ	Ⓒ
2	Ⓐ	Ⓑ	Ⓒ
3	Ⓐ	Ⓑ	Ⓒ
4	Ⓐ	Ⓑ	Ⓒ
5	Ⓐ	Ⓑ	Ⓒ

❷ Listening Dictation 139

Listen. Write the sentences you hear.

1. _____

2. _____

3. _____

4. _____

5. _____

❸ Grammar Review

Circle the correct answer: *A, B,* or *C.*

1. We usually _____ at 7:00 A.M.

 A. getting up
 B. got up
 C. get up

2. We saw Jim _____ week at school.

 A. last
 B. ago
 C. past

3. _____ the coffeepot before you leave.

 A. Do you unplug
 B. Unplugs
 C. Unplug

4. _____ the television.

 A. Don't turn on
 B. Turn on not
 C. Not turn on

5. We called 911 two hours _____.

 A. ago
 B. then
 C. soon

6. I _____ out the trash yesterday.

 A. take
 B. took
 C. taken

LEARNING LOG

I know these words:

○ ambulance
○ attach
○ bathtub
○ Celsius
○ climb
○ clothes dryer
○ cover
○ crawl
○ drain
○ drawer

○ evacuate
○ Fahrenheit
○ faucet
○ fire escape
○ firefighter
○ fire truck
○ hair dryer
○ hose
○ hydrant
○ key

○ ladder
○ lock
○ overflow
○ overheat
○ overload
○ pick up
○ pipe
○ plug in
○ put away
○ put back

○ rescue
○ roof
○ shut off
○ sink
○ sliding door
○ smoke
○ space heater
○ spray
○ take out
○ temperature

○ toaster oven
○ toilet
○ turn down
○ turn off
○ turn on
○ unlock
○ unplug
○ valve
○ window

I can ask:

○ What's the matter?
○ What can I do for you?
○ Could you please come over and look at it?

I can say:

○ I'm calling to report a fire.
○ Don't take the elevator.
○ I turned off the lights.

I can write:

○ a maintenance request
○ a story about an emergency
○ an emergency plan

Work-Out CD-ROM

Unit 9: Plug in and practice!

THINGS TO DO

① Learn New Words 🎧 140

Look at the pictures. Listen to the words. Listen again and repeat. Which words are new to you? Circle them.

② Talk About the Pictures

Work with a partner. Which job(s)

1. involve numbers?
2. involve sick people?
3. is/are in a restaurant?
4. involves electrical problems?
5. Your idea: _____.

③ Listen and Circle 🎧 141

Listen to the conversation. Circle the correct words.

1. A salesperson **has to / doesn't have to** talk to people.
2. A bricklayer **has to / doesn't have to** be strong.
3. A welder **has to / doesn't have to** be a man.
4. An accountant **must / doesn't have to** wear safety equipment.
5. An accountant **has to / doesn't have to** have a special certificate.

Listen again and check your answers.

④ Find Someone Who

Talk to your classmates. Find someone who answers *yes* to your question. Write the person's name in the chart.

A: Do you want to work in an office ?

B: Yes, I do (or No, I don't).

Find Someone Who:	Person's Name
wants to work in an office	_____
likes to work with numbers	_____
likes to work with people	_____
wants to work outside	_____
wants to work in health care	_____
wants to work at night	_____

Administration / Clerical

① **computer programmer**

② **accountant**

③ **administrative assistant**

Target Grammar

Have to, don't have to, and *must*   page 197

Building and Construction

⑨ **painter**

⑪ **bricklayer**

Health Care

4 home health aide

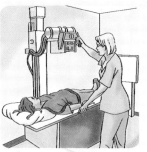

5 X-ray technician

6 nursing assistant

Manufacturing

7 assembler

8 machine operator

OCCUPATIONS OR JOBS

Hospitality

13 chef

14 restaurant manager

10 electrician

12 welder

15 hotel desk clerk

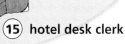

Work-Out CD-ROM

Unit 10: Plug in and practice!

Evaluating Job Skills

THINGS TO DO

❶ Learn New Words 🎧 142

Look at the pictures. Listen to the words. Listen again and repeat.

❷ Listen and Check 🎧 143

Listen to the conversation. Check (✔) the skills the person has.

- ○ communicate ideas well
- ○ resolve conflicts
- ○ organize information
- ○ have computer skills
- ○ work well with others
- ○ help other people
- ○ work independently
- ○ manage time well
- ○ follow directions

❸ Practice the Conversation 🎧 144

Listen to the conversation. Listen again and repeat.

A: I'm interested in the bricklayer position.

B: Do you follow directions well?

A: Yes, I do.

B: Excellent. That's what we need.

Practice the conversation with a partner. Use these ideas.

1 manager	2 accountant	3 front desk receptionist
know how to resolve conflicts	work independently	work well with people

4 administrative assistant	5 electrician	6
organize information well	manage time well	

❹ How About You?

Rate yourself on a scale of 1–5.

	No skills	Not very good	Okay	Very good	Excellent
Organizing information	○	○	○	○	○
Managing time	○	○	○	○	○
Helping others	○	○	○	○	○
Using the computer	○	○	○	○	○

① communicate ideas effectively

④ have computer skills

⑦ work independently

Target Grammar

Adverbs of manner *page 199*

(2) resolve conflicts

(3) organize information

(5) work well with others

(6) help other people

(8) manage time efficiently

(9) follow directions

LESSON 3

At a Career Center

THINGS TO DO

❶ Learn New Words 145

Look at the picture. Listen to the words. Listen again and repeat.

①	career center	⑤	interview	⑨	day shift
②	career counselor	⑥	job applicant	⑩	evening shift
③	application	⑦	full time	⑪	night shift
④	résumé	⑧	part time	⑫	appointment

Which words are new to you? Circle them.

❷ Talk About the Picture

Write 5 things about the picture. Share your ideas with the class.

Example: *James is a job applicant.*

Mia

❸ Practice the Conversation 146

Listen to the conversation. Listen again and repeat.

A: Do you have any experience as an electrician?

B: Yes, I do. I worked as one in my country.

A: Are you good at working on a team?

B: Yes, I am. I had to work on a team in my last job.

A: Would you like to work the day shift or the night shift?

B: I'd like the day shift, but I can work either one.

Practice the conversation with a partner. Use these ideas.

1 an accountant / working independently	**2** a hotel desk clerk / solving problems
work independently	solve problems
full time or part time	the evening shift or the night shift
full time	the night shift

3 a chef / working quickly	**4** a painter / following directions
work quickly	follow directions
days or evenings	full time or part time
evenings	part time

Target Grammar

Compound sentences with *and*, *but*, and *or*   *page 201*

City Works, Inc.

• 7 FULL TIME: Welder, 40 hours per week. More than 40 hours = overtime pay.

• 8 PART TIME: Machine operator, 20 hours per week, 3 - 7 P.M.

—Chicago—
JOB SERVICES

7 A.M. - 3 P.M.
3 P.M. - 11 P.M.
11 P.M. - 7 A.M.

Job Tips

THINGS TO DO

❶ Preview

Look at the pictures and the title of the reading. What is the article about? Check (✔) your guess.

○ Things a nursing assistant does on the job
○ Things you should and shouldn't do at work
○ Things you should do to find a job

❷ Read and Take Notes

Read the article. Take notes in the chart. Write things you should do and things you shouldn't do on your first day at a new job.

Things You Should Do	Things You Shouldn't Do
Be on time.	

❸ Write

Write a story about someone's first day on the job. Read your story to the class. Let your classmates tell what the person did right and wrong.

Example: *On Nancy's first day of work, she arrived early. She met many coworkers. She couldn't remember all their names. She ate lunch at her desk. She called her sister to tell her about the new job. Her supervisor didn't tell her what to do, and her coworkers didn't either. But Nancy was too nervous to ask questions.*

WRITING TIP
When you tell a story, add as many details as you can.

It's important to make the right impression when you start a new job. Here are some tips to help you on your first day.

Dress appropriately. Before your first day, find out if your new job has a dress code (rule about what you can wear to work). If so, be sure to follow it. No matter what*, always be neat and clean.

  Target Grammar

Negative compound sentences   *page 202*

FIRST DAY ON THE JOB

Get to work on time.

Employers value employees who come to work on time. Give yourself an extra 15 minutes to make sure you arrive on time.

Pay attention to introductions.

Your supervisor may introduce you to coworkers. These coworkers will be important to you. They will answer your questions when the boss is not around. Try to remember their names.

* **no matter what:** in any situation

Ask plenty of questions.

Make sure your supervisor tells you what he or she expects of you. Learn your job duties as soon as possible. Set goals for yourself.

Do not take too long for lunch.

Find out about the lunch-hour policy at your new job. Ask if people eat at their desks or take a full hour outside the workplace. No matter what, never take longer than the time allowed.

Do not make personal telephone calls.

You should never make personal phone calls to your friends and family unless it is an emergency.

WINDOW ON MATH

Overtime Pay

A Read the information below.

When an employee works more than 40 hours a week, the extra hours are paid as overtime. Overtime pay is called "time and a half." For every extra hour worked, the employee gets the regular hourly rate plus one half the regular rate.

Example: *Tom earns $10 an hour. If he works more than 40 hours, he should get $10 + $5, or $15, for each hour of overtime.*

B Answer the word problems.

1. Jan earns $12 an hour. Last week she worked 46 hours. How much money did she earn?

2. Mr. Li earns $20 an hour. If he works 50 hours this week, how much will he earn?

Communicating with an Employer

❶ Practice Pronunciation: Intonation in *Yes/No* and *Wh-* Questions 147

When we ask a *yes/no* question, our voices go up at the end.
When we ask *wh-* questions, our voices go up, then go down a little.

A. Listen to the questions. Listen again and repeat.

Intonation in *Yes/No* Questions	Intonation in *Wh-* Questions
Are you applying for this position?	Why are you applying for this position?
Did you work before?	Where did you work before?
Did you travel?	What did you do?
Did you supervise others?	How many people did you supervise?
Do you have any questions?	What questions do you have?

B. Write 3 more questions of each type that an employer might ask in an interview.

Yes/No Questions	*Wh-* Questions
1._____	1._____
2._____	2._____
3._____	3._____

C. Work with a partner. Role play a job interview. Ask and answer the questions.

❷ Practice the Conversation: Describing Skills and Experience 148

Listen to the conversation. Listen again and repeat.

A: Why are you applying for this position?

B: I enjoy working with people .

A: Are you willing to travel ?

B: Yes, I am. In my last job, I had to travel .

A: I see. Tell me about your experience with office work .

B: I worked as an administrative assistant for three years.

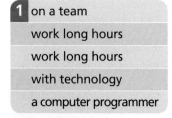

Practice the conversation with a partner. Use these ideas.

1 on a team	**2** with my hands	**3** independently	**4** with people
work long hours	work weekends	work the night shift	talk to customers
work long hours	work weekends	work the night shift	talk to customers
with technology	in construction work	with electrical work	in hospitality work
a computer programmer	a bricklayer	an electrician	a hotel desk clerk

❸ Practice the Conversation: Phoning in an Excuse 149

Listen to the conversation. Listen again and repeat.

A: Hello. Is this Mr. Roberts?

B: Yes, it is.

A: This is Magda Perkins. I'm sorry, but I can't come in today. I'm really sick.

B: I hope you feel better.

A: Thank you.

Listen to these expressions. Listen again and repeat.

Oh, I'm sorry. I hope we'll see you later. / That's terrible, I hope she's okay. / That's too bad. Take it easy. / Okay. We'll see you when you get here.

Practice the conversation with a partner. Use these ideas.

1 I'll be late this morning. I had a car accident.	**2** I have to miss work tonight. My daughter is in the hospital.	**3** I can't work today. I sprained my ankle.	**4** I'll be late today. I missed the bus.
Oh, I'm sorry. I hope we'll see you later.	That's terrible. I hope she's okay.	That's too bad. Take it easy.	Okay. We'll see you when you get here.

❹ Practice the Conversation: Talking About Work Schedules 150

Listen to the conversation. Listen again and repeat.

A: Ms. Garcia, can I talk to you for a minute?

B: Sure. What is it?

A: I usually have Mondays off, but can I have Tuesday off this week?

B: Is it important?

A: Yes, I have a doctor's appointment.

B: OK. I'll see what I can do.

A: Thank you. I appreciate it.

Listen to these expressions. Listen again and repeat.

I'll try. / I'll work something out. / I think I can arrange that. / We'll figure something out.

Practice the conversation with a partner. Use these ideas.

1 Thursday / my daughter is visiting	**2** Friday / I have to go out of town	**3** Saturday / I'm going to a wedding.	**4** Wednesday / I have an appointment.
I'll try.	I'll work something out.	I think I can arrange that.	We'll figure something out.

Understanding Job Ads and Applications

❶ Read and Identify

Read the job ads. Check (✔) your answers. You may check more than one job.

	Job A	Job B	Job C	Job D	Job E	
1.	○	○	○	○	○	is in health care.
2.	○	○	○	○	○	pays well.
3.	○	○	○	○	○	has night shifts available.
4.	○	○	○	○	○	requires computer skills.
5.	○	○	○	○	○	requires good people skills.
6.	○	○	○	○	○	requires travel.
7.	○	○	○	○	○	requires previous experience.
8.	○	○	○	○	○	has part-time positions.

D **Restaurant Staff**

Now hiring
chefs, servers, manager.

Apply in person (M–F) at
Mac's Restaurant, 134 Main St.
Day, evening, and part-time shifts.

E **Office Assistant**

Needed for medical office.
Must be flexible and a team player.
Must have excellent computer skills.
Good salary, great benefits.

Call (510) 555-9774.

A **Nursing Assistants Wanted**
Needed for home care. Spanish-speaking NAs needed for Hispanic cases. All shifts available. Great benefits. Must be punctual and good with people. Call ReLease Nurses at (601) 555-4800.

B **EXPERIENCED CONSTRUCTION WORKERS NEEDED**

Painters, carpenters, bricklayers. Good pay. Travel required. Some long hours. Please contact Building Personnel at (336) 555-4670.

C **Machine operators wanted.**
All shifts, experience with computers a plus. Good benefits and pay. Send résumé to: J. Medford, P.O. Box 312, Harrisburg, PA.

❷ Check *True* or *False*

Read the job application on page 141. Check (✔) *True* or *False*. Correct the false sentences.

	True	False
1. Oscar Garcia has a high school diploma.	○	○
2. He studied to be a computer programmer.	○	○
3. He went to college for three years.	○	○
4. He would like to work full time.	○	○
5. He would rather work the second shift.	○	○
6. At McHale Textiles, his starting salary was $9 an hour.	○	○
7. He supervises one person at McHale Textiles.	○	○
8. He worked at Gould before he worked at McHale.	○	○
9. He worked at Gould for more than a year.	○	○

APPLICATION FOR EMPLOYMENT

Last Name _Garcia_   First _Oscar_   Middle _Manuel_

Position Desired _Machine Operator_

Do you want to work: [X] Full time?   [ ] Part time?   What shift? [X] 1st [ ] 2nd [ ] 3rd

When will you be available to begin work? _in two weeks_

EDUCATION

School	Name and Location	Course of Study	Number of years completed	Did you graduate?	Degree or Diploma
College	Central Community College, Covina, California	Electronic technology	1.5	[X] yes [ ] no	Certificate in electronic technology
High	Covina High School, Covina, California	Tech course	4	[X] yes [ ] no	Diploma
Other	Cedar Adult Program Ontario, California	Auto mechanics	2	[ ] yes [X] no	NA

EMPLOYMENT Please give complete full-time and part-time employment record. Start with present or most recent employer.

Company Name	Telephone
McHale Textiles	(703)555-9282

Address	Employed (Month and Year)
1320 West Avenue, Springfield, VA, 22151	From: 7/08 To: present

Name of Supervisor	Hourly Pay
Joe Lewis	Start: $12 Last: $14

State Job Title and Describe Your Work — Reason for leaving NA
Machine Operator/Team Leader. Monitor machinery, do quality checks, complete daily operating reports, supervise 5 people.

Company Name	Telephone
Gould Technical Fabrics	(626)555-8776

Address	Employed (Month and Year)
467 Bates Parkway, Covina, CA, 91722	From: 2/04 To: 7/08

Name of Supervisor	Hourly Pay
Anthony Delaney	Start: $9 Last: $11

State Job Title and Describe Your Work — Reason for leaving
Machine Operator
Set up and operated machinery. Packaged and labeled products.   Company closed

LESSON 7

What Do You Know?

1 Listening Review 🎧 151

You will hear a question. Listen to the conversation. You will hear the question again. Then choose the correct answer: *A*, *B*, or *C*. Use the Answer Sheet.

1. A. He's a bricklayer.
B. He's a construction worker.
C. He's an accountant.

2. A. at a garden center
B. at a restaurant
C. at a school

3. A. She is good at helping people.
B. She is good at organizing information.
C. She is good at following directions.

4. A. an assembler
B. two years
C. three years

5. A. The caller is sick.
B. The caller is late.
C. The caller's car broke down.

Answer Sheet

1	Ⓐ	Ⓑ	Ⓒ
2	Ⓐ	Ⓑ	Ⓒ
3	Ⓐ	Ⓑ	Ⓒ
4	Ⓐ	Ⓑ	Ⓒ
5	Ⓐ	Ⓑ	Ⓒ

2 Listening Dictation 🎧 152

Listen and write the sentences you hear.

1. _____

2. _____

3. _____

4. _____

5. _____

❸ Grammar Review

Circle the correct answer: *A*, *B*, or *C*.

1. An accountant ____ work with numbers.
   A. has to
   B. doesn't have
   C. have to

2. A teacher _____ wear safety equipment.
   A. doesn't have to
   B. have to
   C. must

3. She doesn't work with people. She works ____.
   A. independent
   B. independently
   C. dependable

4. I work ____ with people.
   A. well
   B. good
   C. bad

5. I like to organize things, _____ my sister doesn't.
   A. and
   B. or
   C. but

6. I didn't get the job, _____ Paul didn't either.
   A. or
   B. usually
   C. and

LEARNING LOG

I know these words:

- ○ accountant
- ○ administrative assistant
- ○ application
- ○ appointment
- ○ assembler
- ○ bricklayer
- ○ career center
- ○ career counselor

- ○ chef
- ○ communicate ideas effectively
- ○ computer programmer
- ○ day shift
- ○ electrician
- ○ evening shift
- ○ follow directions

- ○ full time
- ○ have computer skills
- ○ help other people
- ○ home health aide
- ○ hotel desk clerk
- ○ interview
- ○ job applicant
- ○ machine operator

- ○ manage time efficiently
- ○ night shift
- ○ nursing assistant
- ○ organize information
- ○ painter
- ○ part time
- ○ resolve conflicts

- ○ restaurant manager
- ○ résumé
- ○ welder
- ○ work independently
- ○ work well with others
- ○ X-ray technician

I can ask:

- ○ Are you willing to travel?
- ○ Do you have experience as a welder?
- ○ Can I have Tuesday off?
- ○ Would you like to work the day shift or the night shift?
- ○ Are you good at organizing information?

I can say:

- ○ I would like to work in health care someday.
- ○ I have experience as a ...
- ○ I enjoy working with people.
- ○ I worked as a ... for three years.
- ○ I can't come in today.
- ○ I'll be late this morning.

I can write:

- ○ about my skills and abilities
- ○ a list of job dos and don'ts
- ○ a short description of a day at work

Work-Out CD-ROM

Unit 10: Plug in and practice!

UNIT 1 DESCRIBING PEOPLE

Simple Present of *Be*

Statements			Negative Statements			
I	**am**	happy.	I	**am**		sad.
You	**are**	a student.	You	**are**		a teacher.
He She It	**is**	tall.	He She It	**is**	**not**	short.
We You They	**are**	teachers.	We You They	**are**		students.

Contractions

I am	→	I'm	I am not	→	I'm not
you are	→	you're	you are not	→	you're not / you aren't
he is	→	he's	he is not	→	he's not / he isn't
she is	→	she's	she is not	→	she's not / she isn't
it is	→	it's	it is not	→	it's not / it isn't
we are	→	we're	we are not	→	we're not / we aren't
they are	→	they're	they are not	→	they're not / they aren't

1 Look at the driver's licenses. Complete the sentences with *is, isn't, are,* or *aren't.*

1. Mayra ____is____ five feet six inches tall.
2. Janet's date of birth ___is___ 08-26-13.
3. The licenses ___aren't___ from the state of Texas.
4. Janet's weight ___isn't___ 120 pounds.
5. Janet's address ___is___ in New York.

6. Janet and Mayra ___are___ women.
7. Janet's last name ___is___ Guan.
8. Janet's eyes ___aren't___ brown.
9. Mayra's hair color ___is___ blonde.
10. Mayra's eyes ___aren't___ blue.

Simple Present of *Have*						
Statements			**Negative Statements**			
I You	**have**	brown hair. a small car.	I You	**don't**	**have**	blonde hair. a big car.
He She It	**has**		He She It	**doesn't**		
We You They	**have**		We You They	**don't**		

1 **Complete the sentences with *have* or *has*. Then check *True* or *False*.**

	True	False
1. My teacher _____has_____ blue eyes.	○	○
2. I _____ curly hair.	○	○
3. All of my classmates _____ dark brown hair.	○	○
4. The person next to me _____ a beard.	○	○
5. I _____ a middle name.	○	○
6. My teacher _____ gray hair.	○	○
7. All of my classmates _____ a book.	○	○
8. My teacher _____ long hair.	○	○

2 **Write sentences about yourself and your class. Use *have*, *don't have*, *has*, and *doesn't have*.**

1. I _____don't have a mustache_____.

2. I _____.

3. My teacher _____.

4. My teacher _____.

5. All of my classmates _____.

6. The person next to me _____.

Simple Present, Questions pages 8–9

Yes/No Questions with *Be*

Questions				Answers				
Am	I			I	am.		I	'm not.
Are	you			you	are.		you	aren't.
Is	she he it	late?	Yes,	she he it	is.	No,	she he it	isn't.
Are	we they			we they	are.		we they	aren't.

Wh- Questions with *Be*

Questions			Answers		Questions		Answers
What	is	your name?	Lisa.	What		their names?	Jon and Jake.
Where		the book?	In my car.	Where	are	the books?	In my car.
When		our class?	At 4:00 P.M.	When		our classes?	On Monday.

1 Complete the questions with *am, is* or *are*. Then match the questions and answers.

___d___ **1.** _____Are_____ you tired?

_____ **2.** When _____ the party?

_____ **3.** _____ I tall?

_____ **4.** _____ Robert and Tom tall?

_____ **5.** What _____ your phone number?

_____ **6.** _____ you happy?

_____ **7.** _____ Joe bald?

_____ **8.** Where _____ the school?

a.   No, I'm not. I'm sad.

b.   No, you aren't. You're short.

c.   No, he's not. He has short hair.

d.   Yes, I am. I got up early this morning.

e.   No, they aren't. They're medium height.

f.   555-1945.

g.   It's on Oak Street.

h.   On Saturday.

2 Unscramble the words to make questions. Write your answers. Then practice with a partner.

1. middle name / is / What / your / ? → _____

Your answer: _____

2. you / bored / Are / ? → _____

Your answer: _____

3. are / Where / your books / ? → _____

Your answer: _____

Simple Present - *Yes/No* Questions

Questions				✱	Answers				
Do	I you			✱ Yes,	I you	**do.**	✱ No,	I you	**don't.**
Does	she he it	**like**	milk?	✱	she he it	**does.**	✱	she he it	**doesn't.**
Do	we they			✱	we they	**do.**	✱	we they	**don't.**

Simple Present - *Wh*-Questions

Questions			✱	Questions			Answers
What		you **need?**	✱	**What**		she **need?**	A pen.
Where	**do**	they **live?**	✱	**Where**	**does**	he **live?**	In Boston.
When		we **leave?**	✱	**When**		she **leave?**	At 1:00 P.M.
Who		you **live** with?	✱	**Who**		he **live** with?	A friend.

3 **Read the information. Then answer the questions.**

Ahmed works at a restaurant. He is a waiter. He likes to talk to customers. His customers like him too. He goes to work at 4:00 P.M. every day. He likes to go to bed late at night and wake up at noon, so the hours are good for him.

1. Where does Ahmed work? _____

2. Do his customers like him? _____

3. What is his occupation? _____

4. When does he work? _____

5. Does he like his job? _____

4 **Complete the questions with *do* or *does*. Then ask a partner. Write his or her answer.**

Your partner's answer

1. _____Do_____ you like American music? _____

2. Who _____ you eat dinner with? _____

3. When _____ you eat lunch? _____

4. _____ you have a driver's license? _____

5. Where _____ your father live? _____

6 _____ your classmates live nearby? _____

7. _____ your teacher have long hair? _____

8. _____ you walk to school? _____

Simple Present - Statements

We use the simple present to describe daily habits or usual activities.

Statements			Negative Statements			
I You	speak		I You	don't		
She He	speaks	Spanish.	She He	doesn't	speak	French.
We You They	speak		We You They	don't		

---

1 **Complete the sentences. Use the verbs in parentheses.**

1. My teacher _____wants_____ a new car. (want)

2. Kris _____ in Texas. (live)

3. I _____ to school every day. (go / not)

4. Many people _____ in apartments. (live)

5. Bill _____ to play soccer. (like)

6. We _____ homework tonight. (have / not)

7. You _____ a new book. (need)

2 **Unscramble the words to make sentences.**

1. doesn't / Chinese / He / speak /.

   He doesn't speak Chinese.

2. like / They / cold weather / don't /.

   _____

3. don't / need / I / a car /.

   _____

4. lives / She / in New York /.

   _____

5. swimming / like / don't / We /.

   _____

6. ice cream / We / want /.

   _____

3 Rewrite the sentences in the negative. Use contractions.

1. I like ice cream. → _I don't like ice cream._

2. They wear glasses. → _____

3. He needs a high school diploma. → _____

4. Matt and Kelly live in Florida. → _____

5. Monica speaks Korean. → _____

6. I need a driver's license. → _____

7. We like music. → _____

8. Joe wants a motorcycle. → _____

9. Rich hates flying. → _____

10. I need a job. → _____

11. We live in Texas. → _____

12. Nicole speaks German. → _____

4 Write sentences about you and a friend. Use the verbs in the list.

	Me	My Friend	My Friend and I
1. like	I like pizza.	Julia likes rice.	We like ice cream.
2. like / not			
3. speak			
4. speak / not			
5. need			
6. need / not			
7. want			
8. want / not			
9. live			
10. live / not			

Present Continuous - Statements

We use the present continuous to talk about what is happening now.

Statements			Negative Statements		
I	am		I	'm not	
You	are		You	aren't	
He She It	is	working.	He She It	isn't	working.
We You They	are		We You They	aren't	

1 Complete the sentences. Use the present continuous form of the verbs in parentheses.

1. Julia is at the bank. She _____is cashing_____ (cash) a check.

2. We _____ (eat / not) dinner right now.

3. My car _____ (work / not) today.

4. He _____ (walk) home from school with his friends.

5. Bob _____ (watch / not) TV right now. He _____ (play) a computer game.

6. I _____ (buy / not) stamps. I _____ (mail) a letter.

7. They are at a restaurant. They _____ (get) something to eat.

8. You _____ (do / not) your homework. You _____ (socialize)!

9. Tomas and Sarah are at the library. They _____ (study).

2 Finish the sentences about people in the room right now. Use the present continuous.

1. My teacher _____.

2. I _____.

3. The person next to me _____.

4. My classmates _____.

5. My friend _____.

5A

Present Continuous - *Wh*-Questions

Questions						Answers
What		she **buying**?	What		you **buying**?	Stamps.
Where	is	he **going**?	Where	are	they **going**?	To the library.
Who		she **talking** to?	Who		they **talking** to?	Lilia.

3 **Complete the questions. Then match the questions and answers.**

1. __b__ Where _____*are you going*_____? (you/go)   a. We're buying groceries.

2. __e__ When _____? (it /close)   b. I'm going to the medical center.

3. __d__ Who _____? (she/visit)   c. They're going to the restaurant.

4. __a__ What _____? (we / buy)   d. She's visiting her mother.

5. __c__ Where _____? (they /go)   e. It's closing at 10:00 P.M.

4 **Complete the conversations. Write questions.**

1. A: _____*What are you eating?*_____

   B: I'm eating a sandwich.

2. A: _____

   B: We're going into the supermarket.

3. A: _____

   B: The cashier is helping a customer.

4. A: _____

   B: He's socializing in the cafeteria.

5. A: ____*what are they buying*____

   B: They're buying medicine.

6. A: _____

   B: I'm mailing packages.

7. A: _____

   B: She's talking to the doctor.

Prepositions of Place

next to	across from	between	over	under
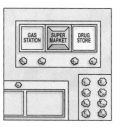			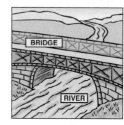	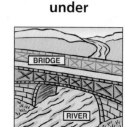
The supermarket is **next to** the drugstore.	The post office is **across from** the bank.	The supermarket is **between** the drugstore and the gas station.	The bridge goes **over** the river.	The river is **under** the bridge.

1 **Look at the map and read the sentences. Fix the sentences so that they are true.**

next to

1. The police station is ~~across from~~ the fire station.

2. The senior center is between the drugstore and the park.

3. The post office is under the bank.

4. The medical center is across from the police station.

5. The fire station is between the bank and the community center.

6. The supermarket is over the senior center.

7. The library is next to the drugstore.

2 **Write a description of where these places are in your city. Use prepositions of place.**

1. The bank is _____.

2. The supermarket is _____.

3. The post office is _____.

4. The fire station is _____.

5. The library is _____.

Prepositions of Direction

through	toward	away from	into	out of
		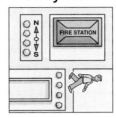		
The cars are going **through** the tunnel.	The man is walking **toward** the fire station.	The man is walking **away from** the fire station.	Jane is walking **into** the bank.	Jane is walking **out of** the bank.

3 Write sentences about the pictures. Use the present continuous and prepositions of direction.

1. Tina and Maura (go) _are going into the community center_

_____.

2. Jeff (run) _____

_____.

3. Barbara (walk) _____

_____.

4. The train (go) _____

_____.

5. Joshua and Zoe (walk) _____

_____.

Wh- Questions

Information Needed	Question Word	Question	Short Answer
THING	**What**	do you want for your birthday?	A camera.
PLACE	**Where**	can I buy a ticket?	At the ticket office.
PEOPLE	**Who**	is he talking to?	His father.
TIME	**When**	is your birthday?	May 2.
CLOCK TIME	**What time**	does the library open?	10:00 A.M.
REASON	**Why**	is she going to the train station?	To pick up her friend.
FREQUENCY	**How often**	do you go to the shopping center?	Every weekend.

1 **Match the questions and the answers.**

1. ____d____ When is the first day of school?
2. _____ Why are you nervous?
3. _____ Where is the post office?
4. _____ Who is your neighbor?
5. _____ What time is your English class?
6. _____ How often do you eat out?
7. _____ What's in your backpack?

a. Because I have a big test tomorrow.
b. 7:00 P.M.
c. Once a week.
d. September 7.
e. Susan Johnson.
f. A laptop.
g. It's on Orange Street.

2 **Answer the questions. Then share your answers with a partner.**

1. When is your birthday? _____.

2. How often do you study for English class? _____.

3. Where do you live? _____.

4. Who is your favorite singer? _____.

5. What is your favorite kind of food? _____.

6. What time do you usually wake up in the morning? _____.

7. Why are you studying English? _____.

8. Where do you shop? _____.

9. What do you usually eat for lunch? _____.

10. How often do you use a computer? _____.

Prepositions of Time

We use **at** to talk about time of day.	
• The train leaves **at** 5:30 P.M.	• I'm going to lunch **at** 12:00 P.M.
We use **on** to talk about days and dates.	
• Joe starts a new job **on** Monday.	• I'm going to New York **on** November 3.
We use **in** to talk about months, years, seasons, and periods of time in the day.	
• Sue was born **in** 1989.	• I will visit you **in** April.
• There is no school **in** the summer.	• I take the bus home **in** the afternoon.
We use **from . . . to** to talk about periods of time that have a set beginning and an end.	
• I'll be in Peru **from** May 3rd **to** 8th.	• I will be busy **from** 2:00 **to** 4:00 P.M.

❶ Finish the sentences. Use the correct prepositions of time and the information in parentheses.

1. There is no school (Friday) _____ on Friday _____.

2. Sandy is going to China (June) _____.

3. The bus arrives (3:30 P.M.) _____.

4. I have class (6:00 P.M. / 8:00 P.M.) _____.

5. Juan moved to Los Angeles (2003) _____.

6. Tom is having a party (December 31) _____.

7. The party is (7:00 P.M. / 9:30 P.M.) _____.

8. We have dinner (6:30 P.M.) _____.

❷ Finish the sentences about you. Use the correct preposition of time.

1. I usually go to bed _____.

2. My English class is from _____.

3. I don't usually go to school _____.

4. I was born _____.

5. I usually eat lunch _____.

6. The school has a vacation _____.

7. My birthday is _____.

8. I usually sleep _____.

Simple Past - Statements

We use the simple past to describe events that began and ended in the past.

Statements		Negative Statements		Simple Past Spelling Rules
I You He She It We You They	**worked** yesterday.	I You He She It We You They	**did not work** **didn't work** yesterday.	• Verbs that end in *e*: add *d*. Example: like → liked • Verbs that end in consonant + *y*: change the *y* to *i*, then add *ed*. Example: try → tried • Verbs that end in consonant + vowel + consonant: double the last consonant, then add *ed*. Example: hop → hopped

1 **Complete each sentence. Use the simple past.**

1. I usually cash my paycheck on Friday, but last week I _____ cashed _____ it on Saturday.

2. She usually deposits her paycheck into her checking account, but yesterday she _____ it into her savings account.

3. We usually endorse our checks on Friday, but last week we _____ them on Thursday.

4. The bank usually opens at 10:00 A.M., but yesterday it _____ at 8:00 A.M.

5. The bank teller usually helps me, but yesterday the bank officer _____ me.

6. The bank usually closes at 12:00 P.M. on Saturday, but last Saturday it _____ at 1:00 P.M.

7. I usually study English at night, but last night I _____ math.

8. That bank teller usually works until 4:00 P.M., but yesterday she _____ until 5:00 P.M.

2 **Write sentences to complete the chart.**

Statements	Negative Statements
1. She opened a checking account.	She didn't open a checking account.
2. They waited in line for 15 minutes.	
3.	I didn't ask you a question.
4. I endorsed my paycheck.	
5.	We didn't talk to the bank teller.
6.	We didn't stop to use the ATM.

Irregular Verbs in the Simple Past

Present	Past		Present	Past		Present	Past
buy	bought		go	went		put	put
come	came		have	had		spend	spent
do	did		make	made		take	took
eat	ate		pay	paid		write	wrote

3 **Finish the sentences in the simple past. Then check *True* or *False* for you.**

	True	False
1. I _____went_____ to the bank last week. (go)	○	○
2. I _____ a car last year. (buy / not)	○	○
3. I _____ a check yesterday. (wrote)	○	○
4. I _____ dinner last night. (make / not)	○	○
5. I _____ a shower yesterday. (take)	○	○
6. I _____ cereal for breakfast today. (eat)	○	○
7. I _____ my bills last week. (pay)	○	○
8. I _____ money yesterday. (spend / not)	○	○

4 **Change the words in bold from simple present to simple past.**

    wanted
John **wants** to withdraw money from his checking account. He **goes** to the ATM. First he **puts** his ATM card into the machine. Then he **types** in his PIN. The machine **asks** him how much money he **wants**. John **types** in $100. Five 20-dollar bills **come** out of the machine. He **takes** the money and **puts** it in his wallet. The machine **asks** if he **wants** a receipt. John **presses** the button for "yes." John **takes** the receipt. He **checks** the receipt. Then he **puts** it in his wallet with his $100.

5 **Write sentences about what you did yesterday.**

1. _____
2. _____
3. _____

Simple Past of *Be*, Statements pages 34–35

Simple Past of *Be*

Statements			Negative Statements		
I	was		I	wasn't	
You	were		You	weren't	
He			He		
She	was		She	wasn't	
It		hungry.	It		hungry.
We			We		
You	were		You	weren't	
They			They		

1 **Complete the paragraph below. Use *was, were, wasn't* or *weren't*.**

Yesterday I had a very bad experience at the bank. The ATM _____was_____ broken, so I went
                                                                    (1)

inside. The bank _____ very busy. Twenty people _____ in line, but only one
                    (2)   **(3)**

bank teller _____ there. She _____ friendly, and she _____ fast. But all
            (4)   **(5)**   **(6)**

of the customers _____ tired. I waited 20 minutes in line. I _____ angry. The bank
                 (7)   **(8)**

officer _____ helpful. He said the other bank tellers _____ sick. When I got home,
        (9)   **(10)**

I _____ tired. It _____ a good afternoon.
  (11)   **(12)**

2 **Write sentences using a word or phrase from Group A and B. Use *be* in the simple past.**

Group A			Group B		
He	My teacher	The restaurant	angry	crowded	nervous
I	The streets	They	bored	dirty	strong
~~My mother~~	The sun	You	busy	hot	~~tired~~

1. _____ My mother was tired last night. _____

2. _____

3. _____

4. _____

5. _____

Simple Past, *Yes/No* Questions pages 36–37

Simple Past - *Yes/No* Questions

Questions			Answers					
Did	I you he she we you they	**work** yesterday?	Yes,	I you he she we you they	**did.**	No,	I you he she we you they	**didn't.**

1 Complete the *yes/no* questions. Use the verb in parentheses and the simple past. Then ask a partner the questions and check their answers.

			Yes, I did.	No, I didn't.
1.	_____Did you use_____	a credit card yesterday? (use)	○	○
2.	_____	any cash yesterday? (spend)	○	○
3.	_____	a car payment yesterday? (make)	○	○
4.	_____	a check yesterday? (write)	○	○
5.	_____	a check yesterday? (cash)	○	○
6.	_____	a money order yesterday? (buy)	○	○
7.	_____	to the bank yesterday? (go)	○	○
8.	_____	a bill yesterday? (pay)	○	○

2 Change the sentences into *yes/no* questions in the simple past.

1. John cashed a check yesterday. → _____Did John cash a check yesterday?_____

2. They opened an account yesterday. → _____

3. I bought a car last week. → _____

4. We paid our bill. → _____

5. Alison used the ATM yesterday. → _____

6. Jacob talked to a bank officer. → _____

7. You endorsed your check. → _____

8. They made a withdrawal last week. → _____

Simple Past of *Be* - *Yes/No* Questions

Questions				Answers					
Was	I			you	were.		you	weren't.	
Were	you			I	was.		I	wasn't.	
Was	he	late?	Yes,	he	was.	No,	he	wasn't.	
Were	we			we	were.		we	weren't.	
	they			they			they		

3 Write a *yes/no* question in the simple past using the words in parentheses. Then look at the picture and write the answer to the question.

1. (Gina / sad) _____ Was Gina sad? _____

Yes, she was. _____.

2. (the flowers / red)_____

_____.

3. (he / relaxed) _____

_____.

4. (Jason / thirsty) _____

_____.

5. (it / sunny) _____

_____.

6. (they / happy) _____

_____.

وابست

Simple Past - *Wh*-Questions

Wh-Questions				Answer
Where		I	go?	To the bank.
Who		you	talk to?	The bank teller.
When	did	she	arrive?	Yesterday.
Why		he	go?	To get cash.
How much		we	pay?	$100.
What		they	say?	Hello.
Wh-Questions with *Be*				Answer
Who	was	he	with?	His father.
What	was	it?		An airplane.
Why	were	you	angry?	Because I was late.
When	were	they	here?	Last week.

1 Finish the questions using the verbs in parentheses in the simple past. Then match the questions and answers.

1. Where ____did____ they ____buy____ their car? (buy)   a. _____ 45 dollars.

2. Who _____ Maria _____ dinner with last night? (have)   b. _____ Eggs and toast.

3. How much _____ your electric bill last month? (be)   c. _____ Amy.

4. Why _____ Mike nervous? (be)   d. _____ Yesterday.

5. What _____ he _____ for breakfast? (eat)   e. __1__ New Jersey.

6. When _____ they here? (be)   f. _____ Because he had a big test.

2 Unscramble the questions. Then answer the questions.

1. did / Who / call / last week / you /?

   _____ Who did you call last week? _____   I called my mother. _____

2. you / Where / last year / did / live /?

   _____

3. pay / last month / did / for groceries / you / How much /?

   _____

4. on Friday night / do / What / you / did /?

   _____

UNIT 4 PLANS AND GOALS

LESSON 1

Want to, Like to, Would Like to

pages 46–47

Want to, Like to, Would Like to		
We use **to** + **verb** after verbs like **want, like, need,** and **would like.**		
I	**want**	**to buy** a new car.
She	**needs**	**to improve** her English.
He	**hates**	**to get up** early.
They	**like**	**to play** soccer.
We	**would like**	**to get** good grades.

Note: *Would like* means *want.* It is very polite.

When we speak, we usually say: **I'd** *like* instead of *I would like.*

1 **Complete the sentences. Use *to* and a verb below.**

study	do	buy	get	start	~~be~~	graduate	become

1. I want _____to be_____ a good parent.

2. Paul needs _____ a job.

3. Laura hates _____ housework.

4. Ming would like _____ a business.

5. They want _____ a house.

6. Danielle wants _____ from a university.

7. I would like _____ a U.S. citizen.

8. I like _____ English.

2 **Write true sentences about you.**

1. I want to _____.

2. I need to _____.

3. I like to _____.

4. I hate to _____.

5. I would like to _____.

6. My best friend needs to _____.

7. My teacher likes to _____.

162 TARGET GRAMMAR: UNIT 4

Future with *Be going to*

We use ***be going to*** + verb to talk about the future. We use it to talk about future plans.

Statements				
I	am			
You	are			
He				
She	is	going to	**come** tomorrow.	
It				
We				
You	are			
They				

Negative Statements				
I	am not			
You	aren't			
He				
She	isn't	going to	**come** tomorrow.	
It				
We				
You	aren't			
They				

1 **Complete the sentences. Use *be going to* and the verbs in parentheses.**

1. He _____is going to become_____ a doctor next year. (become)

2. I _____ a lot of money next year. (save)

3. We _____ to the party tonight. (not / come)

4. My friends _____ in June. (get married)

5. Maria _____ next year. (not / teach)

6. Sofia and Wilma _____ in May. (not / graduate)

7. Huang _____ a U.S. citizen this year. (become)

8. You _____ something new in this class. (learn)

2 **Finish the sentences with your own ideas. Use the future with *be going to*.**

1. _____ tonight.

2. _____ tomorrow morning.

3. _____ next weekend.

4. _____ next week.

5. _____ next summer.

Be going to – Yes/No Questions

We use **be going to** to ask questions about the future.

Questions					Answers				
Am	I				I	am.		I	'm not.
Are	you				you	are.		you	aren't.
Is	he she it	**going to**	**come** tomorrow?	Yes,	he she it	is.	No,	he she it	isn't.
Are	we you they				we you they	are.		we you they	aren't.

❸ **Unscramble the questions. Then ask a partner and write the answers.**

1. you / to / Are / dinner / cook / going / tonight /?

Question: _____*Are you going to cook dinner tonight?*_____

Your partner's answer: _____

2. to / tomorrow morning / you / wake up early / going / Are /?

Question: _____

Your partner's answer: _____

3. next year / to / Are / going / you / English / study /?

Question: _____

Your partner's answer: _____

4. you / tonight / see / to / your family / Are / going /?

Question: _____

Your partner's answer: _____

5. going / Are / to / come to your house / your friends / next weekend /?

Question: _____

Your partner's answer: _____

6. rain / going / Is / it / tonight / to /?

Question: _____

Your partner's answer: _____

7. we / in this class / going / Are / learn something new / to /?

Question: _____

Your partner's answer: _____

Future with *Will*

We use *will* + **verb** to make a promise, to offer help, or to make a prediction.

Statements			Negative Statements		
I You She We They	will 'll	**come** back soon.	I You She We They	will not won't	**be** away for long.

Yes/No Questions with *Will*

We use *will* + **verb** to ask questions about promises and about the future.

Questions			Answers					
Will	I you she we they	**be** here tomorrow?	Yes,	I you she we they	will.	No,	I you she we they	won't.

❶ **Complete the sentences. Use *will/'ll* or *won't*. Then check *promise, offer,* or *prediction*.**

	Promise	Offer	Predict
1. Don't worry. I _____won't_____ open the present until you're here.	✓	○	○
2. I'll call you when I get home. I _____ forget!	○	○	○
3. That box looks heavy. I _____ carry it for you.	○	○	○
4. We don't have any food in the house! I _____ go to the store after work.	○	○	○
5. Wear a warm coat. It _____ be cold tonight.	○	○	○
6. It's dark outside. We _____ drive you home.	○	○	○

❷ **Write short answers. Use *will/'ll* or *won't*.**

1. Will you become a U.S. citizen next year? _____

2. Will your parents come to visit soon? _____

3. Will your best friend get married this year? _____

4. Will you go to school tomorrow? _____

Because for Reason

Notes	Examples
We use *because* + clause (subject + verb) to give a reason.	She went home **because** she was sick. REASON
We use *because* to answer a question with *Why*.	**Why** is she happy? She's happy **because** she's on vacation. REASON

1 Use *because* to give the reason why each action is happening.

1. A: He is taking English classes.

   B: Why?

   A: He wants to get a promotion.

He's taking English classes because he wants to get a promotion.

2. A: I'm eating lunch early.

   B: Why?

   A: I didn't eat breakfast.

_____

3. A: He's going to be late.

   B: Why?

   A: The roads are snowy.

_____

4. A: They are studying hard.

   B: Why?

   A: They want to get good grades.

_____

5. A: He reads to his children every day. _____

   B: Why?

   A: He wants to be a good parent.

_____

6. A: I'm not going to go work today. _____

   B: Why not?

   A: I'm sick.

_____

2 Answer the questions. Use complete sentences and *because*. Then ask and answer the questions with a partner.

1. Why do you study English?

_____

2. Why do you live in this city?

_____

3. Do you want to live in another country? Why or why not?

_____

4. Are you working? Why or why not?

_____

To for Reason

Notes	Examples
We use **to** + verb (infinitive form) to explain a purpose or reason.	He went to the bank **to open** a savings account.
	REASON
We use **to** + verb to answer a question with why.	**Why** did she go to the store?
	She went to the store **to buy** milk.
	REASON

3 Complete the sentences. Use the infinitive form of a verb in the box.

buy	~~get~~	learn	save	sign up	spend	visit

1. My parents moved to the United States _____ to get _____ better jobs.

2. She went to the community college yesterday _____ for classes in the spring.

3. We went to the post office _____ stamps.

4. She went to New York _____ her parents.

5. I shop at Price Giant Supermarket _____ money. They have the lowest prices!

6. They went to Mexico _____ Spanish.

7. Miguel is working fewer hours _____ more time with his children.

4 Answer the questions. Use *to* for reason. Then ask and answer the questions with a partner.

1. Why do you take English classes?

_____

2. Why do you save money?

_____

3. Why do you watch TV?

_____

4. Why do you do your homework?

_____

Go + Verb-*ing*

We use **go + verb-*ing*** to talk about leisure activities.

go bicycling	go dancing	go running	go sightseeing
go bowling	go hiking	go sailing	go skiing
go camping	go horseback riding	go shopping	go swimming

We can also use *go* + verb-*ing* in simple past or future.

I **went bowling** last night. (simple past)   Maya **is going to go shopping** tonight. (future)

1 Look at the pictures. Complete the sentences with the correct verb phrase from the chart above.

1.  Miranda likes to

<u>go horseback riding</u> .

2.  They want to

_____

_____.

3.  Tom often

_____

_____.

4.  Last weekend, I

_____

_____.

5.  Last weekend, we

_____

_____.

6.  They're

_____

next weekend.

2 Complete the sentences with information about you. Use *go* + verb-*ing*.

1. I like to _____

2. I don't like to _____

3. Last weekend, I _____

4. Last summer, I _____

5. Next weekend, I _____

Comparative Adjectives pages 62–63

Comparative Adjectives

We use **comparative adjectives** to talk about the differences between **two** things.

Type of Adjective	How to Form	Adjective	Comparative Adjective
One-syllable adjectives	Add **-er**	tall	tall**er**
		cheap	cheap**er**
One-syllable adjectives ending in a single vowel and a consonant	Double the consonant and add **-er**	big	big**ger**
		fat	fat**ter**
Two-syllable adjectives ending in **-y**	Change the **-y** to **-i** and add **-er**	happy	happ**ier**
		funny	funn**ier**
Two or more syllable adjectives	Add **more**	athletic	**more** athletic
		beautiful	**more** beautiful
Irregular Adjectives	Change to irregular form	good	**better**
		bad	**worse**
		far	**farther**

❶ Write the comparative form of each adjective.

Adjective	Comparative		Adjective	Comparative
1. happy	_happier_		**6.** bad	_____
2. big	_____		**7.** angry	_____
3. good	_____		**8.** wet	_____
4. new	_____		**9.** beautiful	_____
5. heavy	_____		**10.** modern	_____

❷ Complete the conversations with a comparative. More than one answer is possible. Then practice the conversations with a partner.

1. A: Why did they mail a money order instead of cash?

   B: Because a money order is _____.

2. A: Why did you decide to go to Florida instead of New York?

   B: Because Florida is _____.

3. A: Why did she marry Jim instead of Tim?

   B: Because Jim is _____.

4. A: Why did they use a check instead of a credit card?

   B: Because a check is _____.

Comparatives Adjectives in Sentences

We use comparative adjectives in sentences with **be** and **than** to compare two nouns.

Comparative adjectives with –*er*	I	am	old**er**	**than**	you.
	This coat	is	warm**er**		that jacket.
	These flowers	are	pretti**er**		those flowers.
Comparative adjectives with *more*	I	am	**more** tired	**than**	him.
	A stove	is	**more** important		a blender.
	These shoes	are	**more** expensive		those shoes.

1 Look at the photos. Complete the sentences with the comparative form of the adjectives in parentheses and *than*.

Jessica

John

1. Jessica is _____ *younger than* _____ John. (young)

2. John is _____ Jessica. (serious)

3. Jessica's hair is _____ John's hair. (long)

4. John's hair is _____ Jessica's hair. (short)

5. Jessica is _____ John. (beautiful)

6. Jessica is _____ John. (happy)

2 Use the adjectives to write sentences comparing Jessica and John.

1. (old) _____

2. (mature) _____

3. (tired) _____

4. (relaxed) _____

There	was	a sale	at Le Chic.
There	was	a man	at the door.
There	wasn't	a cloud	in the sky.
There	were	cleaning supplies	under the sink.
There	weren't	many people	at the party.

We use **there was** and **there were** to say that something existed in the past. We also use **there was** and **there were** to talk about where something was in the past.

1 **Look at the picture from the food court last weekend. Finish the sentences with *There was, There were, There wasn't* or *There weren't.***

1. _____There weren't_____ a lot of people there.

2. _____ two workers taking a break.

3. _____ a man selling hot dogs.

4. _____ a man carrying a mop.

5. _____ a place to buy Mexican food.

6. _____ children in the food court.

7. _____ empty chairs.

2 **Write five more sentences about the food court using *There was, There were, There wasn't* or *There weren't.***

1. _____

2. _____

3. _____

4. _____

5. _____

Superlative Adjectives pages 66–67

Superlative Adjectives

We use **superlative adjectives** to compare **three** or **more** things.

Type of Adjective	How to Form	Adjective	Superlative Adjective
One-syllable adjectives	Add **the** and **-est**	tall	**the** tall**est**
		cheap	**the** cheap**est**
One-syllable adjectives ending in a single vowel and a consonant	Double the consonant and add **the** and **-est**	big	**the** big**gest**
		fat	**the** fat**test**
Two-syllable adjectives ending in **-y**	Change the **–y** to **–i** and add **the** and **-est**	happy	**the** happ**iest**
		funny	**the** funn**iest**
Two or more syllable adjectives	Add **the most**	athletic	**the most** athletic
		beautiful	**the most** beautiful
Irregular Adjectives	Add **the** and irregular form	good	**the best**
		bad	**the worst**
		far	**the farthest**

1 Write the superlative form of each adjective.

Adjective	Superlative		Adjective	Superlative
1. pretty	the prettiest		**9.** far	_____
2. new	_____		**10.** loose	_____
3. nervous	_____		**11.** heavy	_____
4. big	_____		**12.** curly	_____
5. exciting	_____		**13.** slim	_____
6. tight	_____		**14.** intelligent	_____
7. bad	_____		**15.** good	_____
8. sick	_____		**16.** angry	_____

2 Complete the sentences. Use *the* and the superlative form of the adjective in parentheses.

1. _____ The oldest _____ American is about 115 years old. (old)

2. Muhammad Ali is perhaps _____ fighter in the world. (famous)

3. The Nile is _____ river in the world. (long)

4. Russia is _____ country in the world. (large)

5. A cheetah can run 46 miles per hour. It is _____ animal in the world. (fast)

6. _____ place in the United States is Yuma, Arizona. (sunny)

7. Cuba is home to _____ bird in the world. (small)

8. Helen of Troy was _____ woman of her time. (beautiful)

9. _____ place on earth is El Azizia, a desert in Libya. (hot)

10. _____ man in the world lives in China. (tall)

3 Complete the questions with *the* and the superlative form of the adjective in parentheses. Then ask a partner the questions. Write your partner's answer.

1. Who is _____ the youngest _____ person in your family? (young)

_____ The youngest person in my family is _____

2. Who is _____ person in your English class? (tall)

_____

3. What is _____ kind of food? (good)

_____

4. What is _____ thing that happened last year? (bad)

_____

5. Who is _____ person you know? (beautiful)

_____

6. What was _____ thing you bought last month? (expensive)

_____

7. Who has _____ hair in your family? (short)

_____

8. What is _____ memory you have? (happy)

_____

9. What is _____ mountain in the world? (high)

_____

10. Who is _____ athlete in the world? (good)

_____

Count and Noncount Nouns

	Notes	Examples
Count nouns	**Count nouns** are things we can count. They have a singular form and a plural form. **Singular** We use **a** and **an** before singular count nouns. **Plural** We use **no article** before plural count nouns.	**one egg / two eggs** **one person / three people** **one chair / four chairs** I have **a computer** at home. Would you like **an apple**? **Apples** are delicious. We love **eggs**.
Noncount nouns	**Noncount nouns** are things we cannot count. They are usually singular. We use **no article** before non-count nouns.	**meat** **peace** **snow** **happiness** **rice** **water** **flour** **coffee** **juice** I love **coffee**. **Water** is good for you.

1 Write the words in the correct column in the chart.

~~banana~~	book	cell phone	house	oil	pen	ticket
basketball	bread	coffee	milk	peace	sugar	tree

COUNT NOUNS	NONCOUNT NOUNS
banana	

2 Write *a, an* or *Ø* (no article).

1. Do you have _____a_____ camera?
2. There's _____ juice in the refrigerator.
3. You need _____ egg to make _____ cookies.
4. I love _____ oranges.
5. Do you want _____ sugar in your coffee?
6. Can you bring me _____ menu?
7. Would you like _____ tea?
8. I would like _____ ice cream cone.

Quantity Phrases

We often use quantity phrases before noncount nouns.

a can of soup	**two cartons of** milk	**a bag of** rice	**two bottles of** oil
three cups of coffee	**a jar of** mustard	**a box of** cereal	**a bowl of** cereal

3 Underline the correct quantity phrase to complete the sentences.

1. I bought (<u>a carton of</u> / a box of) orange juice at the store.

2. We would like (four bowls of / four cups of) tea please.

3. Do we have (a bottle of / a can of) beans?

4. We need to buy (a bag of / a bowl of) flour at the store.

5. Would you like (a bag of / a bowl of) soup with your sandwich?

6. We would like (two bottles of / two bags of) water please.

7. We need to buy (a bag of / a bowl of) sugar at the store.

4 Complete the sentences about the food you have in your kitchen. Use count and noncount nouns.

1. I have a can of _____.

2. I have a carton of _____.

3. I have a bag of _____.

4. I have a _____.

5. I have an _____.

6. I have a bottle of _____.

One, each, some, another and *the other(s)*

We sometimes use the pronouns **one, each, some, another** or **the other(s)** in place of a noun. We do this when it is clear what noun the pronoun is replacing.

1. A: Can you bring me a napkin, please?
   B: Sure. I'll get **one** right away.
   [*one = a napkin*]
	2. A: Do you want a piece of cake or a cookie?
	   B: I'll have one of **each**!
	   [*each = a piece of cake and a cookie*]

3. A: Would you like some tea?
   B: Sure. I would love **some**. Thank you.
   [*some = tea*]
	5. A: Would you like another cookie?
	   B: Sure. I would love **another**. Thanks.
	   [*another = cookie*]

5. A: I can only find one shoe.
   B: **The other** is outside!
   [*the other = the other shoe*]
	6. A: How many apples can I take?
	   B: You can take three. **The others** are for the pie.
	   [*the others = the other apples*]

1 Finish the conversations. Write *one, some, each, another, the other* or *the others*.

1. A: Would you like some water?

   B: Yes, I would love _____some_____. Thank you.

2. A: How many cookies can I eat?

   B: Just one. _____ are for the children.

3. A: Can you bring me a menu, please?

   B: Sure. I'll get _____ right away.

4. A: Would you like another cup of coffee?

   B: Sure. I would love _____. Thank you.

5. A: Would you like an apple or an orange?

   B: I'll have one of _____ !

6. A: Are there any sandwiches left?

   B: No, I'm sorry. Jack had one and I ate_____.

7. A: I would like some orange juice, please.

   B: Sure. I'll get you _____ right away.

8. A: Excuse me. Could you bring me another napkin?

   B: Sure. I'll bring you _____ right away.

9. A: Would you like a bowl of soup with your salad?

   B: Sure. I would love _____. Thank you.

Quantifiers: *some, any , a little*, and *a few*

We use *some, any, a little*, and *a few* to talk about small amounts.

We use **some** with plural count and noncount nouns in positive statements and questions. EXAMPLES: There are **some** people at the door. I'll have **some** coffee. Would you like **some** ice cream?	We use **any** with plural count and noncount nouns in negative statements and questions. EXAMPLES: We don't have **any** tomatoes. I don't have **any** homework. Do you have **any** questions?
We use **a few** with count nouns. EXAMPLES: I have only **a few** pictures of him. **A few** students were sick today.	We use **a little** with noncount nouns. EXAMPLES: There's **a little** sand in my shoe. Would you like **a little** sugar in your coffee?

① **Choose the word in parentheses that best completes the sentences.**

1. I need _____ *a little* _____ (a little / a few) milk.

2. She ate _____ (a little / a few) apples.

3. There are _____ (some / any) computers in the lab.

4. I don't want _____ (some / any) coffee.

5. Would you like _____ (a little / a few) chicken?

6. Do we have _____ (a little / any) potatoes?

7. There is _____ (a little / a few) ice cream in the freezer.

8. I have _____ (some / any) time if you want to talk.

② **Rewrite the sentences correctly.**

1. INCORRECT: Last night I had a hamburgers and any french fries for dinner.

CORRECT: _____ *Last night I had a hamburger and some french fries for dinner.* _____

2. INCORRECT: You need a few flour and any eggs to make a cake.

CORRECT: _____

3. INCORRECT: I am making any soup so I need a little potatoes.

CORRECT: _____

4. INCORRECT: I had a few cookie this afternoon.

CORRECT: _____

Quantifiers: *many, much, a lot (of)* and *every*

We use *many, much*, and *a lot (of)* to talk about large amounts.

We use *many* with plural count nouns in positive statements and questions. EXAMPLES: We bought **many** groceries last week. Were there **many** people at the store?	We use *much* with noncount nouns in negative statements and questions. EXAMPLES: There isn't **much** rice left. How **much** coffee do you drink every day?

We use **a lot of** with count and noncount nouns.

EXAMPLES:
A **lot of** fruit grows in California.   That's **a lot of** oranges.

We use *every* before a singular count noun when we are talking about all of a group.

EXAMPLE:
Every student needs a book.

❸ Choose the correct word in parentheses to complete the sentences.

1. We don't have _____ (much / many) juice.

2. _____ (A few / A little) oil may be healthy, but _____ (many / a lot of) oil is not.

3. _____ (Every / Some) apple in the bag was bad. We will need to buy _____ (any / some) new ones.

4. I made _____ (many / a little) mistakes on my test.

5. How _____ (many / much) sugar do you want in your coffee?

❹ Answer the questions. Use *many, much, a lot of, some, any, every, a little* or *a few*.

1. What do you usually eat for breakfast?

_____

2. What do you usually eat for dinner?

_____

3. What do you buy at the supermarket?

_____

4. How much sleep do you get every night?

_____

Adjective + Noun

Adjectives describe **nouns**.

An adjective often comes before the noun.

The article or quantifier comes before the adjective.

	Article or quantifier	Adjective	Noun
I never swim in		cold	water.
I had	a	big	meal.
She bought	a few	beautiful	flowers.
She made	some	delicious	soup.

With the verb *be*, the adjective can come after the noun.

EXAMPLES:　　The **meal** was **big**.　　　　The **flowers** were **beautiful**.

1 **Unscramble the sentences.**

1. hot / for dinner / I / night / soup / ate / some / last /.

　　　　I ate some hot soup for dinner last night.

2. in the refrigerator / three / There are / apples / red /.

_____

3. ate / delicious / after dinner / a / dessert / I /.

_____

4. hot / There is / some / in the kitchen / coffee /.

_____

5. at the store / bought / expensive / I / cheese / some /.

_____

6. like / I'd / hot / please / sandwich / a /.

_____

2 **Answer the questions. Use an adjective + noun in your answer.**

1. What do you usually eat for breakfast? _____

_____

2. What do you have in your room? _____

_____

3. What do you look like?_____

_____

It's, its, and 's

We use **'s** as a short way to say **is**.
EXAMPLES: My name**'s** Tina. (My name **is** Tina.) Bob**'s** late. (Bob **is** late.)
We also use **'s** to show possession.
EXAMPLES: This is Tina**'s** cat. (The cat belongs to Tina) Where is Bob**'s** house? (The house that belongs to Bob)
Its and *It's* have different meanings.
EXAMPLES: **It's** hot today! (it's = it is) Look at the car. **Its** door is open! (its = the car's door)

① Circle the *'s* that shows possession and underline the *'s* that means *is*.

My name's Robert and I think my family's great. My mother's name is Maria and my father's name is Peter. I have one sister. Her name's Sonia. She's married and has two children. Her husband's name is Tom. Their son's name is Bobby. He's my nephew. Their daughter's name is Tina. She's my niece. They live in an apartment. It's new but its living room is very small. I live at my parents' house. It's big, so we have room for my sister's family to stay with us when they visit. It's great when they do!

② Read the sentences. Change *its* to *it's* when needed.

1. Its my birthday.

2. Its a beautiful day.

3. Get out a pen. Now take off its cap.

4. I hate my computer! Its not working.

5. Look at that dog. Its foot is hurt.

6. The bird sat on its nest all day.

③ Answer the questions. Use *it's* and *'s* in your answers.

1. What is your mother's name? What is your father's name?

_____

2. What's the weather like today?

_____

3. What does your English book look like?

_____

Possessive Adjectives and Pronouns

We use a **possessive pronoun** in place of a possessive adjective + noun. We use **possessive pronouns** to show ownership.

	Possessive Adjectives			Possessive Pronouns	
That is	my your his her	jacket.	That jacket is It's		mine. yours. his. hers.
Those are	our their	jackets.	Those jackets are		ours. theirs.

1 **Circle the correct possessive adjective or possessive pronoun.**

1. A: Hey, Sara! I think (your / yours) husband forgot (his / he) hat at the wedding. Is this one (his / he)?

   B: I don't think it's (he / his). It might belong to the other man that was at (our / ours) table. What's (his / he) name?

   A: Tom. Maybe it's (he / his).

2. A: Excuse me. Is that (your / yours) car? (Its / It's) lights are on.

   B: No, it's not (my / mine). Did you check with that family over there? I think it's (their / theirs).

3. A: Excuse me, sir. Is this (your / yours) cell phone? I'm trying to find (its / it's) owner.

   B: I'm sorry, but it's not (my / mine). Where did you find it?

   A: I found it outside (my / mine) house.

2 **Rewrite the sentences. Change the underlined possessive adjective + noun to the correct possessive pronoun.**

1. That's not <u>her</u> laptop. It's <u>my laptop.</u>   *That's not hers. It's mine.*

2. That's not <u>our</u> house. It's <u>their house.</u> _____

3. That's not <u>your</u> cell phone. It's <u>my cell phone.</u> _____

4. That's not <u>your</u> gift. It's <u>my brother's gift.</u> _____

5. That's not <u>my</u> car. It's <u>my sister's car.</u> _____

6. That's not <u>my</u> dog. It's <u>my parent's dog.</u> _____

7. He's not <u>our</u> son. He's <u>my sister's son.</u> _____

8. That's not <u>my</u> water. It's <u>my father's water.</u> _____

Object Pronouns

Subject Pronouns			Object Pronouns	
I			me	
You	want water.		you	
He			him	
She	wants water.	He gave	her	some water.
It			it	
We			us	
They	want water.		them	

3 Complete the conversations with the correct object pronoun.

1. A: Are you going out with your coworkers tonight?

   B: No, I'm going out with _____them_____ tomorrow night.

2. A: Did you spend time with your nephew?

   B: Yes, I spent the day with _____.

3. A: Did Tony return our basketball?

   B: Yes, he did. He returned _____ to _____ last week.

4. A: Don't forget to give me my car keys.

   B: I gave _____ to _____ last night. They're in your purse.

5. A: Did you send your parents the gift?

   B: Yes, I sent _____ to _____ last week.

6. A: Did you give your aunt her jacket?

   B: No, I forgot to give _____ to _____.

4 Unscramble the sentences.

1. gave / the / her / present / I /.

_____

2. the / showed / picture / me / Bob /.

_____

3. told / the / them / secret / She /.

_____

4. gave / We / yesterday / it / you / to /.

_____

Indefinite Pronouns: *Someone, Anyone, Everyone*

For people	someone somebody	**Someone** called you earlier. I don't know who it was. (unnamed)
	anyone anybody	There isn't **anyone** on the phone. It's just silent. (negative)
	no one nobody	**No one** called you. The phone didn't ring. (zero)
	everyone everybody	**Everyone** should call you today. It's your birthday. (all)
For things	something	There's **something** in the box. I can't see what it is. (unnamed)
	anything	There isn't **anything** in the box. It's empty. (negative)
	nothing	There's **nothing** in the box. It's empty. (zero)
	everything	**Everything** is in the box. I put it all in there. (all)

1 **Read the story. Write the correct indefinite pronouns on the lines.**

I had a very bad morning. First, I was sleeping when _____someone_____ knocked on the door.
(1)
But when I opened the door, there wasn't _____ there. Then I was hungry, so I decided to eat
(2)
_____. _____ in the refrigerator looked old, so I didn't eat _____ for
(3)   (4)   (5)
breakfast. I was very hungry all morning. When I got to school, _____ was there. Then
(6)
I remembered it was a holiday. _____ was enjoying the day off. They all had plans, but I
(7)
didn't. I had _____ to do. So I went home and got back in bed.
(8)

2 **Answer the questions. Use an indefinite pronoun in your answer.**

1. Who do you ask for advice?

_____

2. Is there anything you want to do tonight?

_____

3. Did you apologize to anyone today?

_____

4. What is something you think everyone should do in their lifetime?

_____

5. Do you take care of anybody? Who?

_____

Can, Could, Would and May for Requests and Offers				
	Examples		**Answers**	**Level of formality**
Requests asking someone *for something*	Can I Could I May I	have another cup of coffee?	Yes, of course. / Sure. Yes, you may. I'm sorry, but I'm using it.	less more
Requests asking someone *to do something*	Can you Will you Could you Would you	open the door, please?	Sure. / Yes, of course. I'd be happy to.	less more
Offers	Can I Could I May I	bring you another cup of coffee?	Yes, thank you. Yes, please. No, thank you.	less more

1 **Read the scenario and circle the best word to finish the sentence.**

1. You are at your best friend's house. You need to use the phone.

You say: (Can I / May I) use the phone, please?

2. You are at a wedding. You are sitting with the grandparents of the groom. You need the salt.

You say: (Can you / would you) pass the salt, please?

3. You are at a nice hotel. You need directions to the train station. You go to the front desk.

You say: (Could you / May you) tell me how to get to the train station, please?

4. You are moving next weekend and need help. You call your brother.

You say: (Can I / Can you) help me move next weekend?

5. You are at an expensive restaurant. You want an extra plate.

You say: Excuse me. (Would I / May I) have an extra plate, please?

6. You are on the train. An elderly woman has her bag on the last seat. You want to sit down.

You say: Excuse me. (Could I / Would I) sit here, please?

2 **Unscramble the sentences. Then write an answer to the request.**

1. have / could / Excuse me, / I / menu / please / a /?

_____Excuse me, could I have a menu, please?_____ Answer: _____Yes, of course._____

2. would / a picture / take / of us / you / Excuse me, /?

_____ Answer: _____

3. borrow / Can / your / please / bike / I /?

_____ Answer: _____

4. help / Could / you / please / me /?

_____ Answer: _____

5. I / Could / you / anything else / bring /?

_____ Answer: _____

6. close / Will / please / the window / you /?

_____ Answer: _____

7. I / you / a few questions / ask / May /?

_____ Answer: _____

3 **Error correction. Rewrite the sentences correctly.**

1. INCORRECT: Can bring you the check?

CORRECT: _____

2. INCORRECT: I may use your laptop, please?

CORRECT: _____

3. INCORRECT: May a bowl of soup, please.

CORRECT: _____

4. INCORRECT: You'll call me later?

CORRECT: _____

5. INCORRECT: Could I saw your driver's license, please?

CORRECT: _____

6. INCORRECT: Can I take your picture, Mr. President?

CORRECT: _____

Can for Ability

We use *can* to talk about ability in the present.

Statements			Negative Statements		
I You She We You They	**can**	**speak** French.	I You She We You They	**cannot** **can't**	**speak** French.

Yes/No Questions			Answers				
Can	I you she we you they	**speak** French?	Yes,	I you she we you they	**can.**	No,	I you she we you they	**can't.**

1 Complete the sentences. Use *can* or *can't* plus the verb in parentheses.

1. Ella's knee is better. She _____ can go _____ (go) running again.

2. The sun is in my eyes. I _____ (see).

3. Susan has a problem with her heart. She _____ (run).

4. Juan has strong muscles. He _____ (move) that refrigerator for you!

5. Maria and Tom have good ears. They _____ (hear) everything!

6. Nadia is a gymnast. She _____ (do) a cartwheel.

7. We are not mechanics. We _____ (fix) your car.

8. Sonia is an excellent writer. She _____ (help) you with your homework.

2 Complete the questions. Use *can* and the verb in parentheses. Then ask a partner the questions. Write your partner's answer.

1. _____ Can you swim _____? (swim)   _____ Yes, I can. _____

2. _____ three languages? (speak)   _____

3. _____ your toes? (touch)   _____

4. _____ a truck? (drive)   _____

5. _____ without glasses? (read)   _____

6. _____ five miles? (run)   _____

Could for Ability

We use ***could*** to talk about ability in the past.

Statements				Negative Statements		
I You She We You They	could	run 10 miles last year.		I You She We You They	could not couldn't	run 10 miles last week.
Yes/No Questions				**Answers**		
Could	I you she we you they	run 10 miles?	Yes,	I you she we you they	could.	No,	I you she we you they	couldn't.

③ Complete the sentences. Use *can, can't, could,* and *couldn't* and the verb in parentheses.

1. When I was young, I had a lot of energy. I _____ could stay _____ (stay) up all night!

2. There was a lot of snow last week. We _____ (go) to school.

3. When I was a small child, I _____ (read), but now I _____.

4. When Sara was young, she _____ (dance) for hours, but now she _____.

5. A: _____ you _____ (do) cartwheels when you were a child?

   B: Yes, I _____.

6. A: _____ they _____ (see) the rainbow?

   B: No, they _____.

④ Correct the sentences. Use *can, can't, could,* and *couldn't.*

1. INCORRECT: When I was young, I can't drive.
   CORRECT: _____ When I was young, I couldn't drive. _____

2. INCORRECT: Yesterday I couldn't remember his name, but now I could.
   CORRECT: _____

3. INCORRECT: William was sick yesterday, so he can't go to work.
   CORRECT: _____

4. INCORRECT: A: Can Joshua speaks Chinese?   B: No, he can.
   CORRECT: _____

5. INCORRECT: A: Could they fixed your car?   B: Yes, they could fix it.
   CORRECT: _____

Should and *Shouldn't* for Advice   pages 104–105

Should and Shouldn't							
We use **should** to give and ask for advice.							
Statements			**Negative Statements**				
I You She We You They	**should**	**take** the job.	I You She We You They	**should not** **shouldn't**		**take** the job.	
Yes/No Questions			**Answers**				
Should	I you she we you they	**take** the job?	Yes,	I you she we you they	**should.**	No,	I you she we you they	**shouldn't.**

❶ Complete the sentences. Use *should* or *shouldn't* plus the verb in parentheses.

1. You have a fever. You _____*shouldn't go*_____ (go) to school!

2. Kevin's cut is bleeding. He _____ (wear) a bandage.

3. I am feeling dizzy. I _____ (sit) down.

4. Terry and Bill have colds. They _____ (drink) a lot of orange juice.

5. A: Tom has a sprained ankle. _____ he _____ (play) basketball tonight?

   B: No, he _____.

6. A: Dinah has a small cut on her knee. _____ she _____ (see) the doctor?

   B: No, she _____.

❷ Complete the sentences and questions with your own ideas. Use the vocabulary from this lesson.

1. Your friend has a high fever. You tell him:

   You should _____

2. Your brother sprained his ankle. He asks you:

   Should I _____

3. Your teacher has a headache. You tell her:

   You should _____

4. You feel nauseous. You go to the doctor. She tells you:

   You should _____

Adverbs of Degree pages 106–107

Adverbs of Degree

Adverbs of degree describe adjectives. They tell how much.

Adverbs	Examples	Degree = How much
a little	I'd like to sit down. I'm **a little** tired.	less
pretty	I don't want to go shopping. I'm **pretty** tired.	
very	I need to sleep now. I'm **very** tired.	
really	I need to go home now. I'm **really** tired.	
too	I can't move. I'm **too** tired.	more
enough	He can go to that movie. He is old **enough**.	= the right amount
	I can't reach the shelf. I am **not** tall **enough**.	= not the right amount

1 Circle the correct adverb of degree in each sentence.

1. Lisa arrived at 9:05 A.M. today. She was (very / a little) late for her 9:00 doctor's appointment.

2. The wait at the hospital was (really long / long enough). We waited for four hours!

3. You must be eight years old to go to that camp. Ian is six years old. He isn't (old enough / too old).

4. I had a (little / really) good day. I saw my friends at school, and we didn't have any tests.

5. Susan's cut was (very bad / a little bad). She had to go to the emergency room for stitches.

6. You bake that cake at 350 degrees. The oven is at 350 degrees. It's (hot enough / too hot).

2 Unscramble the sentences. Then check *True* or *False*.

	True	False

1. have / I / really / right now / fever / high / a /.

_____   ○ ○

2. strong / muscles / are / My / very /.

_____   ○ ○

3. have / really / eyes / good / I /.

_____   ○ ○

4. I can't run very well.
knees / strong / aren't / enough / My /.

_____   ○ ○

5. I can't order from the children's menu.
am / too / I / old /.

_____   ○ ○

Adverbs of Frequency pages 108–109

Adverbs of Frequency

We use **adverbs of frequency** to talk about **how often** something happens. Adverbs of frequency go **before** the verb. We often use adverbs of frequency with verbs in the simple present.

always	all of the time	I **always** eat cereal for breakfast.
usually	most of the time	She **usually** goes to a restaurant for lunch.
often	a lot of the time	We **often** buy fish at the supermarket.
sometimes	not much of the time	They **sometimes** order a pizza.
rarely / seldom	very little of the time	He **rarely** buys red meat.
never	none of the time	You **never** eat fruit.

In statements with the verb *be*, the adverb of frequency comes after *am, is,* or *are*.
EXAMPLES: I **am often** hungry during class.   Mark **is never** late.

1 Check (✓) the boxes about illnesses and injuries.

How often do you _____?	always	often	sometimes	rarely	never
1. get a headache	○	○	○	○	○
2. get a blister	○	○	○	○	○
3. use crutches	○	○	○	○	○
4. go to the emergency room	○	○	○	○	○
5. feel nauseous	○	○	○	○	○
6. get tired during the day	○	○	○	○	○

2 Complete each sentence. Use an adverb of frequency from the box and the verb in parentheses. You can use a word more than once.

never	rarely	sometimes	usually	~~always~~

1. My mother told me I should eat an apple every day so I don't get sick. I think she's right, so
I _____always eat_____ (eat) an apple at lunchtime.

2. I run every day. I _____ run 3 miles, and I _____ run 5 miles. I never run
more than 5 miles.

3. Dennis plays soccer three times a week. He has a weak ankle. He _____ (use) an
ice pack after he plays soccer.

4. Barb is allergic to eggs. She gets a rash if she eats them. So she _____ (eat) eggs.

5. I only see my brother when I go to New York. I go to New York once a year. I _____
(see) my brother.

Questions with Adverbs of Frequency

We use **often** and **usually** to ask about frequency.

A: How **often** do you get sick?

B: I **rarely** get sick.

A: When do you **usually** feel dizzy?

B: I **usually** feel dizzy in the morning.

3 Unscramble the questions. Then ask a partner the questions. Your partner should answer using an adverb of frequency. Write your partner's answer.

1. often / get / How / a cold / you / do /?

How often do you get a cold?

I often get a cold. I get a cold about three times every winter.

2. When / usually / do / get sick / you /?

3. do / medicine / often / take / How / you /?

4. miss / often / do / How / you / school /?

5. usually / When / use / do / an ice pack / you /?

4 Answer the questions. Use an adverb of frequency in each answer.

1. How often do you go to the doctor?

2. How often do you take aspirin?

3. How often does your doctor give you a prescription?

4. How often does a baby get a fever?

5. Do you ever wear a bandage?

Simple Past Review

Statements		Negative Statements	
I You She We They	**left** yesterday.	I You She We They	**didn't leave** yesterday.

Irregular Verbs in the Simple Past

bleed	bled	give	gave	run	ran
cost	cost	go	went	see	saw
cut	cut	hurt	hurt	set	set
drink	drank	leave	left	shut	shut
feel	felt	meet	met	sleep	slept
get up	got up	read	read	write	wrote

For more irregular verbs, see page 221.

1 **Complete the sentences with the simple present or the simple past form of the verbs in parentheses.**

1. I usually _____drink_____ (drink) four glasses of water every day. Yesterday I _____drank_____ (drink) six glasses of water.

2. Jack usually _____ (shut) the bedroom door at night, but last night he _____ (not / shut) it.

3. Maria usually _____ (sleep) for seven hours during the week. But today is Sunday, so she _____ (sleep) for eight hours last night.

4. Did you _____ (shut) off the alarm last night? I usually _____ (shut) it off on the weekends.

5. Betty always _____ (meet) her mother for lunch on Wednesdays. Today is Thursday, so she _____ (meet) her mother for lunch yesterday.

6. Sean usually _____ (see) movies on Friday nights. Last Friday he went out to dinner, so he _____ (see / not) a movie.

2 **Look at the picture. Complete the paragraph with the simple past of the verbs in parentheses. Some of the verbs will be negative.**

Rob _____went_____ (go) to work today. He usually leaves the house at 8:30, but today he _____
    (1)   (2)
(leave) five minutes late. He _____ (be) in a hurry, so he _____ (do) everything
                                (3)   (4)
he usually does. Rob _____ (put) away the milk, but he _____ (put) away the eggs.
                        (5)   (6)
He _____ (eat) breakfast, but he _____ (do) his dishes. He _____
    (7)   (8)   (9)
(turn) off the TV, but he _____ (shut) off the kitchen lights.
                            (10)

3 **Answer the questions about you. Use complete sentences.**

1. What did you do before you left your house today?

_____

2. What did you eat for breakfast?

_____

3. When did you leave?

_____

4. What did you do after you left your house?

_____

5. Who did you see?

_____

Commands

Commands	A Series of Commands
• **Open** the window.	• **Open** the window <u>and</u> **go** down the fire escape.
• **Go** down the fire escape.	• **Call** 911, **open** the window, <u>and</u> **go** down the fire escape.
• **Call** 911.	
Negative Commands	**A Series of Negative Commands**
• **Don't use** the elevator.	• **Don't use** the elevator <u>or</u> **open** the door to the hallway.
• **Don't open** the door.	• **Don't use** the elevator, **open** the door, <u>or</u> **jump** out the window.
• **Don't jump** out the window.	

Inclusive commands

• **Let's call** the manager. I smell smoke.   • **Let's take** the stairs.

1 Give a series of commands or negative commands for each emergency. Join the commands with *and* or *or*.

1. There's a fire in your school building.

<u>Call 911, leave the building, and go outside with your class.</u>

2. Your toilet is clogged.

_____

3. Someone breaks into your house.

_____

4. You're stuck in the elevator.

_____

5. You have a car accident.

_____

6. A bad storm is coming.

_____

2 Write an inclusive command for each situation.

1. There's a big rain storm. The windows are open. → _____ Let's close the windows. _____

2. The sink is leaking. → _____

3. There's a lot of smoke in your kitchen. → _____

4. Your friend falls and hurts her leg. → _____

5. Someone is breaking into your house. → _____

Adverbs of Point in Time (Past)

We use *last* and *ago* to talk about specific times in the past.

We use *last* before a set time.	We use *ago* after a period of time.
• We watched TV **last night**.	• John was here **three weeks ago**.
• I saw him **last Saturday**.	• We went to the movies **two nights ago**.
• Sue went shopping **last week**.	• I got a promotion **a month ago**.

1 Look at Mayta's calendar. Today is Friday, April 17. Complete the sentences using a past adverb of point in time.

APRIL						
Sunday	**Monday**	**Tuesday**	**Wednesday**	**Thursday**	**Friday**	**Saturday**
⑤ Dinner with mom and dad	⑥ doctor's appointment 2pm	⑦ meet Ann and Ted for dinner	⑧ job interview	⑨ movie	⑩ Party at Maria's 8:00	⑪ Soccer game 2:30
⑫ movie	⑬ Concert CANCELLED hurricane!	⑭ Cable and electricity out	⑮ Power back on! Hurray!	⑯ Lunch w/Tim noon	⑰	⑱ Soccer game 1:15
⑲ Lunch w/Henry	⑳ Breakfast meeting at 7 A.M.	㉑	㉒ English test	㉓	㉔ Sara comes to visit!	㉕ movie

1. Mayta had dinner with her parents _____.

2. She met Ann and Ted for dinner _____.

3. She had a soccer game _____.

4. There was a hurricane _____.

5. The power came back on _____.

6. She saw a movie _____ and _____.

2 Answer the questions about you.

1. When did you move to your present home? _____

2. What did you do last night? _____

3. When was the last time you had a home emergency? _____

Adverbs of Point in Time (Future)

We use **in** and **next** to talk about specific times in the future.

We use **next** before a set time.	We use **in** before a period of time.
• We're going to go to the movies **next week**.	• We're leaving **in five minutes**.
• I'm having lunch with him **next Saturday**.	• She's going to go on vacation **in a week**.
• Sue's going to visit **next month**.	• He's going to graduate **in three months**.

3 Look at Mayta's calendar on page 195. Today is Friday, April 17. Complete the sentences using a future adverb of point in time.

1. Mayta will go to the movies _____.

2. Her friend Sara will come to visit _____.

3. She has an English test _____.

4. Her breakfast meeting is going to be at 7 A.M. _____.

5. She's going to eat lunch with Henry _____.

4 Complete your calendar for next week. Add one thing to each day. Then tell a partner about your plans.

Sunday	Monday	Tuesday	Wednesday	Thursday	Friday	Saturday

5 Answer the questions about you.

1. When is the next time you are going to eat?

_____

2. When is the next time you are going to go on vacation?

_____

3. When is the next time you are going to see your family?

_____

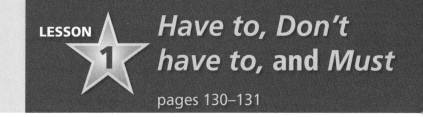

Must for Necessity and Prohibition

We use *must* to talk about necessity. We use *must not* to say something is not allowed.

Necessity			Prohibition		
I You She We You They	must	get a driver's license.	I You She We You They	must not	smoke in the lab.

Have to and *Don't Have to* for Necessity

We use *have to* to talk about necessity. We use *don't have* to say something is not necessary.

Statements			Negative Statements			
I You	have to	get a driver's license.	I You	don't	have to	have a degree to be a cashier.
She	has to		She	doesn't		
We You They	have to		We You They	don't		

1 Read the memo. Then complete the sentences with *have to, has to, must, don't have to,* or *must not*. More than one choice may be correct.

Memo

To: All Employees

From: Management

We want you to be safe at work. Please remember the following policies:

Do:

- Report unsafe situations immediately.
- Wear your safety equipment in work areas at all times. If you do not, you will be fined.
- Eat and drink only in the break room.
- Turn machines off when not in use.
- Take a ten-minute break every two hours.

Don't

- Work when you are tired.
- Work after drinking alcohol.
- Enter work areas without the proper safety equipment, including hard hat and goggles.
- Let machines run without supervision.

1. Workers _____*must*_____ take breaks every two hours.

2. They _____ wear safety equipment in the break room.

3. They _____ eat in work areas.

4. Workers _____ let machines run without supervision.

5. Walter is going to lunch. He _____ turn off his printing machine.

6. Workers _____ drink alcohol at work.

7. Everyone _____ report a safety problem right away.

8. Workers _____ take a break every hour.

2 **Complete the sentences with *have to, has to, don't have to, doesn't have to, must,* or *must not.* More than one choice may be correct.**

1. The teacher _____*has to*_____ work on Mondays.

2. I _____ go to work on Tuesdays.

3. I _____ wear safety equipment at my job.

4. We _____ do homework in class every day.

5. People who live in the United States _____ follow the laws.

6. If you don't work in the United States, you _____ pay U.S. taxes.

7. You _____ drive to school. You can take the bus.

8. Teachers and accountants _____ have college degrees.

9. Truck drivers _____ know how to cook.

10. A nurse _____ follow a doctor's instructions.

11. A salesperson _____ talk to people.

12. An electrician _____ be a man.

13. A chef _____ know how to cook.

3 **Answer the questions.**

1. What do you have to do today?

_____

2. What's one thing you must not do in school?

_____

3. What do you have to do every night?

_____

Adverbs of Manner pages 132–133

Adverbs of Manner

Adverbs of manner tell how we do something. They come after verbs. We form most adverbs of manner by adding **–ly** to an **adjective**.

Adjective	Adverb of Manner	Examples	Irregular Adverbs	Examples
careful	careful**ly**	I listened to the report **carefully**.	good → **well**	Alex writes **well**.
polite	polite**ly**	Jack speaks **politely**.	hard → **hard**	He worked **hard**.
slow	slow**ly**	We ate **slowly**.	fast → **fast**	You walk **fast**.

1 Write the adverb form of the adjectives below.

1. appropriate   _appropriately_

2. careful

3. early

4. efficient

5. fast

6. good

7. hard

8. independent

9. intelligent

10. loud

11. neat

12. polite

13. slow

14. thorough

2 Complete the sentences. Use the adverb form of one of the adjectives in the box.

appropriate	careful	fast	hard	independent	polite	~~slow~~	good

1. Jim works very _____ _slowly_ _____. It takes him a long time to finish projects.

2. He answers customers' questions _____. He says "please" and "Thank you."

3. He can work _____. He doesn't need someone to tell him what to do.

4. He drives too _____. He has gotten several speeding tickets.

5. Nancy works _____. She never takes a break.

6. She writes very _____. She almost never makes a mistake.

7. Nancy doesn't dress _____. Her skirts are too short.

8. She doesn't communicate _____ with her supervisor. She doesn't ask questions or express her opinions.

3 You are the supervisor of Jim and Nancy. Use the information from Activity 2 on page 199. Write down the positive (good) and negative (bad) infomation in the correct place on the chart.

Name	Positive evaluations	Negative evaluations
Jim		
Nancy		

4 Answer the questions with your own ideas.

1. Do you prefer to work independently or with a group of people?

_____

2. Do you think it's more important to work thoroughly or quickly?

_____

3. What do you think it means to communicate well?

_____

4. Why is it important to dress appropriately at work?

_____

5. What is one problem with working too fast?

_____

Now practice asking and answering the questions with a partner. Write your partner's answers on another piece of paper.

LESSON 3

Compound Sentences
with and, but, and or pages 134–135

	To connect two Sentences with:		Compound Sentence
and	same ideas	Paula **finished** quickly. Max **finished** quickly.	Paula finished quickly, **and** Max did **too**.
but	different ideas	John **works** slowly. I **don't work** slowly.	John works slowly, **but** I don't.
or	two choices	Do you **work nights**? Do you **work days**? Is he a **chef**? Is he a **painter**?	Do you work nights **or** days? Is he a chef, **or** is he a painter?

Compound Sentences with *and, but,* and *or*

We use *and, but,* and *or* to combine two sentences into one compound sentence.

1 **Combine the following sentences. Use *but, and ... too,* or *or*.**

1. Michael is an accountant. I am an accountant.

Michael is an accountant, and I am too.

2. Do you want to work the day shift? Would you prefer the evening shift?

_____

3. I was a chef in my last job. You were a chef.

_____

4. Tania likes to work. Luis doesn't like to work.

_____

5. Henry traveled a lot as a salesperson. Martha traveled a lot as a salesperson.

_____

6. Did he quit? Was he fired?

_____

7. Will you start next week? Do you have to wait for paperwork?

_____

8. I worked very hard. I didn't get a promotion.

_____

Negative Compound Sentences pages 136–137

Negative Compound Sentences			
We use **and... not either** and **not... or** to combine two negative sentences into one compound sentence.			
	To connect two negative ideas with:		**Compound Sentence**
and ... not either	different subjects	**Paula** didn't finish quickly. **Max** didn't finish quickly.	Paula didn't finish quickly, **and** Max did**n't either.**
not...or	the same subject	**I** don't work on a team. **I** don't talk to customers.	**I** do**n't** work on a team **or** talk to customers.
		Ann isn't strong. **Ann** isn't healthy.	Ann is**n't** strong **or** healthy.

❶ Combine the sentences below with *and ... not either*, or *not ... or*.

1. An accountant doesn't have to be strong. A teacher doesn't have to be strong.

_____ *An accountant doesn't have to be strong, and a teacher doesn't either.* _____

2. I can't drive a forklift. I can't use a computer.

_____

3. Marcia didn't get to work on time. Marcia didn't dress appropriately.

_____

4. Linda's supervisor didn't welcome her on the first day. Her co-workers didn't welcome her on the first day.

_____

5. Karl doesn't work full-time. Greg doesn't work full-time.

_____

6. The company doesn't give us computers. The company doesn't give us telephones.

_____

7. My co-workers don't work quickly. I don't work quickly.

_____

❷ Work with a partner. List three things you don't do at work or at home. Write compound sentences.

1. I don't answer phones or talk to customers. _____

2. _____

3. _____

4. _____

ALL-STAR STUDENT BOOK 2 AUDIO SCRIPT

Note: This audio script offers support for many of the activities in the Student Book. When the words on the Student Book page are identical to those on the audio program, the script is not provided here.

PRE-UNIT

Activity 2: Complete the Conversations (page 2)
Use a question or sentence from the box to complete the conversations. Listen again and check your answers.

1. A: What's your name?
   B: Keiko.
   A: How do you spell that?
   B: K-e-i-k-o.

2. A: Where are you from?
   B: I'm from Mexico. What about you?
   A: I'm from China.

3. A: What languages do you speak?
   B: Russian, French, and English.
   A: Really? That's interesting!

4. A: Do you like to watch flicks?
   B: I'm not sure. What is a flick?
   A: It is a movie.
   B: Then yes, I do.

5. A: Please turn to page 12.
   B: Could you repeat that?
   A: Please turn to page 12.

6. A: Would you be interested in studying tomorrow?
   B: I'm sorry. I don't understand your question.
   A: Do you want to study with me tomorrow?
   B: Yes, thank you.

Activity 3: Follow Instructions (page 3)
Look at the pictures. Listen to the classroom instructions. Listen again and repeat.

1. Listen to the words.
2. Say, "Hello."
3. Write your name.
4. Sign your name.
5. Check (✔)True or False.
6. Take out a piece of paper.
7. Practice the conversation.
8. Raise your hand.
9. Underline the word.
10. Circle the word.
11. Hand in your homework.
12. Listen and repeat.

UNIT 1

Lesson 1, Activity 1: Learn New Words (page 4)
Look at the pictures. Listen to the words. Listen again and repeat.

1. birth certificate	It's a birth certificate.
2. birthplace	His birthplace is Kingsville, Texas.
3. date of birth	His date of birth is March 2, 1975.
4. first name	His first name is Robert.
5. middle name	His middle name is Manuel.
6. last name	His last name is Garza.
7. sex	His sex is male.
8. driver's license	It's a driver's license.
9. address	His address is 1521 Market Street, San Francisco, California, 94821.
10. hair color	His hair color is brown.
11. eye color	His eye color is brown.
12. height	His height is 5'10".
13. weight	His weight is 160 pounds.
14. diploma	It's a high school diploma.
15. signature	There's a signature on the diploma.
16. employee I.D. badge	It's an employee I.D. badge.
17. occupation	His occupation is nursing assistant.

Lesson 1, Activity 5: Circle *True* or *False* (page 4)
Listen. Then circle True *or* False.

1. Robert's middle name is Manuel.
2. His birthplace is New York.
3. He is a high school student.
4. His eyes are brown.
5. He is five feet nine inches tall.
6. Robert is a nursing assistant.

Lesson 2, Activity 1: Learn New Words (page 6)
Look at the picture. Listen to the words. Listen again and repeat.

1. long hair	She has long hair.
2. short hair	He has short hair.
3. straight hair	He has straight hair.
4. curly hair	She has curly hair.
5. bald	He is bald.
6. beard	He has a beard.
7. mustache	He has a mustache.
8. tall	He is tall.
9. medium height	He is medium height.
10. short	He is short.
11. slim	She is slim.
12. heavy	He is heavy.
13. blond	His hair is blond.
14. light brown	Her hair is light brown.
15. dark brown	His hair is dark brown.
16. gray	Her hair is gray.

Lesson 2, Activity 2: Listen and Write (page 6)
Listen. Write the correct name under each picture.

1. Robert is slim. He has short curly hair and a mustache.
2. Lisa has long blond hair and she's medium height.
3. Estela is short and slim.
4. Rick is short and heavy.
5. Dan is heavy, and he has short straight hair.
6. Paul has dark brown hair, and he is slim.
7. Sam has long straight hair, and he is tall.

Lesson 3, Activity 1: Learn New Words (page 8)
Look at the picture. Listen to the words. Listen again and repeat.

1. happy	He looks happy.
2. relaxed	He looks relaxed.
3. sad	She looks sad.
4. nervous	He looks nervous.
5. afraid	She is afraid.
6. bored	He looks bored.
7. angry	She looks angry.
8. tired	He looks tired.
9. radio	She has a radio.
10. slide	It's a slide.
11. swing	It's a swing.
12. basketball	He has a basketball.
13. camera	He has a camera.
14. toy	It's a toy.
15. laptop	He has a laptop.
16. cell phone	She has a cell phone.

Lesson 4, Activity 1: Learn New Words (page 10)
Look at the pictures. Listen to the words. Listen again and repeat.

1. music	She likes music.
2. swimming	She likes swimming.
3. loud noises	She doesn't like loud noises.
4. soccer	He likes soccer.
5. baseball	He doesn't like baseball.
6. housework	He doesn't like housework.
7. motorcycles	He likes motorcycles.
8. pets	He doesn't like pets.

Lesson 4, Activity 2: Read and Take Notes (page 10)
Listen to the poems. Then read the poems and take notes in the chart.

1.

Yuko
my classmate
brown hair, brown eyes, intelligent
likes music, swimming, and Japanese food
doesn't like pets, loud noises, and the color yellow
speaks Japanese and English
a student
Tanaka

2.

Paul
my friend
tall, slim, good-looking
likes cars, loud music, and soccer
doesn't like baseball, housework, and homework
speaks Chinese, French, and English
a student
Ho

3.

Abel
my husband
tall, dark, handsome
likes cameras, motorcycles, and good food
doesn't like American coffee, alarm clocks, and pets
speaks Spanish and English
a businessperson
Diaz

Lesson 5, Activity 1: Practice Pronunciation: Vowel Sounds in *Slip* and *Sleep* (page 12)
A. Listen to the words. Listen again and repeat.

1. this	9. feet
2. these	10. slim
3. meet	11. slip
4. live	12. sleep
5. fifth	13. is
6. leave	14. easy
7. me	15. he
8. fit	16. his

Circle the words with the long vowel E sound.

B. Listen to the pairs of sentences. Listen again and repeat.

1. This is for you.	These are for you.
2. Did you slip yesterday?	Did you sleep yesterday?
3. I want to live.	I want to leave.
4. Is he shopping?	Easy shopping?

Lesson 6, Activity 3: Listen and Write (page 15)
Listen to the phone conversation. Complete the message form. Use the information in the box.

Woman: Hello? Adult Learning Center.
Man: Hi. Could I speak to Ms. Morgan?
Woman: Sorry. Lena is not here right now. Can I take a message?
Man: Yes. This is Henry Temple. I'm calling from the Reseda Adult School. I want to talk to her about her class.
Woman: Okay, Mr. Temple. I will have her call you back. What's your number?
Man: My number is 947-555-7855. Thank you!
Woman: You're welcome. Good-bye.

Lesson 7, Activity 1: Listening Review (page 16)
Listen to the question and choose the correct answer: A, B, or C. Use the Answer Sheet.

1. What color is your hair?
   A. My hair is long.
   B. My hair is curly.
   C. My hair is brown.

2. What's your last name?
   A. Robert Manuel Garza
   B. Garza
   C. California

3. How are you today, John?
   A. Oh, that's nice.
   B. How did you do it, Ms. Johnson?
   C. Fine, thanks. How are you?

4. Would you give this book to Maya?
   A. She has curly brown hair.
   B. That's a good book.
   C. I'm sorry. I don't know Maya.

5. Is Sara bored?
   A. Yes, she is.
   B. No, thank you.
   C. That's too bad.

Lesson 7, Activity 2: Listening Dictation (page 16)
Listen and write the sentences you hear.

1. A: What color are your eyes?
   B: They're brown.

2. A: You look happy!
   B: I am. I just got good news!

3. A: Hi, I'm José. I'm from Chile.
   B: Nice to meet you, José. My name is Barbara.

4. A: What does Tara look like?
   B: She is tall and heavy. She has short brown hair.

5. A: What's your middle name?
   B: It's Maria.

UNIT 2

Lesson 1, Activity 1: Learn New Words (page 18)
Look at the pictures. Listen to the words. Listen again and repeat. Which words are new to you? Circle them.

1. library	There are many books at the library.
2. study	Tom studies at the library every day.
3. check out books	Janet often checks out books from the library.
4. post office	They sell stamps at the post office.
5. buy stamps	Carlos buys stamps at the post office.
6. mail letters	Maria mails letters at the post office.
7. mail packages	Barb mails packages at the post office.
8. bank	I have money in the bank.
9. get cash	Lee gets cash at the bank.
10. cash a check	Sue cashes her check at the bank.
11. drugstore	They sell medicine at the drugstore.
12. buy medicine	Ana buys medicine at the drugstore.
13. supermarket	They sell food at the supermarket.
14. buy groceries	Laura and Sofia buy groceries at the supermarket.
15. medical center	Doctors work at the medical center.
16. see a doctor	Jack sees a doctor at the medical center.
17. community center	There are many activities at the community center.
18. socialize	Greg and Emily socialize at the community center.
19. take classes	Luz takes classes at the community center.
20. restaurant	I like to eat dinner at a restaurant.
21. get something to drink	Pamela often gets something to drink at a restaurant.
22. get something to eat	Pat often gets something to eat at a restaurant.

Lesson 1, Activity 2: Listen and Write (page 18)
Look at the pictures. Listen and write the names.

1. He is at the restaurant. He is getting something to eat.
2. She is at the community center. She is taking classes.
3. They are at the supermarket. They are buying groceries.
4. She is at the post office. She is mailing packages.
5. She is at the library. She is checking out books.
6. They are at the community center. They are socializing.
7. He's at the library. He's studying.
8. He's at the medical center. He's seeing a doctor.
9. She's at the drugstore. She's buying medicine.

Lesson 2, Activity 1: Learn New Words (page 20)
Listen to the words. Find the places on the map. Listen again and repeat.

on a map

1. avenue	The restaurant is on Central Avenue.
2. boulevard	The fire station is on Adams Boulevard.
3. block	The hotel and the shopping center are on the same block.
4. street	The library is on River Street.

describing location

5. on the corner of	The park is on the corner of Grove and Bristol.
6. between	The library is between the park and the drugstore.
7. next to	The police station is next to the community center.
8. across from	The post office is across from the police station.

giving directions

9. go north	Go north on Low Street.
10. go east	Go east on Adams Boulevard.
11. go south	Go south on Low Street.
12. go west	Go west on Adams Boulevard.
13. take a right	Take a right on Adams Boulevard.
14. take a left	Take a left on Scott Street.
15. go straight	Go straight on Diamond Street.

Lesson 2, Activity 2 Circle *True* or *False* (page 20)
Listen to the sentences. Look at the map. Circle True or False.

1. A: Excuse me. Where's the fire station?
   B: It's on Adams Boulevard.

2. A: Excuse me. Where's the library?
   B: It's next to the drugstore.

3. A: Excuse me. Where's the medical center?
   B: The medical center is between Central and Green.

4. A: Excuse me. Where is City Bank?
   B: City Bank is just north of the post office.

5. A: Excuse me. Where's the Community Center?
   B: It's across from the gas station.

6. A: Excuse me. Where's the hotel?
   B: It's on the corner of Green Avenue and Low Street.

7. A: Excuse me. Where's the train station?
   B: It's east of Diamond Street.

8. A: Excuse me. Where's the shopping center?
   B: It's on Green Avenue between Elm Street and Low Street.

Lesson 3, Activity 1: Learn New Words (page 22)
Look at the picture. Listen to the words. Listen again and repeat.

1. ticket machine	Where's the ticket machine?
2. ticket office	Where's the ticket office?
3. platform	Where's the platform?
4. track	Where's the track?
5. snack bar	Where's the snack bar?
6. newsstand	Where's the newsstand?
7. information desk	Where's the information desk?
8. waiting area	Where's the waiting area?
9. baggage check	Where's the baggage check?
10. buy a ticket	Who is buying a ticket?
11. wait for a train	Who is waiting for a train?
12. read a train schedule	Who is reading a train schedule?
13. make a phone call	Who is making a phone call?

Which words and phrases are new to you? Circle them.

Lesson 4, Activity 1: Practice Pronunciation: Word Stress (page 26)
B. Listen to the conversations. Circle the correct time or number.

1. A: What time is it?
   B: It's 10:15.

2. A: What time does the train leave?
   B: It leaves at 9:30.

3. A: What time is it?
   B: It's 12:40.

4. A: When's the next bus?
   B: 6:13.

5. A: How late is the bus to New York?
   B: 16 minutes.

6. A: When's the next train to Los Angeles?
   B: 8:50.

7. A: How old is Bob?
   B: Seventeen.

8. A: When's the next train?
   B: In 14 minutes.

Lesson 7, Activity 1: Listening Review (page 30)
Look at the pictures and listen. Choose the correct answer: A, B, or C. Use the Answer Sheet.

1. A: Where's Donna?
   B: She's at the medical center. She's seeing a doctor.

2. Tony is mailing a package.

3. Go north and take a left on Park Street.

4. A: When's the next bus?
   B: 5:50.

5. A: Excuse me. Where can I get a train schedule?
   B: At the information desk.

Lesson 7, Activity 2: Listening Dictation (page 30)
Listen. Write the words you hear.

1. A: Excuse me, where's the bank?
   B: It's on Main Street.

2. A: Where's Tina?
   B: She's at the library. She's studying.

3. A: What time does the train arrive in New York?
   B: It arrives at 4:50.

4. A: Can I help you?
   B: Yes, I'd like a one-way ticket to San Diego, please.

5. A: Excuse me, how do I get to the drugstore?
   B: Just go south on Elm St. and take a left on Center St.

UNIT 3

Lesson 1, Activity 1: Learn New Words (page 32)
Look at the pictures. Listen to the words. Listen again and repeat.

1. groceries	How much do you spend on groceries?
2. recreation	How much do you spend on recreation?
3. toiletries	How much do you spend on toiletries?
4. bus fare	How much do you spend on bus fare?
5. car repairs	How much do you spend on car repairs?
6. car payments	How much do you spend on car payments?
7. rent	How much do you spend on rent?
8. utilities	How much do you spend on utilities?
9. gas	How much do you spend on gas?
10. electricity	How much do you spend on electricity?

11. cash	Do you pay your rent by cash?
12. credit card	Do you pay your rent by credit card?
13. personal check	Do you pay your rent by personal check?
14. money order	Do you pay your rent by money order?
15. electronic debit	Do you pay your rent by electronic debit?

Lesson 1, Activity 2: Listen and Write (page 32)
Listen. How much did Lei spend last month? Fill in the chart.

Man: How much did you spend on groceries last month?
Woman: Last month? Let's see . . . My family visited me, so I spent a lot on groceries.
Man: How much did you spend on recreation?
Woman: Oh . . . not very much. Maybe ten dollars.
Man: How much did you spend on toiletries?
Woman: I spent an average amount.
Man: Okay. And how much did you spend on bus fare?
Woman: I took the train last month, so not very much.
Man: What about rent? How much did you spend on rent last month?
Woman: Our rent is very expensive, so I spent a lot on rent.

Lesson 2, Activity 1: Learn New Words (page 34)
Look at the pictures. Listen to the words. Listen again and repeat.

1. toothbrush	Dana bought a toothbrush yesterday.
2. razor	Sam bought a razor yesterday.
3. shaving cream	Sam bought some shaving cream yesterday.
4. shampoo	Jim bought some shampoo yesterday.
5. toothpaste	Jim bought some toothpaste yesterday.
6. penny	The customer's change was a penny.
7. nickel	The customer's change was a nickel.
8. dime	The customer's change was a dime.
9. quarter	The customer's change was a quarter.
10. dollar	The customer's change was a dollar.
11. five dollars	The customer's change was five dollars.
12. ten dollars	The customer's change was ten dollars.
13. twenty dollars	The customer's change was twenty dollars.
14. fifty dollars	The customer gave the cashier fifty dollars.

Lesson 2, Activity 2: Check *True* or *False* (page 34)
Listen to the sentences. Look at the pictures. Check (✓) True or False.

1. Dana bought a toothbrush.
2. Dana gave the cashier $20.
3. Sam gave the cashier $50.
4. Sam's change was 30 cents.
5. Jim bought a razor and shaving cream.
6. Jim's change was 50 cents.

Lesson 3, Activity 1: Learn New Words (page 36)
Look at the picture. Listen to the words. Listen again and repeat.

1. bank officer	The bank officer's name is Marie.
2. bank teller	Ali is a bank teller.
3. safe-deposit box	The safe-deposit boxes are near the exit.
4. ATM	There is an ATM at the front door of the bank.
5. check register	It's a check register.
6. checkbook	It's a checkbook.
7. deposit slip	It's a deposit slip.
8. withdrawal slip	It's a withdrawal slip.
9. savings account	She has a savings account.
10. debit card	He has a debit card.
11. monthly statement	It's a monthly statement.
12. paycheck	It's her paycheck.
13. endorse a check	You need to endorse a check to cash it.
14. make a deposit	He wants to make a deposit.
15. make a withdrawal	She wants to make a withdrawal.
16. open a checking account	He wants to open a checking account.

Lesson 4, Activity 1: Learn New Words (page 38)
Look at the pictures. Listen to the words. Listen again and repeat.

1. check register	It's a check register.
2. transaction amount	The transaction amount is $60.
3. balance	The balance is $385.89.
4. check number	The check number is 326.

Lesson 4, Activity 3: Read and Take Notes (page 38)
Read the personal checks and deposit slips and complete Al's check register on page 39. Listen again and check your work.

Check number: 326. Date: 9/16. Description: Veritas Telephone Company. Transaction amount: $42.76. Balance: $228.38.

Date: 9/17. Description: deposit. Deposit amount: $312.00. Balance: $540.38.

Check number: 327. Date: 9/18. Description: Bank Two. Transaction amount: $356.76. Balance: $183.62.

Date: 9/26. Description: Cash withdrawal. Transaction amount: $50.00. Balance: $133.62.

Date: 9/30. Description: deposit. Deposit amount: $850.00. Balance: $983.62.

Lesson 5, Activity 1: Practice Pronunciation: *Ng* versus *Nk* (page 40)
C. Now listen again. You will hear one question from each pair in Activity B. Circle the correct answer.

1. What is that bang?
2. Do you have a sink?
3. Now think. What do you want?

Lesson 5, Activity 2: Listen and Write: Listening to an Automated Phone System (page 40)
Listen and write the missing words. Listen again and check your answers.

Thank you for calling Horizon Bank. For existing account information, press 1. For all other services, press 2. To speak to a customer service specialist at any time, press 0.

For checking accounts, press 1. For savings, press 2. For credit cards, press 3.

Please enter you checking account number followed by the pound sign.

For personal accounts, please enter the last four digits of your Social Security number followed by the pound sign.

Your available balance is $886.59.

Lesson 7, Activity 1: Listening Review (page 44)
You will hear a question. Listen to the conversation. You will hear the question again. Choose the correct answer: A, B, or C. Use the Answer Sheet.

1. How did the person pay the bill?
   A: What are you doing?
   B: I'm paying the electric bill.
   A: I paid it yesterday with a check.

How did the person pay the bill?
   A. the electric bill
   B. with a check
   C. with a money order

2. How much money did she spend on groceries?
   A: How much money did you spend on bus fare last month?
   B: A lot. How much money did you spend on groceries last month?
   A: Not much.

How much money did she spend on groceries?
   A. A lot.
   B. An average amount.
   C. Not much.

3. What was the correct amount of change?
   A: Your change is $12.25.
   B: Hmmm. I thought it was $12.50.
   A: Oh, sorry. You're right.

What was the correct amount of change?
   A. $12.15
   B. $12.25
   C. $12.50

4. Where can you get a withdrawal slip?
   A: Did you fill out a withdrawal slip?
   B: A withdrawal slip?
   A: Yes. You can get one from a teller.

Where can you get a withdrawal slip?
   A. a withdrawal slip
   B. from a teller
   C. from an ATM

5. How much is the money order worth?
   A: I'd like to buy a money order.
   B: How much do you want it for?

A: Two hundred fifty dollars.
B: Okay. Your total is two hundred fifty-five dollars.

How much is the money order worth?
   A. $215
   B. $250
   C. $255

Lesson 7, Activity 2: Listening Dictation (page 44)
Listen and write the sentences you hear.

1. A: How much did you spend on recreation last month?
   B: I didn't spend very much.

2. A: How did you pay the gas bill last month?
   B: I paid with a money order.

3. A: The total is $8.95.
   B: Can you change a fifty?
   A: Sure. Your change is $41.05.

4. A: I'd like to make a withdrawal.
   B: Did you fill out a withdrawal slip?
   A: Yes, I did.

5. A: I'd like to buy a money order.
   B: How much do you want it for?
   A: Four hundred fifty dollars.

UNIT 4

Lesson 1, Activity 1: Learn New Words (page 46)
Look at the pictures. Listen to the words. Listen again and repeat.

Personal Goals

1. become a U.S. citizen	He would like to become a U.S. citizen.
2. get married	They would like to get married.
3. buy a house	She would like to buy a house.
4. be a good parent	She would like to be a good parent.
5. be a good citizen	He would like to be a good citizen.

Educational Goals

6. get good grades	He would like to get good grades.
7. get vocational training	They would like to get vocational training.
8. graduate from a university	She would like to graduate from a university.
9. get a GED	He would like to get a GED.
10. learn something new	She would like to learn something new.

Work Goals

11. get a job	He would like to get a job.
12. get a raise	She would like to get a raise.
13. get a promotion	He would like to get a promotion.
14. start a business	She would like to start a business.
15. win an award	He would like to win an award.

Lesson 1, Activity 2: Listen and Write (page 46)
Listen to people talk about goals. Look at the pictures. Write the correct number.

   a. Carla would like to graduate from a university.
   b. Sonia would like to be a good parent.
   c. I would like to win an award at work.
   d. Bob would like to learn something new.
   e. José would like to get married.
   f. John would like to get a job.

Lesson 2, Activity 1: Learn New Words (page 48)
Look at the pictures. Listen to the words. Listen again and repeat.

1. go back to school	She is going to go back to school.
2. take a business course	She is going to take a business course.
3. save money	She is going to save money.
4. learn to use a computer	She is going to learn to use a computer.
5. take a writing course	She is going to take a writing course.
6. learn more English	He is going to learn more English.
7. vote	He is going to vote.
8. do volunteer work	He is going to do volunteer work.
9. read to your children	Are you going to read to your children?
10. spend time with your children	Are you going to spend time with your children?

Lesson 3, Activity 1: Learn New Words (page 50)
Look at the picture. Listen to the words. Listen again and repeat.

1. office manager	He is an office manager.
2. office worker	He is an office worker.
3. designer	He is a designer.
4. bookkeeper	She is a bookkeeper.
5. salesperson	He is a salesperson.
6. supervisor	He is a supervisor.
7. mechanic	She is a mechanic.
8. late	He is late.
9. on time	He is on time.
10. organized	He is organized.
11. disorganized	He is disorganized.
12. good with people	He is good with people.
13. hardworking	He is hardworking.
14. lazy	He is lazy.
15. bad attitude	He has a bad attitude.
16. good attitude	She has a good attitude.

Lesson 4, Activity 1: Learn New Words (page 52)
Look at the pictures and photos. Listen to the words. Listen again and repeat.

1. gymnastics	She is doing gymnastics.
2. gold medal	She won a gold medal.
3. coach	She likes to coach.

Lesson 5, Activity 2: Listen and Write: Listening to a Recorded Message (page 54)
Listen and write the missing words. Listen again and check your answers.

Welcome to Westville Adult School. Sorry we missed your call. For information about adult ESL classes, press 1. For information about vocational training, press 2. For information about the computer classes, press 3. To register for a class, press 4. To hear this message again, press 5.

Lesson 7, Activity 1: Listening Review (page 58)
Look at the pictures and listen. Choose the correct answer: A, B, or C. Use the Answer Sheet.

1.A: What's your goal?
   B: I would like to get a raise.

2.A: What's your goal?
   B: I have a personal goal. I would like to buy a house.

3.A: What's your goal?
   B: My goal is to be a good parent, so I'm going to read to my children every day.

4.A: Who do you think will get the new job as a salesperson?
   B: I think Liz will. She's good with people.

5.A: You look happy. What's up?
   B: I just got a promotion.

Lesson 7, Activity 2: Listening Dictation (page 58)
Listen. Write the words you hear.

1.A: What are your goals?
   B: I would like to become a U.S. citizen.

2.A: What is your goal?
   B: I have a work goal. I would like to start a business.

3.A: What is your goal?
   B: I would like to get a promotion, so I'm going to go back to school.

4.A: Who do you think will get the job as the new office worker?
   B: I think Sara will get it. She's hardworking.

5.A: You look happy. What's up?
   B: I just learned to use a computer.

UNIT 5

Lesson 1, Activity 1: Learn New Words (page 60)
Look at the pictures. Listen to the words. Listen again and repeat. Which words or phrases are new to you? Circle them.

1. pair of athletic shoes | I need to get a pair of athletic shoes.
2. jacket | I need to get a jacket.
3. heavy coat | I need to get a heavy coat.
4. pair of boots | I need to get a pair of boots.
5. washing machine | I need to get a washing machine.
6. dryer | I need to get a dryer.
7. refrigerator | I need to get a refrigerator.
8. stove | I need to get a stove.
9. dishwasher | I need to get a dishwasher.
10. dish soap | I need to get some dish soap.
11. broom | I need to get a broom.
12. mop | I need to get a mop.
13. bucket | I need to get a bucket.
14. vacuum cleaner | I need to get a vacuum cleaner.
15. coffeemaker | I need to get a coffeemaker.
16. blender | I need to get a blender.
17. toaster | I need to get a toaster.
18. can opener | I need to get a can opener.
19. peeler | I need to get a peeler.
20. cutting board | I need to get a cutting board.

Lesson 1, Activity 3: Listen and Take Notes (page 60)
Amanda is moving into a new apartment. Listen to her talk about what she has and what she wants to buy. Complete the chart.

A: Hi, Amanda. Do you want to go shopping together for your new apartment?
B: Sure! That sounds like fun!
A: What do you need to get?
B: Well, let's see. There is already a refrigerator and a stove, but I need to get a washing machine.
A: Okay. Do you have a toaster and a coffeemaker?
B: I have a toaster, but I don't have a coffeemaker. I want to buy one.
A: Do you have a blender?
B: No, I don't, but I don't use blenders, so I don't want to buy one.

Lesson 2, Activity 1: Learn New Words (page 62)
Look at the pictures. Listen to the words. Listen again and repeat.

1. carry | What is Jim carrying?
2. take a break | Who is taking a break?
3. go out of business | Which store is going out of business?
4. jewelry store | Where's the jewelry store?
5. go into | Which store is Carla going into?
6. toy store | Where's the toy store?
7. push a stroller | Who is pushing a stroller?
8. furniture store | Where's the furniture store?
9. sale | What's on sale at Arches Shoe Store?

10. demonstrate | What is Lola demonstrating?
11. mall directory | Where's the mall directory?
12. appliance store | Where's the appliance store?

Lesson 2, Activity 2: Check *True* or *False* (page 62)
Listen to the sentences about the mall. Look at the picture. Check (✓) True or False.

1. Le Chic Clothing is busier than Gemma's Jewels.
2. A lot of people are buying hot dogs.
3. Frank is pushing a stroller.
4. Don bought a bike for his son.
5. Arches is bigger than May's.
6. The mall opens earlier on Sunday than it does on Saturday.

Lesson 3, Activity 1: Learn New Words (page 64)
Look at the picture. Listen to the words. Listen again and repeat.

1. refund | He got a refund for the toy.
2. exchange | He exchanged the jacket for another one.
3. receipt | You need a receipt to make an exchange.
4. regular price | The regular price of the coffeemaker is $24.99.
5. marked down 50 percent | Whirley vacuum cleaners are marked down 50 percent at Al's Superstore.
6. half price | Sierra Stoves are half price at Al's Superstore.
7. 20 percent off | Ovay coffeemakers are now 20 percent off.
8. clearance sale | There was a clearance sale.

Lesson 7, Activity 1: Listening Review (page 72)
You will hear a question. Listen to the conversation. You will hear the question again. Choose the correct answer: A, B, or C. Use the Answer Sheet.

1. What does the woman need to buy?
   A: Where are you going?
   B: I'm going shopping. I need to get a washing machine.

What does the woman need to buy?
   A. She's going shopping.
   B. a washing machine
   C. a dishwasher

2. How much was the discount on the toaster?
   A: Did you get a new toaster?
   B: Yes, I got one on sale at Kitchens Galore. It was 15 percent off.
   A: That's great!

How much was the discount on the toaster?
   A. 15 percent off
   B. 50 percent off
   C. half price

3. What's wrong with the athletic shoes?
   A: Can I help you?
   B: Yes, I want to return these athletic shoes.
   A: Is there something wrong with them?
   B: Yes, they are too small.

What's wrong with the athletic shoes?
A. athletic shoes
B. They are too small.
C. They are too big.

4. What does the woman want?
A: Can I help you?
B: I want to return this coat. It's too small.
A: Do you want to exchange it for a bigger one?
B: No, thank you. I just want a refund.

What does the woman want?
A. to buy a jacket
B. to exchange a jacket
C. to get a refund for a jacket

5. Where does the man usually shop?
A: Where do you buy furniture?
B: I like Ben's Furniture Store.
A: Is Ben's better than May's?
B: I think so. They have nicer salespeople.

Where does the man usually shop?
A. furniture
B. Ben's
C. May's

Lesson 7, Activity 2: Listening Dictation (page 72)
Listen. Write the sentences you hear.

1. A: Where are you going?
B: I'm going shopping. I want to get a new heavy coat.

2. A: Where did you buy your vacuum?
B: At May's department Store. There was a sale.

3. A: Were they having a sale at Jingle's?
B: No, but there were a lot of people there!

4. A: Is CompWorld better than ElecUSA?
B: I think so. They have cheaper prices.

5. A: Why do you always shop at May's?
B: I like shopping at May's because they have the biggest selection.

UNIT 6

1 Lesson 1, Activity 1: Learn New Words (page 74)
Look at the pictures. Listen to the words. Listen again and repeat. Which words are new to you? Circle them.

1. red meat	Did you eat any red meat yesterday?
2. poultry	Did you eat any poultry yesterday?
3. fish	Did you eat any fish yesterday?
4. eggs	Did you eat any eggs yesterday?
5. milk	Did you drink any milk yesterday?
6. ice cream	Did you eat any ice cream yesterday?
7. cheese	Did you eat any cheese yesterday?
8. oil	Did you eat anything with oil in it yesterday?
9. fruit	Did you eat any fruit yesterday?
10. peanuts	Did you eat any peanuts yesterday?
11. vegetables	Did you eat any vegetables yesterday?
12. sugar	Did you eat any sugar yesterday?
13. flour	Did you eat anything with flour in it yesterday?
14. cereal	Did you eat any cereal yesterday?
15. soft drinks	Did you drink any soft drinks yesterday?
16. coffee	Did you drink any coffee yesterday?

Lesson 2, Activity 1: Learn New Words (page 76)
Look at the picture. Listen to the words. Listen again and repeat.

1. counter	They are sitting at the counter.
2. menu	She is looking at a menu.
3. waiter	The waiter is wearing a white shirt.
4. check	The waiter is giving her the check.
5. booth	They are sitting in a booth.
6. hostess	The hostess is seating them at a table.
7. tray	He is carrying a tray.
8. plate	There is a plate on the table.
9. bowl	There is a bowl on the table.
10. napkin	There is a napkin on the table.
11. serve food	She is serving food.
12. take an order	She is taking an order.
13. pour	She is pouring water.
14. trip over	He tripped over a purse.
15. fall off	The glass is falling off his tray.
16. set the table	He is setting the table.
17. clear the table	She is clearing the table.
18. spill	He is spilling his milk.

Lesson 2, Activity 2: Write the Names (page 76)
Listen to the sentences about the picture. Write the person's name.

1. A: Have you seen our waiter?
B: She's over there. She's clearing a table.

2. A: Have you seen our waiter?
B: She's over there. She's taking an order.

3. A: Have you seen our waiter?
B: He's over there. He just tripped over a bag.

4. A: Have you seen our waiter?
B: She's over there. She's pouring water.

5. A: Have you seen our waiter?
B: She's over there. She's serving food.

6. A: Have you seen our waiter?
B: He's over there. He's setting the table.

Lesson 3, Activity 1: Learn New Words (page 78)
Look at the menu. Listen to the words. Listen again and repeat. Which words are new to you? Circle them.

1. appetizers   What's your favorite appetizer?
2. soups   What's your favorite soup?
3. salads   What's your favorite salad?
4. main dishes   What's your favorite main dish?
5. sandwiches   What's your favorite sandwich?
6. side orders   What's your favorite side order?
7. desserts   What's your favorite dessert?
8. beverages   What's your favorite beverage?

Lesson 3, Activity 2: Complete the Chart (page 78)
Listen to the people ordering at the Casa Alberto Restaurant. Check (✓) the types of food they order.

1.
A: Are you ready to order?
B: Yes. I'd like a small garden salad and the spaghetti and meatballs.
A: Do you want something to drink with that?
B: Yes. I'd like some ginger ale.
A: Large or small?
B: Large, please.

2.
A: Are you ready to order?
B: Yes. I'll have a large chicken soup and the rice pudding.
A: Do you want something to drink with that?
B: Yes. I'll have some tea.
A: Large or small?
B: Small, please.

3.
A: Are you ready to order?
B: Yes. I'd like to start with a shrimp cocktail and then have the chicken in a basket as my meal.
A: Do you want something to drink with your meal?
B: No. Water is fine for me, but I'll have a cup of coffee after my meal.
A: Large or small?
B: Large, please.

4.
A: Would you like to order any dessert today?
B: Yes. I'll have the cake.
A: Would you like any ice cream with that?
B: No. Just the cake is fine. And I'll have some coffee with it.
A: Large or small?
B: Small, please.

5.
A: Are you ready to order?
B: Yes. I'll have the steak and a small garden salad.
A: Do you want something to drink with that?
B: Yes, I'll have some cola.
A: What size cola?
B: Large, please.

Lesson 4, Activity 1: Learn New Words (page 80)
Look at the pictures. Listen to the words. Listen again and repeat. What words are new to you? Circle them.

1. fry   You can fry an egg.
2. bake   You can bake bread.
3. boil   You can boil water for tea.
4. cut up   You cut up vegetables to cook them.
5. slice   You can slice meat.
6. mix   You mix ingredients.
7. peel   You can peel a potato.
8. mash   You can mash a potato.
9. heat   You heat soup in a pan.

Lesson 5, Activity 2: Listen and Write (page 82)
Listen to three people ordering at a deli. Check (✓) what each person orders. Then write the total you hear for each order.

1.A: Can I help you?
B: Yes, I'd like a steak sandwich, please.
A: Do you want something to drink with that?
B: Yes, I'll have a large root beer.
A: Okay. That will be $8.00.

2.A: What can I get for you?
B: I'd like a veggie sandwich.
A: Do you want a salad with that?
B: No, thank you.
A: Would you like something to drink?
B: Sure. I'll have a small tea, please.
A: That will be $6.25.

3.A: Can I help you?
B: Yes, I'd like a fruit salad, please.
A: Do you want something to drink with that?
B: Sure. I'll have a small orange soda.
A: For here or to go?
B: To go, please.
A: That will be $7.50.

Lesson 7, Activity 1: Listening Review (page 86)
Listen to the conversation. To finish the conversation, listen and choose the correct answer: A, B, or C. Use the Answer Sheet.

1.Did you eat any eggs yesterday?
A. No, thank you.
B. Yes, I'd like some eggs.
C. Yes, I did. I had some for breakfast.

2.Can you bring me a napkin please?
A. Yes, I'll get one right away.
B. Yes, you can have one.
C. Yes, you are.

3.Are you ready to order?
A. For here, please.
B. Yes. I'd like a small chicken soup and a salad.
C. Yes, it is.

4. Do you want something to drink with your sandwich?
   A. Yes, I'd like some french fries please.
   B. Yes, I'd like some ice cream.
   C. No, thank you.

5. What size lemonade?
   A. Large, please.
   B. No, thank you.
   C. Yes, it is.

Lesson 7, Activity 2: Listening Dictation (page 86)
Listen and write the sentences you hear.

1. A: Can I help you?
   B: Yes, I'd like a turkey sandwich and a small coffee.

2. A: Can you bring me a glass of water, please?
   B: Sure. I'll get one for you right away.

3. A: Are you ready to order?
   B: Yes. I'd like the baked fish dinner and an orange juice.

4. A: Do you want something to drink with your green salad?
   B: Sure. I'll have a cup of tea.

5. A: What size soup would you like?
   B: Large, please.

UNIT 7

Lesson 1, Activity 1: Learn New Words (page 88)
Look at the pictures. Listen to the words. Listen again and repeat.

1. grandparents	Manuel and Maria are Juan's grandparents.
2. parents	Tito and Rosa are Juan's parents.
3. aunt	Lupe is Juan's aunt.
4. uncle	Richard is Juan's uncle.
5. cousin	Marco is Juan's cousin.
6. brother-in-law	Paul is Juan's brother-in-law.
7. nephew	Nick is Juan's nephew.
8. niece	Sofia is Juan's niece.
9. fiancée	Lisa is Juan's fiancée.
10. co-worker	Tom is Juan's co-worker.
11. boss	Mr. Li is Juan's boss.
12. friend	Joe is Juan's friend.
13. neighbors	Mr. and Mrs. Nath are Juan's neighbors.
14. landlady	Mrs. Chen is Juan's landlady.

Which words are new to you? Circle them.

Lesson 1, Activity 2: Listen and Circle True or False (page 88)
Listen to Juan describe his family relationships. Circle true or false.

My name is Juan. I'm going to tell you about my family.

1. My grandparents' names are Manuel and Maria.
2. One of their children is my Aunt Lupe.
3. Lupe is married to my uncle. His name is Marco.

4. My Aunt Lupe and Uncle Richard have one son. He is my cousin.
5. I have one brother-in-law. His name is Nick.
6. I have a niece, too. Her name is Sofia.

Lesson 2, Activity 1: Learn New Words (page 90)
Look at the picture. Listen to the words. Listen again and repeat.

1. bride	Where's the bride?
2. groom	Where's the groom?
3. kiss	Who is kissing Marta?
4. musicians	Where are the musicians?
5. in a bad mood	Who is in a bad mood?
6. make a toast	Who is making a toast?
7. gifts	Where are the gifts?
8. photographer	Where's the photographer?
9. in a good mood	Who is in a good mood?
10. dance	Who is dancing?
11. hug	Who is Joe hugging?
12. shake hands	Who is shaking hands with Ron?

Lesson 2, Activity 2: Listen and Circle (page 90)
Listen and circle the correct name.

1. He's in a good mood.
2. She's dancing with Tito.
3. She's the bride.
4. He's standing next to the food.
5. He's kissing Marta.
6. He's shaking Ron's hand.
7. He's talking to the photographer.
8. He is making a toast.

Lesson 3, Activity 1: Learn New Words (page 92)
Look at the pictures. Listen to the words. Listen again and repeat. Which words are new to you? Circle them.

1. ask for advice	He's asking her for advice.
2. take care of	She's taking care of her grandmother.
3. compliment	He's complimenting her work.
4. apologize	He's apologizing.
5. disagree	They disagree about the food.
6. yell at	He yelled at the man to slow down.
7. criticize	He criticized the painter's work.
8. talk back	The boy talked back to his mother.
9. interrupt	He interrupted them.

Lesson 3, Activity 2: Listen and Write (page 92)
Listen to the conversations. Number the words and phrases from 1-5.

1. A: It's time to go to bed now.
   B: No! I want to stay up and play!

2. A: Wow! You look beautiful in that dress!
   B: Thank you!

3. A: You are so lazy! And you are late every day.
   B: I will try to work harder.

4.A: I'm sorry I forgot to call you yesterday.
   B: That's okay.

5.A: I think this is a great car.
   B: Really? I don't like it!

Lesson 7, Activity 1: Listening Review (page 100)
Look at the pictures and listen. Choose the correct answer: A, B, or C. Use the Answer Sheet.

1.A: This is Mrs. Sanchez. She's my landlady.
   B: Nice to meet you, Mrs. Sanchez.

2.A: Where do your grandparents live?
   B: In California.

3.A: Look at Barbara!
   B: Who's that dancing with her?
   A: That's one of her friends.

4.A: Where's the photographer?
   B: She's over there by the gifts.

5.A: How was your day?
   B: Not so good.
   A: What happened?
   B: My daughter talked back to me.

Lesson 7, Activity 2: Listening Dictation (page 100)
Listen and write the sentences you hear.

1.A: How many cousins do you have?
   B: Twelve.

2.A: Who's shaking Bill's hand?
   B: That's Ron.

3.A: Do you know him?
   B: Yes, I do. He's a nice guy.

4.A: How was your day?
   B: Not so good. My boss criticized me.

5.A: Can I help you clean the house?
   B: Thanks for offering, but I'm all set.

UNIT 8

Lesson 1, Activity 1: Learn New Words (page 102)
Look at the pictures. Listen to the words. Listen again and repeat. Which words are new to you? Circle them.

1. brain	It's a brain.
2. lungs	They're lungs.
3. heart	It's a heart.
4. wrist	It's a wrist.
5. skin	It's skin.
6. back	It's a back.
7. tooth*	It's a tooth.
8. muscle	It's a muscle.

9. waist	It's a waist.
10. hip	It's a hip.
11. joint	It's a joint.
12. bone	It's a bone.

Lesson 2, Activity 1: Learn New Words (page 104)
Look at the pictures. Listen to the words. Listen again and repeat. Which words are new to you? Circle them.

1. burn	It's a bad burn.
2. cut	It's a deep cut.
3. fracture	It's a bad fracture.
4. sprain	It's a sprain.
5. bruise	It's a bruise.
6. shock	He got a shock from the electric cord.
7. rash	She has a rash on her leg.
8. fever	She has a fever.
9. cold	Bill has a cold.
10. flu	Sara has the flu.
11. infection	She has an infection on her finger.
12. feel dizzy	Tom feels dizzy.
13. blister	Jacob has a blister on his hand.
14. feel nauseous	Lisa feels nauseous.
15. bleed	The cut on his arm is bleeding.

Lesson 2, Activity 2: Listen and Write, (page 104)
Listen and look at the pictures. Write the name of the person that has the illness or injury.

1.A: Is your cold getting any better?
   B: I don't think so.
   A: Maybe you should go home and rest.
   B: Maybe you're right.

2.A: Are you okay?
   B: No. I'm feeling dizzy.
   A: Maybe you should sit down.
   B: Maybe you're right.

3.A: Your cut is still bleeding.
   B: I know.
   A: Maybe you should put more pressure on it.
   B: Maybe you're right.

4.A: Are you okay?
   B: No. I'm feeling nauseous.
   A: Maybe you should drink some ginger ale.
   B: Maybe you're right.

5.A: Is your flu getting any better?
   B: I don't think so.
   A: Maybe you should see a doctor.
   B: Maybe you're right.

6.A: Is your fever getting any better?
   B: I don't think so.
   A: Maybe you should take some medicine.
   B: I already did.

Lesson 3, Activity 1: Learn New Words (page 106)
Look at the picture. Listen to the words. Listen again and repeat.

1. emergency room   Where's the emergency room?
2. examining room   Where's the examining room?
3. X-ray   He got an X-ray.
4. radiology   Where's the radiology department?
5. stitches   She got stitches.
6. sling   He has a sling.
7. ice pack   He has an ice pack.
8. admissions desk   Where's the admissions desk?
9. splint   He has a splint.
10. wheelchair   He's in a wheelchair.
11. waiting area   Where's the waiting area?
12. crutches   She has crutches.
13. cast   She has a cast.
14. bandage   She has a bandage.

Lesson 3, Activity 2: Listen and Circle *True* or *False* (page 106)
Listen to the sentences and look at the picture. Circle True *or* False.

1. The emergency room is very empty.
2. Alice is in the waiting room.
3. Alex is in the examining room.
4. Nina's ankle looks pretty painful.
5. Ben is in a wheelchair. He has a splint on this leg.
6. Fred is in the waiting room. He is probably waiting to get stitches.

Lesson 4, Activity 1: Learn New Words (page 108)
Look at the medicine labels. Listen to the words. Listen again and repeat.

1. table   Take two tablets.
2. teaspoon   Take two teaspoons.
3. cream   Use the cream two times a day.
4. prescription   You need to see the doctor to get a prescription.
5. OTC   The medicine is OTC.
6. capsule   Take two capsules.

Lesson 5, Activity 1: Practice Pronunciation: Can and Can't (page 110)
B Listen to the sentences. Underline the word you hear.

1. He can't come to school today.
2. She can go back to work.
3. Bob can play soccer today.
4. She can't walk without crutches.
5. I can exercise today.
6. Tara can't take off her bandage.

Lesson 5, Activity 4: Listen and Write (page 111)
Listen to two people making doctor's appointments. Fill out the appointment cards.

1.
A: I'd like to make an appointment with Dr Thomas.
B: What kind of appointment do you need?
A: A routine checkup, please.
B: Let's see. It looks like I have an opening on the 15th at 9 A.M.
A: Great. I'll take it!
B: And your name please?
A: It's Andy Chen. C-H-E-N.
B: Okay Andy, that's 9 A.M. on November 15th with Dr. Thomas. See you then!
A: Thank you!

2.
A: Does Dr. Levine want to see you again?
B: Yes. She said to come back in two weeks.
A: Is it for a follow up appointment or a routine check up?
B: A follow-up appointment.
A: Okay. Let's see. It looks like I have an opening on the 23rd at 2 P.M.
B: That's perfect.
A: And your name please?
B: It's Lily Smith. S-M-I-T-H.
A: Okay Lily, that's 2 P.M. on April 23rd with Dr. Levine. See you then!
B: Thank you!

Lesson 7, Activity 1: Listening Review (page 114)
Look at the pictures and listen. Choose the correct answer: A, B, or C. Use the Answer Sheet.

1. Your brain is in your head.

2. A: is your burn getting any better?
   B: No, I don't think so.

3. A: What happened to your leg?
   B: I sprained my ankle.
   A: You should use an ice pack.

4. A: How often do I take it?
   B: Take one capsule three times a day.

5. A: I'd like to make an appointment as soon as possible.
   B: What's the problem?
   A: I have a rash.

Lesson 7, Activity 2: Listening Dictation (page 114)
Listen and write the words you hear.

1. A: Is your flu getting any better?
   B: No, I don't think so.

2. A: What happened to your hand?
   B: I burned it.

3. A: Did they put an ice pack on it?
   B: Yes, and then they gave me these crutches.

4. A: What happened?
   B: I fell down and hurt my hip.

5. A: How often do I take it?
   B: Take one tablet four times a day.

Lesson 1, Activity 1: Learn New Words (page 116)
Look at the pictures. Listen to the words. Listen again and repeat.

1. shut off	Shut off the alarm clock.
2. plug in	Plug in the coffeepot.
3. pick up	Pick up the newspaper.
4. put away	Put away the dishes.
5. take out	Take out the milk.
6. turn on	Turn on the radio.
7. turn off	Turn off the radio.
8. put back	Put back the milk.
9. turn down	Turn down the heat.
10. lock	Lock the door.
11. unlock	Unlock the door.
12. unplug	Unplug the coffeepot.

Lesson 1, Activity 3: Listen and Write (page 116)
Listen to the instructions. Write the number of the picture.

Thanks, Katia, for checking on the house while I am gone. I'm going to go over some instructions.

First, use this key to unlock the door.

Second, turn on one or two lights. You can leave them on at night.

Third, take out the trash on Tuesday night. Wednesday is trash day.

Fourth, when you leave, make sure you turn down the heat. The thermostat is in the hall.

After that, unplug the coffeepot if you used it.

Finally, the most important thing—remember to lock all the doors.

Call me with any questions. I'll see you on the 19th.

Lesson 2, Activity 1: Learn New Words (page 118)
Look at the pictures. Listen to the words. Listen again and repeat.

Things that leak

1. valve	A valve can leak.
2. faucet	The faucet is leaking.
3. pipe	The pipe is leaking.
4. roof	The roof is leaking.

Things that overheat

5. toaster oven	A toaster oven can overheat.
6. space heater	The space heater is overheating.
7. clothes dryer	The clothes dryer is overheating.
8. hair dryer	The hair dryer is overheating.

Things that clog

9. drain	A drain can clog.
10. sink	The sink is clogged.
11. toilet	The toilet is clogged.
12. bathtub	The bathtub is clogged.

Things that stick

13. window	A window can stick.
14. key	The key is stuck.
15. drawer	The drawer is stuck.
16. sliding door	The sliding door is stuck.

Lesson 2, Activity 3: Listen and Write (page 118)
Listen to the telephone messages. Write the problem.

You have four messages. To listen to your messages, press 1.

First message: Hi. This is the tenant in Apartment 103. We've got a problem. The roof is leaking. Can you come over right away?

Second message: This is John Burke in 210. The clothes dryer is overheating. Could you check it out, please?

Third message: Sorry to bother you, but this is Lisa in Apartment 507. The kitchen sink is clogged again. It's really making a mess.

Fourth message: Hey. I'm the tenant in Apartment 401. My key is stuck in the front door. Would you get it out for me?

Lesson 3, Activity 1: Learn New Words (page 120)
Look at the picture. Listen to the words. Listen again and repeat.

1. smoke	There's a lot of smoke.
2. spray	They spray water on the fire.
3. fire escape	They are going down the fire escape.
4. rescue	He is rescuing the man.
5. climb	The man is climbing down.
6. evacuate	The residents need to evacuate the building.
7. ladder	He is on the ladder.
8. ambulance	The ambulance is in front of the building.
9. cover	The woman covers her mouth.
10. firefighter	The firefighter is spraying water.
11. hose	The hose brings water to the fire.
12. crawl	The man crawls under the smoke.
13. hydrant	The firefighter attaches the hose to the hydrant.
14. attach	The firefighter needs to attach the hose.
15. fire truck	The fire truck is next to the building.

Lesson 4, Activity 1: Learn New Words (page 122)
Listen to the words. Listen again and repeat.

1. overload	Don't overload the outlet.
2. overheat	The space heater can overheat.
3. overflow	The sink overflowed.

4. temperature   The temperature is too high.
5. Celsius   They use the Celsius temperature scale in most countries.
6. Fahrenheit   We use the Fahrenheit temperature scale in the United States.

Lesson 5, Activity 4: Listen and Write (page 125)
Listen to the news report. Write the missing words. Listen again and check your answers.

This is Channel 5 news at 9:00 A.M. We have breaking news of a major fire in the 2000 block of Main Street, at the Landview Apartments. We don't have many details yet, but we do know that 45 families had to leave their homes at 5:30 this morning. Firefighters and other emergency personnel are on the scene. We'll bring you more news as the story develops. Drivers should take North Street instead.

Lesson 7, Activity 1: Listening Review (page 128)

You will hear part of a conversation. To finish the conversation, listen and choose the correct answer: A, B, or C. Use the Answer Sheet.

1.A: Oh, no. We've got a problem.
   A. What's the matter?
   B. I don't know.
   C. Yes, I can.

2.A: What's your location?
   A. There's a fire.
   B. 564 9th Street.
   C. Thank you.

3.A: Could you please take a look at my kitchen sink?
   B: Is it leaking again?

   A. In an hour.
   B. Apartment 13A.
   C. No. This time it's clogged.

4.A: What is the emergency?
   A. Someone had a car accident.
   B. At the corner of Main and Pine Streets.
   C. I don't think so.

5.A: Hi. This is the tenant in Apartment 19B. The sliding door is stuck.
   A. Is it the window again?
   B. Okay. I'll be right over.
   C. Thank you.

Lesson 7, Activity 2: Listening Dictation (page 128)
Listen. Write the sentences you hear.

1. Please turn off the lights.
2. The hair dryer is overheating.
3. The fire truck is next to the hydrant.
4. Don't use the elevator.
5. You can use the fire escape.

UNIT 10

Lesson 1, Activity 1: Learn New Words (page 130)
Look at the pictures. Listen to the words. Listen again and repeat. Which words are new to you? Circle them.

1. computer programmer   He is a computer programmer.
2. accountant   She is an accountant.
3. administrative assistant   She is an administrative assistant.
4. home health aide   She is a home health aide.
5. X-ray technician   She's an X-ray technician.
6. nursing assistant   He is a nursing assistant.
7. assembler   She is an assembler.
8. machine operator   He is a machine operator.
9. painter   He is a painter.
10. electrician   He is an electrician.
11. bricklayer   She is a bricklayer.
12. welder   He is a welder.
13. chef   She is a chef.
14. restaurant manager   He is a restaurant manager.
15. hotel desk clerk   She is a hotel desk clerk.

Lesson 1, Activity 3: Listen and Circle (page 130)
Listen to the conversation. Circle the correct words.

A: What kind of job do you think you want? Something in sales?
B: No, I don't want to be a salesperson. A salesperson has to work with people. I like to work alone.
A: How about something in construction?
B: Well, I'm not very strong.
A: Hmm. A bricklayer must be strong, but what about a welder?
B: But I'm not a man.
A: A welder doesn't have to be a man. A lot of welders are women.
B: I don't think I want to wear a lot of safety equipment. What about an accountant?
A: Sure. An accountant doesn't have to wear safety equipment. But an accountant has to have a special certificate.

Lesson 2, Activity 1: Learn New Words (page 132)
Look at the pictures. Listen to the words. Listen again and repeat.

1. communicate ideas effectively   Are you able to communicate ideas effectively?
2. resolve conflicts   Can you resolve conflicts?
3. organize information   Do you organize information well?
4. have computer skills   Do you have computer skills?
5. work well with others   Do you work well with others?
6. help other people   Do you like to help other people?

7. work independently	Can you work independently?
8. manage time efficiently	Do you manage time efficiently?
9. follow directions	Do you follow directions well?

Lesson 2, Activity 2: Listen and Check (page 132)
Listen to the conversation. Check the skills the person has.

A: I'm interested in the position of administrative assistant.
B: Okay. Do you have any experience?
A: Yes, I do. I was an administrative assistant for five years.
B: What skills do you have for this position?
A: I'm very good at organizing information and managing my time.
B: Do you work well with people?
A: Yes, I do. I like to help people. I'm also good at resolving conflicts.
B: What are some areas you need to improve?
A: Well, I want to improve my computer skills. They could be stronger.
B: Okay. We'll call you with our decision next week.

Lesson 3, Activity 1: Learn New Words (page 134)
Look at the picture. Listen to the words. Listen again and repeat.

1. career center	Where is the career center?
2. career counselor	Who is the career counselor?
3. application	Do you have your application?
4. résumé	Did you bring a résumé?
5. interview	When is your interview?
6. job applicant	Are you a job applicant?
7. full time	Are you looking for a full-time job?
8. part time	Are you looking for a part-time job?
9. day shift	When does the day shift start?
10. evening shift	When does the evening shift start?
11. night shift	When does the night shift start?
12. appointment	Did you make an appointment?

Lesson 7, Activity 1: Listening Review (page 142)
You will hear a question. Listen to the conversation. You will hear the question again. Then choose the correct answer: A, B, or C. Use the Answer Sheet.

1. What is Mark's job?
   A: Hey, Mark. Are you still working in construction?
   B: No, I'm an accountant now.

What is Mark's job?
   A. He's a bricklayer.
   B. He's a construction worker.
   C. He's an accountant.

2. Where does Tina work?
   A: Hi, Tina. What do you do now?
   B: I'm a chef.

Where does Tina work?
   A. at a hospital
   B. at a restaurant
   C. at a school

3. What is Lidia good at?
   A: So, Lidia, I see you work in an office. Are you good at following directions?
   B: Yes, I think so. I follow directions very well.

What is Lidia good at?
   A. She is good at helping people.
   B. She is good at organizing information.
   C. She is good at following directions.

4. How long did the speaker work there?
   A: I worked there for three years.
   B: What did you do?
   A: I was an assembler.

How long did the speaker work there?
   A. an assembler
   B. two years
   C. three years

5. What's the problem?
   A: I'm so sorry. I can't come to work today.
   B: What's the matter?
   A: I'm really sick.

What's the problem?
   A. The caller is sick.
   B. The caller is late.
   C. The caller's car broke down.

Lesson 7, Activity 2: Listening Dictation (page 142)
Listen and write the sentences you hear.

1. A welder doesn't have to be a man.
2. I'm good at helping people.
3. Are you willing to travel?
4. I want to work the day shift.
5. I'm sorry. I can't come to work today.

VOCABULARY LIST

Numbers in parentheses indicate unit numbers.

20 percent off (5)
accountant (10)
across from (2)
address (1)
administrative assistant (10)
admissions desk (8)
afraid (1)
ambulance (9)
angry (1)
apologize (7)
appetizer (6)
appliance store (5)
application (10)
appointment (10)
ask for advice (7)
assembler (10)
ATM (3)
attach (9)
aunt (7)
avenue (2)
back (8)
bad attitude (4)
baggage check (2)
bake (6)
balance (3)
bald (1)
bandage (8)
bank (2)
bank officer (3)
bank teller (3)
baseball (1)
basketball (1)
bathtub (9)
be a good citizen (4)
be a good parent (4)
beard (1)
become a U.S. citizen (4)
between (2)
beverage (6)
birth certificate (1)
birthplace (1)
bleed (8)
blender (5)
blister (8)
block (2)
blond (1)
boil (6)
bone (8)
bookkeeper (4)
booth (6)
bored (1)
boss (7)
boulevard (2)
bowl (6)
brain (8)
bricklayer (10)
bride (7)
broom (5)
brother-in-law (7)

bruise (8)
bucket (5)
burn (8)
bus fare (3)
buy a house (4)
buy a ticket (2)
buy groceries (2)
buy medicine (2)
buy stamps (2)
camera (1)
can opener (5)
capsule (8)
car payments (3)
car repairs (3)
career center (10)
career counselor (10)
carry (5)
cash (3)
cash a check (2)
cast (8)
cell phone (1)
Celsius (9)
cereal (6)
check (6)
check out books (2)
check register (3)
checkbook (3)
cheese (6)
chef (10)
clear the table (6)
clearance sale (5)
climb (9)
clothes dryer (9)
coach (4)
coffee (6)
coffeemaker (5)
cold (8)
communicate ideas effectively
   (10)
community center (2)
compliment (7)
computer programmer (10)
counter (6)
cousin (7)
cover (9)
co-worker (7)
crawl (9)
cream (8)
credit card (3)
criticize (7)
crutches (8)
curly hair (1)
cut (8)
cut up (6)
cutting board (5)
dance (7)
dark brown (1)
date of birth (1)
day shift (10)

debit card (3)
deduct (3)
demonstrate (5)
deposit slip (3)
designer (4)
dessert (6)
dime (10¢) (3)
diploma (1)
disagree (7)
dish soap (5)
dishwasher (5)
disorganized (4)
do volunteer work (4)
dollar ($1.00) (3)
drain (9)
drawer (9)
driver's license (1)
drugstore (2)
dryer (5)
eggs (6)
electrician (10)
electricity (3)
emergency room (8)
employee (3)
employee I.D. badge (1)
endorse a check (3)
evacuate (9)
evening shift (10)
examining room (8)
exchange (5)
eye color (1)
Fahrenheit (9)
fall off (6)
faucet (9)
feel dizzy (8)
feel nauseous (8)
fever (8)
fiancée (7)
fifty dollars ($50.00) (3)
fire escape (9)
fire truck (9)
firefighter (9)
first name (1)
fish (6)
five dollars ($5.00) (3)
flour (6)
flu (8)
follow directions (10)
fracture (8)
friend (7)
front desk receptionist (10)
fruit (6)
fry (6)
full time (10)
furniture store (5)
gas (3)
get a GED (4)
get a job (4)
get a prescription (2)

get a raise (4)
get cash (2)
get good grades (4)
get married (4)
get something to drink (2)
get something to eat (2)
get vocational training (4)
gifts (7)
go back to school (4)
go east (2)
go into (5)
go north (2)
go out of business (5)
go south (2)
go straight (2)
go west (2)
gold medal (4)
good attitude (4)
good with people (4)
graduate from a university (4)
grandparents (7)
gray (1)
groceries (3)
groom (7)
grow up (7)
gymnastics (4)
hair color (1)
hair dryer (9)
half price (5)
happy (1)
hardworking (4)
have computer skills (10)
heart (8)
heat (6)
heavy (1)
heavy coat (5)
height (1)
help other people (10)
hip (8)
home health aide (10)
hose (9)
hostess (6)
housework (1)
hug (7)
hydrant (9)
ice cream (6)
ice pack (8)
in a bad mood (7)
in a good mood (7)
infection (8)
information desk (2)
interrupt (7)
interview (10)
invitation (7)
jacket (5)
jewelry store (5)
job applicant (10)
joint (8)
key (9)

kiss (7)
ladder (9)
landlady (7)
laptop (1)
last name (1)
late (4)
lazy (4)
learn more English (4)
learn something new (4)
learn to use a computer (4)
library (2)
light brown (1)
lock (9)
long hair (1)
loud noises (1)
lungs (8)
machine operator (10)
mail letters (2)
mail packages (2)
main dish (6)
make a deposit (3)
make a phone call (2)
make a toast (7)
make a withdrawal (3)
mall directory (5)
manage time efficiently (10)
marked down (5)
mash (6)
mechanic (4)
medical center (2)
medium height (1)
menu (6)
middle name (1)
milk (6)
mix (6)
money order (3)
monthly statement (3)
mop (5)
motorcycle (1)
muscle (8)
music (1)
musicians (7)
mustache (1)
napkin (6)
neighbors (7)
nephew (7)
nervous (1)
newsstand (2)
next to (2)
nickel (5¢) (3)
niece (7)
night shift (10)
nursing assistant (10)
occupation (1)
office manager (4)
office worker (4)
oil (6)

on the corner of (2)
on time (4)
one way (2)
open a checking account (3)
organize information (10)
organized (4)
OTC (8)
overflow (9)
overheat (9)
overload (9)
painter (10)
pair of athletic shoes (5)
pair of boots (5)
parents (7)
part time (10)
paycheck (3)
peanuts (6)
peel (6)
peeler (5)
penny (1¢) (3)
personal check (3)
pets (1)
photographer (7)
pick up (9)
pipe (9)
plate (6)
platform (2)
plug in (9)
post office (2)
poultry (6)
pour (6)
prescription (8)
push a stroller (5)
put away (9)
put back (9)
quarter (25¢) (3)
radio (1)
radiology (8)
rash (8)
razor (3)
read a train schedule (2)
read to your children (4)
receipt (5)
recreation (3)
red meat (6)
refrigerator (5)
refund (5)
regular price (5)
relaxed (1)
rent (3)
rescue (9)
resolve conflicts (10)
restaurant (2)
restaurant manager (10)
résumé (10)
roof (9)
round trip (2)

sad (1)
safe-deposit box (3)
salad (6)
salary (3)
sale (5)
salesperson (4)
sandwich (6)
save money (4)
savings account (3)
see a doctor (2)
senator (4)
serve food (6)
set the table (6)
sex (1)
shake hands (7)
shampoo (3)
shaving cream (3)
shock (8)
short (1)
short hair (1)
shut off (9)
side order (6)
signature (1)
sink (9)
skin (8)
slice (6)
slide (1)
sliding door (9)
slim (1)
sling (8)
smoke (9)
snack bar (2)
soccer (1)
socialize (2)
soft drink (6)
soup (6)
space heater (9)
spend time with your children (4)
spill (6)
splint (8)
sprain (8)
spray (9)
start a business (4)
stitches (8)
stove (5)
straight hair (1)
street (2)
study (2)
sugar (6)
supermarket (2)
supervisor (4)
swimming (1)
swing (1)
tablet (8)
take a break (5)
take a business course (4)
take a left (2)

take a right (2)
take a writing course (4)
take an order (6)
take care of (7)
take classes (2)
take out (9)
talk back (7)
tall (1)
teaspoon (8)
teeth (8)
temperature (9)
ten dollars ($10.00) (3)
ticket machine (2)
ticket office (2)
tired (1)
toaster (5)
toaster oven (9)
toilet (9)
toiletries (3)
toothbrush (3)
toothpaste (3)
toy (1)
toy store (5)
track (2)
transaction amount (3)
tray (6)
trip over (6)
turn down (9)
turn off (9)
turn on (9)
twenty dollars ($20.00) (3)
uncle (7)
unlock (9)
unplug (9)
utilities (3)
vacuum (5)
valve (9)
vegetable (6)
vote (4)
waist (8)
wait for a train (2)
waiter (6)
waiting area (2)
waiting area (8)
washing machine (5)
weight (1)
welder (10)
wheelchair (8)
window (9)
withdrawal slip (3)
wrist (8)
work independently (10)
work well with others (10)
X-ray (8)
X-ray technician (10)
yell at (7)

IRREGULAR VERBS

Irregular Verbs

Base Form	Simple Past		Base Form	Simple Past
be	was/were		keep	kept
become	became		know	knew
begin	began		leave	left
bleed	bled		lend	lent
break	broke		lose	lost
bring	brought		make	made
buy	bought		meet	met
choose	chose		pay	paid
come	came		put	put
cost	cost		read	read
cut	cut		ring	rang
do	did		run	ran
drink	drank		see	saw
drive	drove		sell	sold
eat	ate		send	sent
fall	fell		set	set
feel	felt		shake	shook
fight	fought		shut	shut
find	found		sleep	slept
forget	forgot		speak	spoke
fry	fried		speed	sped
get	got		spend	spent
give	gave		take	took
go	went		teach	taught
grow	grew		tell	told
have/has	had		think	thought
hear	heard		wear	wore
hold	held		write	wrote
hurt	hurt			

Spin

CREDITS

PHOTO CREDITS

p. 11, (Yuko) Ken Usami/Getty Images; (Paul and Abel) Royalty-Free/Corbis

p. 15, Erica S.Leeds

p. 24, Photodisc/Getty Images

p. 28, (top) Richard Wareham Fotografie/Alamy; (bottom) Keith Brofsky/Getty Images

p. 53, (left) Wally McNamee/Corbis; (center) Getty Images for Laureus; (right) Getty Images

p. 56, Anderson Ross/Getty Images

TEXT CREDITS

p. 25, Southern California Regional Rail Authority. "Southern California Regional Rail Map" by permission of Metrolink.

p. 65, PhotoLink/Getty Images

p. 67, (top left) Getty Images; (center left) The McGraw-Hill Companies, L. Niki; (top right) BananaStock/PunchStock; (center right) 2007 Getty Images; (bottom left) Dynamic Graphics/Jupiter Images; (bottom right) Richard Levine/Alamy

p. 95, (top) Getty Images; (bottom) Pictorial Press Ltd/Alamy

p. 99, Doug Menuezl/Getty Images

p. 113, The McGraw-Hill Companies, Jill Braaten Photographer

p. 127, Jocelyn Augustino/FEMA

SKILLS INDEX

ACADEMIC SKILLS

Grammar

Reading

Writing